Praise for *Real Teachers*

"The point of Stuart Grauer's book is to remind us that Great Teaching, singular, rare, unusual, is something that should be sought after and found. Thank you. It's wonderful, timely, accessible, clear as a bell."

—Richard Dreyfuss
Actor, Oxford scholar, founder of The Dreyfuss Initiative

"Stuart Grauer brings joy, courage, and imagination to the dialogue on education. His stories add inspiration to our sense of possibility."

—Vicki Abeles
Director/Producer, nationwide film *Race to Nowhere*

"A book of wonderful news—a breath of fresh air for classroom teachers and educators. This book evokes the heart of teaching in a clear, compelling, and soulful way. It will help teachers to reinvent the system, find their passion, and stay in the teaching profession."

—Paula A. Cordeiro
Dean, School of Leadership and Education Sciences
University of San Diego

"For the real teacher, the growth is in the plant, not the gardener. In his wise, lyrical, and liberating book, Stuart Grauer shares the harvest of his lifetime in education that truly matters."

—Richard Lederer
Host/originator of NPR's *A Way with Words*
Author of *A Tribute to Teachers*

"Stuart Grauer is a rebel and education is his cause. His beautiful book is both revolutionary and revelatory. *Real Teachers* is a joy-filled adventure that will inspire you to action."

—Jeff Salz
Corporate Anthropologist, Adventurer,
Author of *The Way of Adventure*

"Just what the doctor ordered: a book reminding us what is possible in schooling, and how much it depends on freeing teachers to think big. It's a book full of wonderful tales from the field."

—Deborah Meier
MacArthur Fellowship Recipient, New York University Senior Scholar,
Author, School Founder, Founder of the "Small Schools Movement"

Real Teachers

Real Teachers

True Stories of Renegade Educators

Stuart Grauer

SelectBooks, Inc.

New York

Real Teachers™ is a trademark of Stuart Grauer

This edition published by SelectBooks, Inc.

For information address SelectBooks, Inc., New York, New York.

First Edition

ISBN 978-1-59079-954-3

Cataloging-in-Publication Data

Grauer, Stuart.
  Real teachers : true stories of renegade educators / Stuart Grauer.
  p. cm.
Includes bibliographical references.
  Summary: "Head of private secondary school in Southern California explores the meaning of an authentic education. In his stories of discoveries about teaching, he hopes to inspire students and teachers to transcend the common belief that efficient delivery of a standardized core curriculum is the essential value of educators--and to expect much more from themselves and their schools"--Provided by publisher.
  ISBN 978-1-59079-954-3 (pbk. book : alk. paper)
  1. Teachers--Conduct of life. 2. Teaching--Anecdotes. I. Title.
  LB1775.G675 2013
  371.1--dc23
        2012032852

Contents

Security is mostly a superstition. It does not exist in nature, nor do the children of men as a whole experience it. Avoidance of danger is no safer in the long run than outright exposure. Life is either a daring adventure, or nothing.

—Helen Keller
The Open Door (1957)

Preface

❧

To the Educator

As a college student of economics, I was struck by the concept of *economic determinism*: that no matter what happened in the world it could be interpreted in terms of economics. I came to understand that becoming an economist would entail developing that specific worldview. I did not become an economist, however; I chose teaching, a choice for which I have been richly rewarded.

As we sift through the endless skill set that great teaching requires of us, ultimately we realize that, as with any other complex task, without a compelling perspective and a sense of the whole, our work cannot be fully mastered. More than a skill set, teaching is a way of seeing. In becoming a teacher, I eventually discovered that the great teachers see the entire world in terms of education. For the true teacher, essentially any event, from trivial to universal, can become valuable, regardless of its origin, when viewed fundamentally in terms of its ability to connect us in a lasting way with our students. Over time, a new concept arose in my mind: *educational determinism*. This perspective entails viewing and analyzing life through the eyes of a teacher. But who has those eyes? And where can we get them?

The essays in this collection were gathered in the first decade of the new, third millennium. They were developed and drafted over a seven-month period in relative isolation at Martha's Vineyard, Massachusetts; The Pine

Ridge Indian Reservation, South Dakota; Teahupo'o, Tahiti Iti; Maui, Hawaii; San Juanico, Baja California Sur, Mexico; the Caribbean Sea; Park City, Utah; Whidbey Island, Washington; New York City; and Encinitas, California. Following conventions in creative nonfiction, some names and places were changed as appropriate.

The onset of the third millennium figures so largely for me that this new era seemed to take on the qualities of a character in some of the stories. Youths growing up during this time are referred to as Millennials. Elsewhere in literature they are referred to as Gen Y. The terms come with some baggage, too, often implying enormous changes in ways of thinking and working. It is the generation of the digitally augmented mind.

The essays pay homage to the sensibilities most at risk in an overcrowded, over-institutionalized, "wired" world. There are sensibilities without which we could not aspire to great teaching, that is: as a teacher, your efforts matter, personally and as a member of a team. The stories in *Real Teachers* cover Socratic teaching, regional education, revered teaching traditions, and a general consideration of what characterizes great teaching. The authentic connection between all living things, and in particular, between teacher and student, is the basis for the compassionate education conveyed in these stories. The advancement of this connection has been achieved by people in a variety of roles: religious and spiritual leaders, great organizational and business managers, national leaders, community activists, and many others. But certainly among the foremost of these connectors, awakeners, and leaders has been the teacher. Teaching is a great and noble profession, a profession sought out by those of the highest accomplishment in every civilization throughout history. Let us celebrate teachers and great teaching!

As educational research and practice has shown for many years, the teachers whom students treasure are those who see their purposes as freeing rather than controlling, and they find their work and ideas to be ever connected with larger meanings. Teachers who practice this model long enough find joy and love in their work. The stories in *Real Teachers* are filled with metaphors and images to bring this model to life.

If a specific subject area or profession only practices self-study, its findings may be clever, but it is unlikely that they will be true advances. Solutions to problems that seem entrenched or intractable must come from both within and without. The stories in this collection come from all over the world and from many disciplines, some from unlikely and surprising sources, and yet they each have something essential and enriching to add to our educational practices and perspectives. What my research associates and I found most striking in compiling these essays, was that the majority of topics covered were historically among the most core, essential elements of educational systems, and yet are now largely outside the scope of most formal research being conducted in the United States or addressed in scholarly literature.

Movements in university schools of education and large school district offices indeed suggest new, non-traditional roles for teachers, for instance as reliable deliverers of a modern standardized curriculum and guides of student technology as it is used in a "classroom of the future." Neither of these roles is covered in this collection. These two, incipient models would redefine what it means to become a classroom teacher. In particular, they promote the concepts that a teacher should be more of a sideline coach than an inspirational leader or student mentor, that one is a teacher by virtue of a specific skill set as opposed to the true, traditional value of teaching, which transcends skills and is a cast of mind and heart. Predominant but never, ever stated in teacher education as it stands at the start of a new millennium is the buried presumption that the teachers we need are essentially efficient bureaucrats working within a controlled system. As naturally as this transition is being treated, we can find no precedent for it in the history of education—these are not roles to which we would have historically assigned the name *teacher*.

I will state my perspective up front. I believe if something which is not a machine becomes too much of a system the best challenge we can take on is in throwing it out. Such systems can only originate in the fear of relying on real people, and this can be expected to happen once systems get too big. Although there may be value in the new, systematized roles of teacher as technology assistant and deliverer of standardized curriculum, neither of these roles can be successful in establishing what is most meaningful about scholarship, learning, and educational artistry. Neither role imbues us with the educational deterministic view which has infused the following stories and has been the work of the many teachers whom I have come to know as masters of the Socratic method and educational leaders.

Neither of these two, key roles is inspiring a new generation of educational connoisseurs or aficionados. What we are discovering instead, is that the average new teacher drops out of the profession within five years as a result of being uninspired, frustrated, or simply overwhelmed. This we can now predict clearly: school design that caters to these emerging roles will lead to still more impersonal, bureaucratic schools with even bigger classes. Neither a reliable curriculum nor expertise in a skill set is enough. We will have to look elsewhere and find new visions.

As tempting as it is, we need not bemoan progress, technology, standardization, or the evolving role of the teacher. But give a great student and even a great laptop computer to two teachers—Socrates and a novice teacher—and the student of Socrates will learn better every time. Reflective experience, depth of meaning and relationships, along with the chance to cultivate the imagination are products of real teaching. For this reason, I suggest that before we deem the traditional role of teacher an anachronism, we honor, study, and reward, beyond technology and standardized curriculum, what real teachers must deliver even more of: the growing sense of purpose we get through the development of meaningful human relationships. We are granted this sense of purpose by real teachers, unforgettable in our lives, and it is real teachers whom we encounter in these stories.

In our school, we use the slogan "Learn by Discovery," yet there are always board members, strategic planners, and parents who question this—it sounds too much like elementary school. In the essay "Single Handing It" I ask us to "imagine a world where 'discovery,' the work of Magellan, Einstein, and NASA, are viewed as a better fit for kindergarten and Cub Scout troops—certainly not for high school where we have real tests to pass!" My point here is, the path of "discovery"—and, ultimately, joy—is easily overwhelmed and derailed by huge educational bureaucracies, interest groups, and corporations marketing high stakes, high profit instructional and testing programs. A shift in perspective is needed. With this, we can restore joy, fearlessness, discovery, and authenticity in schooling.

Wonderfully, the interactivity with both teachers and with the natural world around them is still comparatively high in the elementary grades and still seen as feasible by many at this level. However, once students reach secondary school, the need for real teachers becomes increasingly acute. In these upper grades, much in the way of authentic, constructivist, and expeditionary learning is tossed out as non-college preparatory or unmanageable. An insurance risk. A transportation headache. We live in an age of the hidden teen. In my town, parks are routinely built and developed specifically so that they will be utterly unappealing to teens. Even parents seem afraid of them. A good number of them have not had regular, meaningful conversations with an adult, including with a teacher, in years.

I have met a great many teachers at home and abroad. I brought the first American student delegation to set foot on the Shanghai University Attached Middle School, a $20 million rotunda. The principal had gathered a huge U.N. style circle of dignitaries, sat me at the front, and announced to the rapt audience, "Dr. Grauer will now deliver a speech." (To you wishful travelling educators, I can share that carrying with you even a quickly assembled stash of quotes from Confucius, Plato or Socrates, Lincoln, Einstein, Mandela, and the Buddha should take you around the world.)

I've traveled to meet the head of a school for AIDS orphans in northern Botswana, the head of a remote Alaskan village reinstituting native language and culture after twenty years with no salmon, a school high in the Swiss Alps, and the school heads of several desperately poor Indian reservations. I have flown peace kites with students in schools on both sides of the Israeli-Palestinian border. I have shared classes with the heads and founders of these schools in addition to participating with the many ingenious teachers who have taught under the same roof as me throughout the various stages of my career. I have taught sixth graders at the Paopao School in French Polynesia and graduate education courses at two universities. I have chaired school accreditation visits at schools all over the Southwestern United States. I now believe that what makes real teachers is not merely the efficient delivery of an entire curriculum, or even the high scores their students may achieve. Teachers are real, and great, by virtue of their ability to see themselves and their students as mutually connected to the whole of creation. As a result, it often seems as though literally anything can be woven into their teaching.

The real teachers illustrated in these stories find that their classrooms and their students—wherever the setting, rich or poor, ugly or beautiful—are "enough" and not lacking. They find real teaching opportunities and resources wherever they are. They are teachers in the classroom, but they remain teachers at home and at parties, in the desert or out to sea, in retirement or in utter isolation.

These stories are delivered without apology (a claim that could change later), but I confess a bias towards local and regional input into the curriculum and programming of all schools. This is in no way intended as criticism of national, global, or multicultural perspectives, which I have pursued for many years. It is, however, in support of a timeless side of education that, almost suddenly, appears to have little advocacy or political stature, at least at the secondary school level. Hence, all essays are set in local communities, where regional differences are cherished. My goal in taking on this issue is not to lend advocacy to any one perspective, but for the restoration of balance between them.

The main issues facing national educational efforts are not new, nor are they hidden from view. Institutionalization, the over-consolidation of schools and districts into massive entities, overcrowding, the conflict of standardization versus individuality, and so on, all in a giant, often unspoken war between the needs to standardize education to serve the needs of many versus special interest groups that keep gaining in strength—and of course special needs only gain in salience when systems become harder, larger, and more standardized. What's usually missing in the search for answers to these issues is a sensitivity to the values of local communities and, even further under the radar, individual learners of unique and extraordinary capacities. How did we arrive at this system of schooling? What if class size and school design were based on something real—something consciously, intentionally meaningful, something that does more than just augment or reevaluate the thing before it, *the thing that we don't really know how it got this way?*

I wrote these stories because I believe that we all have an outlier in us, and this outlier will provide us with new perspectives and the regeneration of our faith in teachers. Even in our over-augmented school systems which largely attempt to be all things to all people, where standardization appears to be a core value, and where teachers and students can easily feel the constant turning of the competitive treadmill, we can seek our authentic selves. Our secondary school teachers need not act like any of the teachers in these stories to be, in some way, more real. They may be inspired by them to recall that they, too, can be just as real. Nor does it matter if the reader agrees with the conclusions I form, since our beleaguered field will benefit more from passionate disagreement than passive acceptance. To simply be Socratic is an authentic form of activism among teachers because it opens us up to the process of discovery, a process we cannot always control. Hence, these essays, just like the real teachers they portray, will almost certainly be provocative.

Methodology must be well married to content. As a teacher, when you refuse to put a score on an achievement, when you refuse to draw straight lines to the process of discovery, you cannot help but provoke your best students to smiling insurgency, perhaps even of a tribal nature. Data does not really move us, but empathy, the true currency of a real teacher, does. For this reason, this book consists not of controlled empirical research studies, but of true story narratives.

To the empirical researcher, think tank, policy maker, or critic, I have this to offer: I have spent most working days for the past nearly four decades in classrooms and on campuses, interacting personally with students and front-line teachers. This experience includes both teaching and evaluating in public and private settings; United States and abroad; elementary and secondary schools and universities; on faculties and as an outside hired gun.

One of the welcome outcomes of this work would be follow-up studies on any of the many issues suggested, in particular studies on smaller schools and classes and on community-based education. In fact, our organization (Coalition of Small Preparatory Schools) has grant money available for this, and we invite inquiries from students and researchers.

A word on intuition. As it stands, neuroscientists studying primary con-sciousness are attempting to build computer networks which, by the year of this publication, should approach in capacity the number of neuronal con-nections of a common octopus, but still remain orders of magnitude from the complexity of the human mind. While the developing capacity of artifi-cial intelligence has accelerated empirical research into new realms, no form of quantitative study yet rivals the human intuition in its ability to provide meaningful associations and conclusions. The reader will find, throughout the collection, associations made—from the obvious to the unexpected and the bewildering. It is these associations and the sometimes unexpected paral-lels therein which our trial readers, researchers, and editors have appreciated and relished as much as anything in these stories while they were being devel-oped and finalized. At least to us, parallelism in life, when based upon direct human experience, is both more fascinating and more fortuitous in its capac-ity to provide imaginative leadership in education than the correlations found in formal research. As stated, we welcome experimental researchers to create follow-up in the form of data-driven studies on any of the findings herein, and we hope they will.

A final assumption breathing life into the essays is that people are good. We've known all along that those special people, the teachers who students admire most and learn the most from, have a penchant for viewing people in general as able and friendly, and that they feel connected both to their students and to the ever larger purposes in their lives. If we create or develop a social system or institution and a group or individual is not doing well in it, let us not make the assumption that there is something wrong with the group or the individual. These essays honor the individual first and assume that institutions exist to honor them (not vice versa, as teachers, parents, and students may find in larger systems and classes). Although there is a substantial body of work to support it, I hold this assumption to be self-evident—therefore, for the most part, beyond referencing throughout. Like real teaching, it is nothing more than a way of seeing the world.

Introduction

LEARNING TO LOVE EDUCATION AGAIN

The great teachers through the ages have often emphasized that the purpose of life is to awaken happiness for oneself and others. If you set out in search of joy in education, where would you go? Education at its best has often been referred to as "enlightenment." When was the last time you experienced enlightenment? When was the last time you experienced great joy or great listening? Is there time for this in our schools?

In our troubled and busy world, questions like these are easy to give up on. I invite you to revisit them as you read *Real Teachers*. The ten narrative essays in this collection were written for savoring and for inviting open space into your days. The stories in *Real Teachers* are intended to bring teaching to life and to raise stimulating, provocative questions whenever people gather together to discuss schooling. Icons are smashed with love, intractable issues are unhinged, and many questions are set in the balance, demanding our thought and action. They are stories of discovery and possibility rather than of limits and boundaries.

Real teaching is not always so easy or practical. The steady shift to big systems education (bigger classes, bigger schools, etc.) has been accompanied by a shift in the educational research and literature, which has resulted in a dearth of storytelling in the field. Storytelling is a basic part of the creation and continuance of identities, cultures, and traditions. In these narrative essays, we experience communities from around the globe intimately as their purposes, sense of place, and visions of the future are revealed. As well, the stories in *Real Teachers* raise and illustrate compelling issues. I hope these stories will be the subject of great conversations that you will have about great education. I hope you will gain new appreciation for your own stories and journeys.

You will get through this book most easily if you are not multitasking or keeping a close watch on your digital devices. We all benefit from disconnected downtime in our tech-dominated lives, even those of you reading this through a glass screen. I invite you to unplug. Go a little out of bounds as we attempt to rediscover what matters in education and how we can restore authenticity, joy, and gratitude in our roles as educators, students, parents, and concerned community members. Think of these stories as spring break.

1

Real Teachers, Oil on Canvas

HARMENSZOON'S LAST QUESTION

The Socratic Oath

On the way to the museum, walking through Central Park, my wife and I were having a conversation about *real* teachers, about what that meant. We were meandering, taking the long way, and covering the whole idea of authenticity in teaching. (One thing my wife and I share is that we both married a teacher.) We were trying to create verbal paintings, descriptions of those special ones who connect to us in ancient and classic ways, the ways which made the concept and term *teacher* evolve in the first place. It was March, a fair coverage of snow was on the ground, and the day was hazy and dull and beautiful, like a glaze had been brushed over it.

Manhattan Island is where I was born and where, thirty-five years ago, I took my first "straight" job, teaching art history at the Dwight School, not far from the location of our stroll. What a town in which to teach art history!

We had returned to the city for our twentieth wedding anniversary. We stopped for brunch in a delicatessen near the Frick Collection, an old haunt of mine, where they were featuring our all-time favorite artist. Anticipating Rembrandt, we finished up our bagels and lox and were on our way. As though on cue, a man outside on the sidewalk clothed in a shiny suit said into a cell phone, "My people can get those same shirts for $160 and $190." So we were back in New York.

The show at the Frick was entitled *Rembrandt and His School*. We were struck by the concept of Rembrandt as *teacher*. So, we were discussing what to call those special ones. Did *teacher* have the same meaning now as it did in the old days? All the same baggage? Was there a better term that conveyed real teachers? "Mentor," "facilitator," "leader," "professor," and "coach" all came up. "Trainer?" (Ughh!) "Educator?" (Not bad).

Guru is a Sanskrit word long used for those regarded as having great knowledge, wisdom, and authority, and that word came up, too. ("What does guru mean?" we had once asked a Hindu friend, hoping for enlightenment. "*Guru?*" she considered. "Well, that means: *teacher*.")

Jesus of Nazareth was called *rabbi*, so we looked up the meaning (I had an iPad). It means, in translation, "*teacher*." *Sensei* has an exotic tone to it: teacher, or master, is what it means. *Master* is used much in Europe and South America, as in the Italian word *maestro*, meaning teacher. What about the word *Lama*, which is used in Tibet? It also refers to a teacher (of the Dharma)—maybe a tall order.

Forsaking the chance to be called "His Excellency" as is common among African heads of state, Tanzania's president Kikwete took the revolutionary step of placing the esteemed title "Mwalimu" before his name: *teacher*.

Who are the real teachers in these uncertain times of competing agendas? Are they in our schools? What do they do? Teach like gurus in the old days? Teach as instruments of the state or of bureaucracy?

We interview a number of teachers each year and it can be disappointing meeting the ones who present themselves as curricular delivery systems. "I see you love gardening," we said recently to a young lady interviewing as a biology teacher. "Would you be able to use this expertise with your students?" "If it is part of the curriculum," she answered, as if her own personal skills and loves ought naturally to be segregated from her development as a teacher and regulated by the state. Many young teachers we met took pride in this passive, subservient role because they believed it would make them appear reliable and trustworthy. While these are excellent traits for a young teacher to have, at some point the authentic life of openness and discovery and the need to conform and be reliable must synthesize.

I read hundreds of articles on teaching every year and most of them are, by far, about the same thing: the effort to replace real teachers with a system or program. Often, school teachers do not appear to be *masters*, but rather workers who carry out the expectation of the *real experts* from afar. In our world of accelerating systematization, I get the sense that *Teaching for Dummies,* would easily outsell *Teaching for Experts.*

I know there is good cause for some aspects of this shift. But I also know there are many *maestros* still in our classrooms, continuing to search and ask questions. These are people who create open environments where students can deepen their inquiries rather than race through them; these are the connoisseur teachers who understand the fearless role models who inhabit our vision of the past, but are also adaptive, creative, and visionary. It is up to us to become both.

What does it mean to be a member of this noble or once noble profession? Who practices such an art and science? Is the title *teacher* earned from below or assigned from above?

Research has identified the manager teacher, the planner teacher, the standards-based teacher, the teacher as judge, the subject area expert teacher, the didactic teacher, the Socratic teacher. These incredibly giving people are in a wide-open, historically rich field, each one fulfilling their given purpose in life. There is even a field of research that studies teacher research. But there is scant research on those *real teachers* who understand that their job, and its value, is intergenerational and that their teaching practice is inseparable from their free and independent life and the way they live it. Just as Socrates conducted his teaching practice around questions, we can learn that the real teacher exists independently of the curriculum and course content.

In finding teachers, we hardly know what to look for. They are flexible or unyielding, disciplined or wild, and they rarely appear to have a lot in common. How does my history teacher compare with Aristotle or Socrates? And why are the most famous teachers in history men from over two thousand years ago? In every other field these iconic figures are being regularly replenished.

Sometimes nothing is the best teacher, as in Zen, or in a green grotto filled with the white noise of a stream falling down and through and not a soul around for miles. Teachers tend to fill in our unexpected moments, as though a rock cracked open in our minds or hearts and a ray of light came through from some world we had never thought of. Sometimes the greatest teacher is the one who gets out of the way and allows his students to learn. Great teachers embrace not only discourse but silence. Just as medicine has a Hippocratic

Oath, "First, do no harm," teaching needs a Socratic Oath, "First, do not prevent learning."

If you are a teacher, you have chosen a noble profession, possibly one of the world's oldest professions. Perhaps our dreams of our achievements will be widely lauded, since our labors may be unfulfilled. Yet history convinces us that perseverance and courage shift the odds greatly in our favor. Another name for *teacher*, historically, is "lord," described in the Gospel of Luke in the Bible as one who has disciples, those who must remain alert and awake for His coming. In this sense, to be a real teacher, guru, rabbi, or mentor is such an esteemed thing as to be almost unattainable. From this point, when we become aware that everything and everyone has the potential to be a teacher, we start to become real students. This is the window into becoming a real teacher.

Studies conducted in the field of brain research have revealed that humans have a negativity bias. Watch a teacher or parent scan down a student report card. Their finger will stop at the lowest (not the highest) grade practically every time. But my own observations reveal that real teachers may not have this bias. The greatest teachers see first and primarily that which is good and worthwhile in their students. They listen their students into goodness, they are kid whisperers. The simple but profound capacity to listen, notes William Isaacs, is very difficult to achieve on an ongoing basis. This is the heart of Socratic dialog. That white noise of empathic listening seems to filter out all the pathology flowing into discussions, so that what real teachers hear from their students and fellow teachers is that which is hopeful and worthwhile. How do they do it? They just do it. I've observed great teachers doing this with students thousands of times. Maybe they have taken the Socratic Oath and don't even know it.

Teaching and Paradox

The Frick exhibit was called *Rembrandt and His School*. A featured painting was a former Rembrandt. This painting had recently been downgraded from an authentic work of the master and reattributed to the "School of Rembrandt." The downgraded painting was called "Old Woman with a Book," which is a painting Henry Clay Frick himself once exalted as "one of the finest Rembrandt's in existence," and it is also a work that the curator of this new show called "a work by one of Rembrandt's minor pupils."

Hence, a painting that had been labeled a Rembrandt for over three centuries is at last attributed to one of his students, a member of his *school*. One question never asked is: is this a downgrade or an upgrade? Through some formula, art historians have determined that, although Rembrandt certainly had a hand in designing "Old Woman with a Book," and even added some brush strokes to the old woman, a student had done most of the work. At last students were getting the credit they deserved.

I wonder how Rembrandt would feel about this. Would he be happy for the work of his school? I hope so. Despite the attraction of the Great Man Theory, it is never the lone genius who advances civilization. The great ideas of these "great men" advance civilization only to the extent to which they are taught. In great schools, scholarly research bears out in such a way that ideas proliferate so naturally that oftentimes no one can even identify their source—not the principal or the marketing department. (Although sometimes certain people believe it was their idea from the start.) In the *good, at best* organization, the attribution of good deeds and ideas is fought over or claimed privately in small pockets or dyads; in the *great* ones it is embraced and understood as a shared product of the whole.[2] These schools must have great and humble teachers to allow this distinction between the role of teacher and student to be genuinely shared if not entirely blurred. And indeed in the presence of great and transcendent masterworks, it can feel ridiculous to call ourselves *teacher* or *master*—we can only be *student*.

In this way, Rembrandt's sketches and etchings mimicked the masters before him (Titian, for example). In the same way, Rembrandt's studies eventually became the model for his students, who copied him and his copies. When we give an honest account of all the passing along, copying, and competing, we can only lose sight of the difference between the students and the teachers. Notwithstanding the paradox and pervasiveness of plagiary, we can identify real teachers as people of curiosity and gratitude, people who share, and who pass along wisdom.

Ultimately, no one owns wisdom. As the teacher withdraws his or her role as an individual, the teacher is no more; there is only the teaching relationship and mentorships. The teacher and student are vital in an organization where there is constant flow, and such an organization would be called "*school*" if the name "school" wasn't already taken.

Rembrandt and His School challenges our presumptions about what it means to be a teacher and how to define a school.

History's Most Fabled Student-Teacher Relationship

Always up for a challenge, the next morning we sat at Café Sabarsky drinking thick Viennese coffee, feeling Old World, and planning our approach to the Metropolitan Museum of Art; the Met. By opening time, we were caffeinated and prepared to view what we thought might be the greatest portrait ever painted—of a teacher. We entered the Met and set out on the labyrinthine path towards the Dutch rooms. En route, almost as if on script, we passed right by the famous Jacques-Louis David painting, "The Death of Socrates," possibly the most famous portrait ever painted of history's most fearless teacher. My hero. But David could never do what Rembrandt could. The depth is not there. (I could copy the image of "The Death of Socrates" herein, but you could probably Google a view of it more easily.) We pressed on.

My pulse quickened as we sensed the dark tones of the Dutch Masters through a doorway. We reached the Rembrandt room, and I began to study the eyes of each piece. There were all sorts of eyes: anxious, scrutinizing, non-descript, or empathic; sadly inquisitive eyes. Eyes of pure delight. (Later, a quick scan of several glossy magazines at a corner stand in Columbus Circle would prove that even the top supermodel's eyes were nowheresville compared to Rembrandt eyes.) There was even a Rembrandt with the exact same slight smirk as the Ben Franklin portrait in the other wing—each pair of eyes and each expression revealing a distinct world, like a Shakespeare play. Then, through a doorway and across the next gallery room—so dark you could miss it—perhaps the most revealing, alluring expression we'd ever seen on a teacher: Aristotle.

Contemplating a bust. A mouth that faintly smiles. The melancholic yet egocentric, lost-in-thought eyes that slant down and into the eyes of the blind poet. Homer. Homer's vacant eyes, slanting up towards Aristotle and slightly to the side—a hint of skepticism, as though hinting: "This means nothing." Then, at an equal downward slant—as if reflecting off of Homer's eyes—a medallion on a thick, intricately carved gold chain draped about Aristotle and hanging to his waist. On the medallion is the likeness of a hero, believed to be Alexander the Great. We think: *Imagine being Alexander the Great's teacher, imagine teaching the great warrior-emperor!* But the blind Homer cares no more for Aristotle's medallion than he does for his hubris. He is in equal parts blind and unimpressed.

Communing with the scene in the dark richness of oil and canvas, in this room virtually inhabited by Rembrandt, the mind begins to wonder: How can Homer be so unmoved by the great Aristotle? How can he be so utterly unimpressed by the greatest, most fabled student-teacher relationship in the history of civilization? It is as if the great poet's reserve reminds Aristotle, the rock-star teacher, that neither his epic success as a teacher of emperors, nor the successes of his great warrior-conqueror student are real. They are great, and yet at the same time they are merely stories. The painting's plot is formed by a geometric relationship, a reunion of the broken parts of this epic triad. The constellation of poet-scholar, teacher-philosopher, and epic warrior-student is complete. The triangle is nature's power formation (basic feng shui) and we see in this teaching triad that no part has depth without the other. Rembrandt has constructed a master lesson on the essential quality of the Socratic teacher, played here by Homer: he is a cornerstone of humility.

This geometry is probably as old as humankind. Through time, coinciding with or subsequent to their greatest achievements, history's geniuses, as a matter of personal evolution, have become teachers. Einstein attended the Polytechnic School in Zurich to study to become a teacher and, only after a failed, two-year search for a teaching position, began work at the Bern patent office. It was only after his greatest work as a physicist that he at last became a teacher, and he remained so for the rest of his days. Socrates, Jesus, Confucius, —all infuriated people or terrified them with the magnitude of their life questions and, after their great quests, as a final culmination of their life's work, eventually became teachers. After Confucius's great work as a state magistrate reached wide acclaim, he left office to travel throughout China, teaching. Sitting Bull, after his youth as a warrior, would also later accept the role of teacher. Because of his renown as a teacher, Rembrandt's studio was filled with pupils. None of these real teachers wrote much down, but their followers did; an example of how great teaching, once delivered, takes on a life of its own. In this way, we may never know the world's great teachers; we can only know how their teaching refracts through their students, and the students of those students.

Like real teaching, real art is an agent of transformation. Real teaching is what resonates between the teacher and the student. It does not reside in an individual, it resides in a relationship. As teachers, our impact can be measured in the transformation of our students as they transform and redefine us.

A Real Teacher

The concept that teaching cannot be embodied in an individual but only as a relationship between the people may not be desirable or acceptable to some, and I spent considerable time journaling about it back at the hotel. Consider the case of Rembrandt.

Over the past generation, emerging scholarship and cataloguing techniques have caused art historians to determine that hundreds of "Rembrandts" were indeed drawn by the hands of others. The reason for all the confusion: Rembrandt had one of the largest teaching practices in his day, with at least fifty pupils studying closely alongside him in his sprawling Amsterdam studio. Rembrandt taught his students to draw in his style, as they sketched side by side.

Fifty is a relatively large student count for a school with one teacher. As the head of a school, I currently employ around thirty-five teachers. Although I can feel sure that most are within my sphere of influence and that we share common values, there is always some teaching being done that represents neither me, nor any unified school of thought of which I know. In some cases, young teachers establishing their independence and trying out their own theories or the theories of their graduate school professors are not ready to contain themselves or their energies within a specific school of thought or practice, perhaps for the better!

It takes time to understand what a school is, what it stands for, and what its methodologies are. Some teachers learn these methodologies only to realize that they do not want to live with them. Some of these teachers stay and some go. As a young teacher in the 1970s in a public high school with seventy-five teachers, I confess I was not even remotely influenced by the philosophy or practices of the principal of that school. I don't remember a word he said, only that one day I showed him how to fillet a trout. To me, his interest in this demonstrated a kind of philosophy, but I had no idea what larger purposes he had in his role as a principal or what his school meant to him. In that school, I informally placed myself under the mentorship of an assistant principal, but belonged to no suborganization, tribe, or even subculture. I have never taught, much less sketched, side by side in the classroom with any principal or educational mentor beyond a semester of student teaching almost forty years ago.

On the contrary, in my current school, I have spent many years teaching side by side with promising teachers in training, often for a year at a time, and stay in dialog with them thereafter. Some have been receptive and furthered our mutual efforts. Some have become better mentors than I have. Some have, of course, left disenfranchised. Some have subsequently started their own schools or studios. Over time, a core group of educators has developed, advancing a shared and identifiable style of education right on our campus: *a school.*

In the 2012 New York art scene, the artist Damien Hirst staged a show of formulaic art (consisting of simple dots) wherein he claimed, as though it were a concept transcending the oil and canvas he used, that few of the paintings in this show were actually executed by his own hand and brush. Instead, they were done by "employees"—not even "students."[3] I hope this is not a futuristic metaphor for the diminishing role of real teachers, or for a passionless American teacher filling in the state and district mandates almost as if by proxy.

Rembrandt began accepting students at the age of nineteen or twenty-one (depending on the source) and taught for the rest of his life. As the Rembrandt School grew, the number of brushstrokes he put on canvass decreased as his efforts in great teaching and mentorship increased. So which is his legacy—his art or his teaching? Some of his pupils, like Nicolaes Maes, not only embodied Rembrandt's vision and skill, but advanced it in their own ways after the master was gone. The school lived on as others embraced Rembrandt's techniques well after his death.[4]

No epitaph reads: "Rembrandt Harmenszoon van Rijn, Teacher." The gentle, broken master was buried in an unmarked grave. At his height, his work became manifest in the triads he formed with his students and patrons. His students were not only grinding his colors and filling in his backgrounds, but increasingly sharing everything they could with him, until the distinction between pupil and teacher—and even observer—dissolved, transformed into a school of thought and action. I believe this to be a goal to aspire to, for any *teacher*, for any *school.*

In many places in the world there is nowhere to write things down and no schools. There are wars or civil wars, miles to walk to find a classroom, no technology, a history of suffering, and no opportunity. But even in those places, a real relationship with another, with a respected, caring other, is the only pathway to real education. Even in those places, perhaps especially in those places, there are real teachers. Where teaching relationships are not strong, connected, respectful, and enduring, we can expect decline, be it in a family, a community, or a whole culture.

Crossing the line into self-sustaining teaching relationships and classes can be tricky. There is a letting go process that the traditional teacher and the class may have to acknowledge, and when we try to force it and make the class be autonomous just for the sake of having a theory, it will become unstable and our students and patrons will begin to complain and fragment. When a teacher becomes Socratic and expects his students to become equal partners in the development of their own education, students can become frustrated or insecure; there can be power struggles or vacuums. It's an iterative, gradual process. We give out too much control, we pull back a little; then we give out a little more, pushing, pulling, eventually reaching a new kind of Socratic equilibrium.

It is our students who define our teachers, make them successful, embrace or disturb their teachings, act out their philosophies, and maybe even fillet their fish for them. Our graduates are ready to graduate only when they have become our partners in teaching as well as in their own scholarship, so that they too may pass it along.

Gratitude

There at the Frick last spring, the 1658 "Self-Portrait" of the fully mature Rembrandt had just come on display after a long absence, newly refurbished to all its original depth and sheen. We began making our way back to it, walking down Fifth Avenue. Even in a town where, within moments of a walk in Central Park you can stand in the presence of "Starry Night" or Jackson Pollack's "No. 5," the anticipation of encountering arguably the greatest portrait ever painted was incomparable. We entered the Frick atrium, passed through the marble columns in walking meditation, the garden court, and into the storied Oval Room.

There on canvas sat the heavily robed Rembrandt before only himself, confident but not vain. To those so inclined, I recommend spending some time communing with this creation. (An Internet likeness is wholly inadequate.) Every Rembrandt portrait expresses its own, distinct value, but this one is a world beyond. Here the master has transformed from *artist* into *teacher,* holding worlds of power in reserve, power so unnecessary that it seems tragic.

The Dutch masters, and Rembrandt most of all, created moist eyes for their portraits and, after a while, as the viewer searches these eyes with increasing depth and openness, his own eyes become this way. We are drawn in. The eyes, mouth, expression—so powerful, so grand, so monumental as to be beyond "teacher," travelling into a realm of presence one might call "real." This artistic expression appears and feels beyond the ego, connected to something universal. Studying this portrait, we can find it all—the personal losses and unbearable tragedy, financial ruin, the arrogance of his youth gone; the trumpeter's widow, the adoration of his students—all there. To study the very eyes and tones that Rembrandt himself had studied is an homage to human perseverance.

Leaving the museum, leaving New York where I had started my career a generation ago, where I took off on a sailing voyage only to return to a dean recommending I get out of the field, where I had wandered endlessly through the museums searching for I have no idea what, I take a master lesson with me as I go. We are broken, some, and we are beyond vulnerable at the same time. As teachers, our impact is determined by the extent to which our students search for meaning in our methods and worldview. Our students' expectations for great teachers expose crack after crack in our goodness, intelligence, competency, and faith, and I thank my students for that. Eventually, as our students become teachers themselves, we cede control of them and our teachings take on lives of their own. This can be frightening or humiliating.

Study the eyes long enough and you will see everything. This is where centuries of students have found themselves drawn in by Rembrandt's ancient message: *We are not the owners of our own wisdom, we are only its recipients. Thought and expression are only real teaching if they can connect us to other generations. Our gratitude for whatever wisdom we manage to discover in our students is our ultimate act of teaching and this fascination, which we call the Socratic Method, is pure art.*

In the end, Rembrandt leaves us with a question, left unanswered now for twice seven generations: could there ever be a greater human aspiration than to be called *teacher?*

2

Digging a Hole

CLINICAL TEACHING ON EXPEDITION IN MEXICO

*As educators and students, what gets us ready to commit to an
endeavor—to a class or study, to a purpose, rather than grazing
half-heartedly through it? What makes us tap into something
larger? What causes us to cast off our timid shadows and engage
fully in life and the largest purposes we can find for it?*

A cherrywood conference table. Fake mahogany desk. Oak and cherry book-shelves stuffed with lesson plan files, books on teaching methodology, and planners. All the things in my classroom are purchased to look businesslike, having no particular origin, selected for their invisible Southern California essence. There are even a few pieces laden with meaning, like the beautiful Hawaiian o'o digging stick and a cherrywood curio cabinet, both excellent decorations, and I admit I'm attached to them. But in the corner is a rough, hand-hewn wooden pickaxe with a pig iron head that does not match anything at all, and if pickaxes could talk, I think this one could offer up some true things about leadership in education.

It was already ten years ago, and since then we've travelled the world building schools and homes and gardens. We've had some colorful journeys, journeys that might lend themselves to teaching stories more easily than the one I am about to relate. But who can say which things will become enduring and rich memories of friendship and which remain mere colorful decorations on the wall? And I have yet to experience any lesson more complete than that one journey to central Mexico where our students' full labors amounted to little more than digging a hole.

Day 1. Anticipatory Set: The First Kiss

We—ten students and three teachers—signed on to a house-building trip to rural, central Mexico. Months of study in Spanish language and culture struck me as superficial preparation. We had looked at the brochures and had a series of student and parent meetings. We were essentially putting ourselves at the mercy of Habitat for Humanity to pave the way for a safe trip, having at best only a vague idea what it was really like down there. The consideration of what matters in the lives of Mexican campesinos was not in our realm of cognition. To tell more truth, we had barely talked to any of the students on a personal or individual level about our trip and I was hardly getting a sense of fire in the belly or burning humanitarian conviction from them. It's not their fault; in fact, it is probably our fault, for making service seem like a stepping-stone to college rather than a genuine act of compassion. The expedition began to unfold in accordance with *best practice* lesson planning.

> *"Clinical teaching" typically breaks each lesson down into five parts to ensure a complete learning experience; so each lesson is a model journey that we move through.*

> *The typical lesson plan breaks the lesson, or journey, down into stages, starting with the development of a sense of anticipation. Wise educators develop an "anticipatory set" for students in order to ensure their readiness for any lesson at hand. For our part, we had students develop proposals defending their rationale for attending this trip, but we got the sense that they "knew the drill"—their proposals were academic and devoid of real anticipation or pathos.*

> *Teachers and students alike can easily confuse anything presented in school with just another required part of the curriculum. The assumption that causes this confusion is simple: "You have no choice if you want to pass, so just sit down and do the work." Or, "You have no choice if you want your pick of colleges." Nobody says these things; they are just understood.*

> *"Why is this lesson important?" we might ask our class in an effort to support a more balanced purpose and a clearer intent.*

> *"Because it's required!" is the presumption on the days when bureaucracy takes over. "Because we are told to do it by the right people."*

Presented this way, the lesson stimulates the anticipation of the most compliant in the room rather than the most genuinely curious.

"Why is this important?" we will ask on a better day. The real teacher will be thinking differently this time. It is important:

"Because I know you will find it beautiful."

"Because it creates change for the better."

"Because it is so funny you will never forget it!"

"It will put food on the table someday."

And for those special ones: "It is a deep and universal truth." "It brings about transformation." At some point, we believe that probably all the best lessons really are journeys; we hope that our students can somehow experience new worlds and that a great lesson is like an expedition. And at this point, we have anticipated such an expedition extremely well.

But where to start? How to start?

The sombreros, burros, craggy mountain passes, and turning, hot southern sun we were envisioning from north of the border vaporized as we got into a real airplane, the first of three. There was no anticipating the storm on our plane's decent into the León City airport on that dark night. Passing through a siege of lightening bursts, it was like finding a forbidden hole in the cosmos— we were all moving into another realm. I welcomed this chaos, capable of creating a common experience to connect our group (so long as we survived).

Now intensifying, the lightning and instantaneous thunder cracked open the sky. As the wings tremored, we knew then for certain that the plane would be engulfed. For any future life beyond that, we could have only gratitude and no further entitlements. Colin, grade nine, normally rendered passive in affect from a computer-gaming addiction, pulled out our brochure from Millard Fuller, founder of Habitat for Humanity, which provided a wider perspective. "Building a solid foundation and a solid house is about the same as building a good life. You are safe from the elements." The plane touched down. No one spoke. We were paying attention now.

It got worse as our cab snaked and wound down rainy streets into the blackness of the gorge called Ciudad de Guanajuato, down through its underground, cloistered streets—this cab could not possibly have had brakes. In the back row of this scene huddled Adam, eleventh grade, round eyes wide and contemplative; Colin, eating snacks compulsively; Alexis, eleventh grade, arms crossed tightly in terror and eternal judgment as we fell down the abyss; and, at last, the cab driver, who cried out in crazed joy, "There's a street in Guanajuato called 'Callejon de Veces,' and it is so narrow you have to kiss to pass by!"

These essential experiences served to prepare us for entry into the new environment far from California's domain, for the sacred or profane. There can be no significant journey, or none I've seen, without a front-end barrier to break through, whether the barrier is wasps, borders with machine guns, one-wheel landings, lost passports, or defiant students. Or the other kind of border, which allows only those with resolution and courage, or those who will gain it, to pass through, to have readiness, and to be game for anything. We arrived at the hotel quieter, more observant. Travis (eleventh grade) translated the "Rules of the Casa Kloster Hotel": "Number four: *No escupar las paredes, ni pisos*" (Travis: "Don't spit on the walls or floors"), and all other rules were off. We peeked out into the plaza. Guanajuato is a European-style, winding-street-filled town with thick, carved doorways and plazas of cobblestone or grass, international students drinking coffee under umbrellas, and always a disco a block away. Our students' anticipation was as thick as the disco crowd.

But now it was very dark, and late, and we assumed everyone was exhausted. The two chaperones and I were relieved to show everyone to their rooms, threaten them with an early start the next day, and go off to sleep.

The students snuck out.

*   *   *

"I couldn't believe so many people were dancing and having such a crazy time and we were out of the United States," said Dennis, twelfth grade, at the bus the next morning. (Dennis would have another crazy time in college the next year, drop out and work for two years, then finally return to college and get on the straight path.)

> *The master lesson does not need to teach a useful skill. It does not need to be any more "relevant," than kissing a pretty girl or listening to ocean waves. Who cares if beauty is relevant or irrelevant! It is beauty. And it*

starts merely with a state of receptivity we call "anticipatory." A lesson clearly and well-anticipated has a chance of becoming a masterpiece.

We mulled over our coffee and cocoa as though last night were a past life and we were trying to find some new presence. Now it was time to raise the big process questions: How will Encinitas, California, behaviors cut it around here? What are you meant to care about down here? What matters? Are we here to meet our needs or theirs? Will Travis get kissed in narrow streets?

It was time to move the lesson along.

Day 2. Beginning the Instruction: Digging

We have come a long way and there are important instructions to give. The next part of our journey or lesson entails getting our students the information they will need to go about their task and achieve their mission. This is the information download, the story. It is the most teacher-, book-, or media-centric part of the lesson. Students need background content to apply later, just as a sculptor needs clay to shape.

Carissa, another chaperone, begins the lesson, detailing that Valle is a city of seven tall church spires surrounded by seven volcanoes capable of engulfing us at any minute. We will have a guided tour. Sunday nights the town singles gather in the large, green town square before the Baroque-style cathedral; she will take us there. The *singlas* (girls) step obediently around the entire square, counterclockwise, while caballeros, all appearing to be twenty-something, walk clockwise in a courtly fashion, like a folk dance. (Or is it that folk dances are like this?) The paisanos love the square like they love Benito Juarez. Every town, if it is a good town, must somehow love something in this way.

It was time to travel to our worksite in San Vicente de Garma. We passed great fields of towering corn and sorghum deep in the country, lush and overgrown, the sprawling, government irrigation infrastructure barely visible—pure observers. A burro-drawn cart passed by, chickens hustled out of a clearing where the road opened up to the farming village, small brick houses lining narrow streets, no cars running. The bus pulled up in front of a walled compound, a classic Central American *finca*, still occupied by the village founders, the Garzas. We stepped out of the bus. It was hot and white in the sun. From there, we passed slowly through tiny dirt alleyways, at last reaching a small, oval compound of five minute homes in various stages of shade under eucalyptus trees and a few oaks.

The settlement, an extended family, was stocked with chickens, a few goats, a couple of cows and a bull, a family of white turkeys, two stables, vegetables growing on vines—all of this rising up out of packed dirt—and a pack of roaming, dark-brown-haired, coffee-skinned kids. The youngest of them, with a Flintstones tee and sleepy eyes, clasped (like a teddy bear) a large box of "SnackWells," Nabisco's sodium-intensive paean to the global corn monocrop. In the picture we took, a burro stands chewing from a pile of corn husks next to a yoke and cart that also served as a slide for the kids. As always, the bass line from a nearby radio pulsed through the air, the lyrics faint: disco punk mariachi.

The students huddled together before fumbling through the entryway to the compound. Inside a dark shack, an aproned, expressionless woman cooked masa over a wood fire. Outside of the worn-out shacks were mainly piles of volcanic rock. The walls consisted of piles of concrete slabs with curtains for doors and windows. Corrugated fiberglass had been thrown overhead to serve as roofs, secured by tires and, on one, an old bicycle, to prevent them from blowing away. Across the enclosure, a new brick house was in progress. "This is our house," said a bowlegged man in Wranglers and a straw cowboy hat, pointing up the narrow compound and piles of brick. The foreman. Our teacher.

Funds donated by our student travelers and the school enabled the purchase of that brick. Had we donated just a bit of it we would not be here, but we had purchased all of it—the price of being allowed to help. Our students wandered in with caution, largely ignored by the laborers but for their brand-new, rawhide work gloves, which suddenly seemed like they were made from Day-Glo. As inconspicuously as possible, the students began to find stray jobs.

Say what you will, but most students are accustomed to being told exactly what do to, and to do nothing until such instruction is given, especially with teachers. Add to this that our group was too culture shocked to say much, and none of the on-site workers or locals said much either. Our students drifted in clusters amongst the native work crew. A couple mixed concrete with shovels right on the dirt, glopping it into the wheelbarrow. One helped the mason. One or two carried bricks to the house. Some were told to start digging a hole in the ground, three meters by three meters by three meters.

The students began to move, slowly, insecurely, remotely, as invisibly as possible, leaving consciousness out of it, entering the new world and the new lesson, passively at first.

Work proceeded with little talk. Sometimes one student or another could find a niche in brick laying, trenching, or wheelbarrow work, but mainly what our volunteers were best qualified for was digging. This freed up the locals to make the intelligent decisions and provide for any task requiring actual skill.

These country laborers and their family members have skills that could easily fetch five dollars a day on the market, when work is available. Grauer School skills, from the most winning soccer player's kick, to the highest student SAT score, to the highest faculty graduate degrees, are not worth mole around here. If intelligence is sensitivity to the environment, we were the least intelligent in the village. Mercifully, the campesinos paid us little mind.

Our morning pace remained slow as the sun got higher. Gabe, eleventh grade, was helping the mason and Alicia stood by or sat on the bench looking fragile, but everyone else was digging in shifts. Spanish teacher and trip translator Carlos, the fittest among us, was pickaxing in the new pit like it was a race. Adam, tenth grade, was at the wheelbarrow removing dirt from the hole and Colin was digging. Noelle (tenth grade, who loved sculpting and all visual arts) was waiting for the chance to mix cement.

When it comes to service, the problem of how to help is not always easy—outside of a few specialty areas that we each have, helping can be frustrating or even, as we would soon learn in Guanajuato, completely humiliating. So it was good to be digging. "What are we digging?" Alicia asked, but no one even cared and the shovels kept slamming into the dirt. The students dug in with muscle and conviction soon followed as we began to make way.

Lunchtime arrived and we gathered around a wooden table. The bright, matte orange of the bricks lying in a pile next to our lunch table did not remind us of the brochures we'd reviewed together. Somehow, all that we had discussed in California had no relation to any of this. The need for our journey was, so far, a presumption created by Habitat for Humanity's glossy brochures. At some point, a student must independently develop his own case for being a humanitarian, in order to construct his own meaning and purpose.

The lesson continued. Carissa explained that if these villagers could get a house with rooms and drainage and didn't need to walk a quarter mile to the nearest water closet, maybe they wouldn't have to deal with squalor every day and they could focus on tending to the fields and market. They would not have to spend their whole lives looking up at a good, self-sufficient life perpetually just slightly out of reach. They could get a leg up on survival and have more time for luxuries like education, packaged food, and even pottery and the arts.

San Vicente de Garma is not that bad off for a place that needs houses. If you join Habitat for Humanity and go to Africa, say, the outskirts of Durban, you are liable to work with families still festering from apartheid days, families who have been forcibly uprooted and relocated. Habitat builds houses for these families who are faced daily with the task of dragging out the family's sewage bucket, digging a hole, dumping it in, and burying it. For many, even a mud hut that doesn't collapse every time it rains would be an upgrade, and a cinder block hut would be Freedom. For some, the poverty line is a dollar and a quarter a day and any formal education at all is a luxury.

"My friend's family was homeless—they spent the night in their car after they lost their lease," says Dennis. Like every global problem, relative poverty exists a walking distance from practically wherever you live in America. At fancy Southern California prep schools in high-end zip codes you can find it. In our affluent, suburban town, long-time Encinitas local Maggie Houlihan, who served on the mayor's task force on housing, commented: "Many North County people live one paycheck away from homelessness." We have learned lessons in homelessness, although we have not learned clearly what we are doing way down here. Our locals can save a lot on plane fare and still fight homelessness. Why did we really come to San Vicente de Garma to serve?

Day 3. Teacher Presents Guided Practice: We Dig, but Need Leadership

In the best lessons, after having his or her say regarding the subject matter, the teacher must guide the students as they practice creating meaning on their own. This is a test of how with-it the teacher can be, and how attuned he or she is to the students. They can create orally, graphically, or physically, so long as it is genuine—the real teacher honors all learning styles. On expedition, a student's worth and achievement is, of course, not judged by a letter grade, but by how useful or helpful the student appears to be in a given situation. More difficult still, student achievement is rarely clearly quantifiable. As a result, this kind of situation can leave some students feeling confused and insecure. Teacher guidance is paramount at this state. Ironically, in the very best of lessons and journeys, our students have no benchmark to determine the worthiness of a venture. The question, "Is this work even significant?" is one they must answer for themselves, even though they are forever asking their teachers to answer it for them.

The idea of initiative, entrepreneurship, attacking open-ended problems, forming purposes beyond those the size of an algebra problem, etc., are all regular topics of conversation between educators and students. Still, we have no one answer for the question "What motivates students?" except our knowledge that some are more internally driven (intrinsically motivated) and other more externally driven (extrinsically motivated).

Why are we striving so? What makes relationships with students matter? What is noble about this work? If you are a teacher and find these questions coming up often, you are in the right profession.

"They say papaya in the morning calms the stomach," someone says, and everyone who needs to believes it.

Down in Mexico, the open markets are set precisely so that the majority of people must pass by them on their way to work each day. Here, a large smoothie with fresh-cut papaya is fifty cents. Early morning in the countryside is a good time. The goats play in the streets, little local children are on their way to school. Donkeys carry their cartloads of fresh greens. Tractors are quietly waiting, ready at the edges of town. It is not too hot.

After two days, our students are digging peacefully. Eventually, they will come to understand that if the campesinos could live above subsistence, their kids could get some education, enough to understand overpopulation, and enough to be able to plan beyond the next crop.

For now, they are digging to deepen their college applications, or because their parents sent them down here so they could be good parents. And they are digging because there were others digging before them and going along with the program is what they are used to. Digging is connecting. On occasion, a few will dig to uncover the poverty or pain of their own, entitled, suburban existence, a cosmic insurance policy. Whatever the reason each had for their digging, it never appeared that day, at least to me. We were like the singlas and cabelleros stepping around the town square on Sunday nights, moving in time to the music, but not yet connected. The digging proceeded slowly.

In any situation where humans work closely for a while, they naturally divide into roles, and so digging dirt eventually became a classifier of identity and, in a crude way, intelligence. Some stayed close around the pit, swapping between the pickaxes and wheelbarrows. Those more independently disposed began making a game of it, exploring every permutation possible given these crude elements for work and achievement.

Inside the old family hut, which would become a stable when the new house was done, the matron stood over a wood stove, an open fire in the back of the hut (a good way to get lung cancer), and the mole vat. A pile of corn lay on the dirt floor by her feet. "Puede la estudiante usted trabajar?" someone muttered in tortured Spanish. "Can a student help you [make lunch]?"

"No."

The matron was honest and she knew our help would be of no help, that we couldn't even get the head off a chicken. If you wanted to help, you could dig. Alicia hovered around the hut, turned back, and reflected with a bored look for a moment over the hole, then turned back and watched the two women remove the roasting chilies from where they worked over the open fire. The women then added the chilies to the mole vat, shook off the soaked corn husks, and began wrapping the chicken and masa. Tomorrow maybe Alicia would be able to help in the kitchen. We dug or watched digging.

The hole grew to one meter deep, forming a nice striation. Then it happened: we hit rock. Adam and Colin attacked the new layer, and then another rotation of diggers, then another—it looked like the end of the line. At last the locals moved in and chipped a large piece of it off: dark-gray, pocked material. Igneous. A couple concerned students were taken aback: this earth was right out of a volcano, one of the volcanoes we could see from town. The next layer might not be so easy.

The campesino foreman and the mason dug a pit around some of the rocks and the students could see the jagged outlines emerging slowly. Eventually, their pickaxes could leverage them out. Once the rock was almost gone, the men handed back the pickaxes and shovels. The day was growing old, though, and the students were ready to knock off by then. It was good for a third day, and the students were stable in their roles. Their guided practice was coming to a successful close.

Sweaty and ever seeking for ways to disturb the system, I mused, "Is there anything college preparatory about this?"

"Not really," Dennis responded, "you have to use up a lot of energy, not just sit in class and do what the teacher says." University of San Diego, University of California, Chapman, and Purdue would receive some of these students in a year.

"Dennis, you're a good guy, but that's weak," I replied, though I was about to be sorry I had.

Like a game ending, the thought of digging this hole all week suddenly resurfaced. "What are we digging?" "Yea, why are we digging," chimed in Alicia, and I knew the game was over as the others' attentions piqued.

"A sump. It's a sump," I explained to downturned faces. Pause. "A sump hole." And I gave it up at last: "We're digging a hole for their toilet to run to. A sewer."

"We're digging a shithole!" Colin lobbed in, wry and grinning.

"We came all the way down here to dig a . . . ?" Dennis paused.

This was beyond humbling. "Okay. Great. I'll tell you what," I said. No quieting the issue any more. "You guys donated around $3,000 each, mainly for bricks, and you traveled 1,500 miles by shuttle, airplane, bus, taxi, another bus, another shuttle, and then a mile on foot to give pretty much all the help you are qualified to give, to do one of mankind's oldest, most basic tasks: digging a shithole. Now you get to figure out what to tell your parents back home. You gonna write that on your college essays?" Dennis's face froze in the "uncool" position and Colin cracked up.

"But for our next trip, I'll have it all lined up for us to save the forests of the world, okay?"

In legend and life a hole is usually bad news. The King James Bible is full of holes:

"And they shall go into the holes of the rocks . . . for fear of the Lord . . . when he ariseth to shake terribly the earth."

Isa. 2:19

". . . he that earneth wages, earneth wages to put it into a bag with holes."

Hag. 1:6

And so it is in the military: "You'll never get rich / by digging a ditch / you're in the Army now!"

It is among our misfortunes that we do not very well distinguish what is important from what sounds important. "But for now, you characters better brush up on your masonry if you want to do more than dig." It was well after noon and our group was fragmenting, tired, and getting ready to go. A gear was shifting. The little girls in their cotton dresses with crosses around their necks smiled shyly at us as we left for the day. The walk out of the village was slow, and we noticed for the first time a horse and some goats and fowl that stood around like communal property. We noticed the women hanging clothes behind the homes. We stopped for a game of pool with some people in a tienda we passed on the way out. A man guided two donkeys as they pulled a wide furrow maker home from the fields.

Day 4. Students' Independent Practice: With the Skinny One in the Sun

The music starts early in the village. Mexican songs from various radios come on, so that the music keeps changing as you walk down the street. Later, once the work had started, the turkeys would start babbling and the bulls their loud protesting. But, for now, it was all peace as the students began their tread up the now familiar camino real, past the finca, past the tiny shops with their dusty, corrugated aluminum doorways just beginning to slide open, through the worn pathways, and to the construction site. Our students are the only teens in the village, the population consisting of men, women, and young children. We have noticed this shortage of teens in many Central and South American villages, although there seemed to be many in the big cities.

The previous night, the students had slept well with no thought of discos. The sun was as round as a burro's paunch and we were on site early, working our hands and backs, swinging the pickaxes. For whatever reason, the students were starting to gain their own sense of direction and leadership. "Good digging," pitched in the always encouraging senior Sara Z., whose college applications would begin to occupy her time just a couple weeks after her return. "We're past the two meter mark." Sara would eventually get her MBA and become an accountant. She peered down into the rich, dark dirt mixed with igneous clumps. As we worked, we began to notice things in the home-stead that must have eluded our initial glance. All about the worn shacks were plants. Plants sat in a hundred different pots, and flowers of every color were blooming, yellow butterflies nervously flitting throughout. We started noticing the pretty dresses of the little ones playing, the innocent faces. Why did it take three days to begin seeing this?

> *At some point, the student's work transcends the teacher's goals and takes on a life of its own. If it does not do this, the work is merely an act of compliance, which is not education but training at best. If the work does get to this level, it can reach a state of full engagement, perhaps even a flow state. On a bad day, all teachers hit rock and will have to forego the achievement of this level of learning, perhaps instead opting for an "Okay, class, time to hit the workbooks." But on a good day, this is as good as it gets. Students collaboratively or independently pursue tasks or learning that has somehow become real to them, tasks that matter.*

The locals had started early and had already dug a huge rock out of our hole, saving us about an hour of labor. The students, ready to dive in, donned the thick gloves, which were now so dirty they blended into the worksite, and silently approached the hole. By now in the pit, the dirt was neither dark nor moist. It was grayish ash, a mixture of black, gray, and white volcanic rubble. A few other students picked up odd jobs around the skeletal house: making the lentil-shaped supports for framing, lifting, and hauling. The more Spanish you could speak, the more you could help. Those who functioned best in the local language moved up the ladder and became our leaders, or at least found work beyond just digging; but we'd all fallen somewhere in the construction lineup, and we were all players now.

North of the border, at least around Southern California, we are encouraged to "think outside the box." By the end of the fourth day, these creative-analytical, box-impaired students, who know fifty ways to avoid cleaning up their room back home, had their simple labors divided into eight or more specialties: pickaxing, shoveling, scraping, bucket removal, wheelbarrow, management, encouragement, evaluation, and more. One person used the axe, another the sledgehammer. A rhythm emerged, too, and time expanded. In this kind of labor, a collective intelligence forms. Adam and Colin, normally at home on their computers, designed an intelligent bucket and pulley system to get dirt out of the deepening hole. (Adam would eventually graduate from Rice University and become an engineer.)

The actual hole was just a story. It was the process of work that mattered now. The students made progress, and by lunchtime the pit looked to be the size of a royal grave, say, Henry VIII.

Past the black layers of earth, then further down into the igneous layer, hunger overtook us by noon, and we washed our hands clean and dry with the gray, ashy earth.

The corn was picked at the edge of the village. For the first time, Noelle was first to the table, no longer balking at the peasant food. They all made short work of a large bucket of roast corn with limes and chili powder. Kids normally grin when they eat corn, that's a cross-cultural universal, and even Alicia, the most skeptical about food, joined in.

We gathered over fresh tamales with rich, gritty, almost chocolaty mole, our students' first mole, the best food in the world on that day, as the neighborhood elders gathered around the hole and sized it up: "Un metro mas." Still one more meter to dig.

Digging is good work, regardless of its purpose. It is a more focused activity than students normally have when managing the almost unbelievably complex multitasking required by college preparation. In digging, everything is focused on something simple, hour after hour. It becomes perfect, like breathing, beyond thought, a pure existence.

A person walks by and you have a choice; maybe you try to ignore them because they are ruining your rhythm. Too late, now ignoring them is the false choice because you have already been interrupted. So you wave good day to the interloper and just resume digging, resume the rhythm. The simple acknowledgment allows you to let the interruption go peacefully. A real digression is a stone in your path. The task takes on a life of its own. Getting each rock out takes on a moral value and is a success, like getting an A, but no grade is really necessary.

As good as digging is, humiliation is a still better experience, as it exposes a crack in our spirits which only humility can fill. We worked hard and, on that fourth day of digging, reached the rock bottom of the socio-economic scale. We are hole-diggers in practice, social class, and aspiration, nothing more. By lunchtime, the children of the little village joined us and they giggled and played at the foot of the benches where we ate. Every student ate the tamales, as though they had somehow connected us through these good times.

We were in it. We were adapted. The campesinos got the radios going strong, the organ pumping to a deep base line. The balladeers and trumpeters laid it on thick:

On Camino de Michoacan

I pass the time with the skinny one in the sun

After lunch, Colin tapped out a couple steps, then a couple others joined in, as Alicia smiled (sort of) and we had a mini dance-work party. The niños danced to the music, longer than we did, and we grinned and clapped and ate until everyone was stuffed.

Before the bullfight of Vinny Castillo-o

Like almost anyone else from Southern California, these students would be hopeless in trying to live off their own harvest as our new amigos did. Not one of our suburban bodies measured up to that of the smallest campesino at this worksite, even those among us who, a week ago, thought we were fit.

For it is better . . . that wayyyyyyyy.

The song ends and with no instructions everyone happily meanders back to resume the work.

The house had taken shape and was almost ready for roofing, and we had become legitimate, if very quiet, community members. Our group felt the strange dignity of being the lowest in the community, the ones who dig.

Day 5. Lesson Closure: We Are Evaluated

As the great theories have it, human development comes in five stages: we have this in Maslow's hierarchy of human needs, Erickson's stages of psychosocial development, Tuckman's stages of small group development, Kübler-Ross's stages of dying. In fact, story plots are also normally broken down into five parts. There are said to be five stages of love. Even rumors of Apple computer product launches are said to come in five waves. The best things come in stages, and every discipline has its own set of them. In every one of these, by the time we reach the last stage of it, whether it is closure or reward, shipping a product, or expressing our gratitude, we have gone through something substantial and we are changed as individuals and as members of a group. No question, the way things end has a dramatic impact on how we process and learn from them.

The owner of the new home was campesino Alfredo Espinoza, a short, leather-skinned, tough-looking rancher in cowboy clothes. Alfredo had more similarities to suburban American parents than differences, despite his farm roots, and despite the fact that his wife, our cook, had lost their male heir in childbirth five years earlier. He loved to laugh, at least during break time. He loved his children and work well done. But Alfredo had one thing we did not have: a worn-to-smoothness, well-balanced, hand-forged pick with a custom handle he had carved for it out of a branch. Now he clasped it and stretched his hand out toward me, handing it over. I felt like he was awarding me my diploma, that this whole rite of passage made me a real teacher.

While we dug, the petty distractions fled. Our group of disparate, occasionally dissonant individual students had gradually become a team, and we, as chaperones, had become real teachers.

Leadership is the synthesis of our collective goals, realized as a culture all its own. If you find a school or organization riddled with competing agendas or egos, complex challenges, or core functionality issues, go dig a hole together. You could save a lot on consulting fees.

At last we were coming to the end of our trip and now, acclimated somewhere between two worlds, I expected reentry would be the hardest part. It often is, because what makes any lesson great is that we have been transformed.

Our students dug down deeper than any grave. They shed impatience, fear, cliquish behaviors, victim mentality, and the ego that gets in the way of humility and tolerance across cultures. They left all of this in the earth that they had dug together, and then we left.

Though the clinical lesson plan has five standard parts, a great lesson also moves through stages of personal and group transformation. In the end, students become a part of some shared task or purpose that transcends the lesson. We had a history, a team where everyone had an identity, a language, a routine—a culture. If you can get that into your classroom, you should have an A+. Better still, the last stage of all good learning and life is a sense of connection to a larger purpose, a great sense of unity and belonging to all creation.

Most of our well-gloved kids will never again have occasion to stand that deep in real earth that they have dug with their own hands. I packed the pickaxe in my suitcase and, luckily, it made it through security and into my office—that was exactly one year after we were attacked on 9/11. But this only makes it more valuable and more artful an object, and I love handling it, pacing across my office when things seem hard and I need to remember what real work is. It probably looks crazy, but the weighting is just right and the shaft has taken on a wonderful luster, even though it is still impregnated with some of the white, igneous dust from way down there.

Miles of red, green, and yellow fields and the surrounding seven active volcanoes humbled our students as they provided the most basic labor on earth. And, in the end, what we all learned about charity, or even about houses or the digging of holes, doesn't seem nearly as important as the lesson, almost too simple for words, that holes need digging.

Guanajuato, Mexico

3

~

Leaving the John Muir Trail

Authentic Leadership in Education

The Real World

Cathedral Peak is a crown jewel for Yosemite climbers, and its ascent is a coveted achievement. Inclining steeper and steeper on the ascent, it is finally reached by scaling nearly straight up a granite spire, then rolling up and over onto a flat top of no more than five by eight feet, a tiny table perched at well over ten thousand feet in the air. According to climbers who have made this ascent—not me—it can be scary up there, especially when it's windy, but the scarier part is that once there, you have to get down. For many, parenting and schooling evoke similar fears.

Though the John Muir Trail passes right by it, Cathedral is far off the trail map. My nieces Sarah and Emily, my daughter Audrey, and I are camped beneath this peak in Tuolumne Meadows, gazing up to the north, ready to set out in the opposite direction.

I am the uncle and parent out here, though I know my teacher self could get drawn in at any time. We head southward along the Tuolumne River, padding on the soft forest floor. As the trail switchbacks, the path turns to igneous stone crunching under our feet. My niece Sarah observes, "Look at the two colors of rock up there," pointing to a gorgeous rock dome from which a giant slab had been sheared off. She has an eye for color, I think. I ask,

31

"Have you been doing much art?" and she replies, "We only needed one arts elective so I took music." I didn't know we were talking about high school—I thought I was asking about life.

No surprise. For young people, learning and even art can seem reduced to mandates supplied by colleges and departments of education rather than processes for the discovery of self, service, and potentials.[1] In English class, the lockstep, five-paragraph essay has substantially replaced the art of wordsmithing—it's writing as a fill-in activity.[2] For the most part, we can largely thank standardized testing for this. This includes a prosperous interest group called the College Board, home of Scholastic Achievement (college placement) Testing, as well as a handful of government contractors providing testing, all of whose existence depends on their ability to rank students in accordance with standards selected for their ease and reliability in grading more than for their proven worth. The College Board has passed one of the most esteemed tests in marketing itself: most parents and a great many educators who use its products presume that they originate from a government regulatory agency, and they typically presume those products to be intrinsically worthy requirements or givens.

Here in California, despite an unbelievably gifted talent pool of teachers and a burgeoning small schools movement, schools keep getting larger—school systems are engineered to bear their own weight rather than operate in accordance with some larger purpose and vision. Small schools, despite having an absence of virtually all social and safety problems associated with mass schooling, are analyzed as too expensive and often viewed as a threat. It is not politically expedient to factor in dramatic increases in graduation rates, academic achievement, teacher and student connectedness, and college placement, or even to consider the dramatic decreases in violence in schools (or "schools within schools") with fewer than four hundred students.[3]

I say to Sarah, "Can you see what I mean about how much art there is up here?" She answers, "Yes, Uncle Stuart, but I'm talking about art class: *real art.*"

With no hint of irony, across the United States parents and students alike routinely refer to two or three thousand students in a gated compound as "the real world." I look up at the mountain and blue sky, the tiny brook winding down with chilly, clear water and would be the first to call it "unreal." Be that as it may, the story of the "comprehensive school," how each generation is creating larger and less personal schools than the one before it, is being documented by educational experts and universities nationwide. Some of these outside experts are wondering what has happened to things like arts education and outdoor education, devalued because they do not lend themselves to quantitative measurement and are not on the SATs.[4] Red tape makes leaving the school or even the classroom hardly worth it for most teachers.[5]

Imagination is similarly limited. Our consolidated schools aspire to a nonexistent spirituality as school boards and teachers bristle to acknowledge that students might be developing such a thing on their watch. "God forbid" someone mentions the "R" word: religion—squabbling over the nuances of man's supremacy in the cosmos is just as prevalent today as it was when Galileo faced the Inquisition.

We pass over a stream channel with ancient boulders softened with thick moss. "The one who meditates on the Divine is like a tree planted by streams of water," Psalm 1 teaches. We are approaching a deep green, covered rise, and I am wondering if a teacher is allowed to enact Psalm 1 in school, if it's legal. "'The world is a sacred vessel,' it's from the Tao Te Ching," I recite to Sarah. Strangely, I know I could get away with that in school. Asian spirituality is still relatively non-threatening. She replies with her normal, wry grin.

Free Falling

Nationwide, the notable College Board (owner of the heavily marketed "AP" label) is lobbying for Advanced Placement engineering exams while interest groups try to nudge education towards vocational training. Turning robust liberal arts learning into narrow, commercial training is not only bad for education, it's also bad for the economy. Those in our society with the highest abstract thinking skills also generate the most income. Abstract thinking is the engine of curiosity and the precursor of entrepreneurship.

Physical education requirements can now be met in many schools by logging into online, Internet-based, independent physical education—a powerful metaphor for an obese rising generation.[6] Physical education is often the first thing cut when budgets are tight. Obesity among Millennial students has reached an all-time historical high with no end in sight.[7]

Rounding a bend while ascending a thick pine forest, we encounter a small group of day hikers and Emily asks the inevitable question: "Are we almost there?" When the hikers tell us, "I'm sorry to say, no," I want to interject: "Yes, you are 'there,' now. And it will not be on the test." We spent months anticipating *being here now*. It seems like few wise men in all of history, in the East or West, have failed to point out that our lives are enriched along the trail, that happiness is not your end but your journey. I say nothing. For now, Emily needs security, and she needs me to prove to her that we are a fixed point on a line on our hiking map. Compared to the wilderness, school's captivity can be comforting. Out here, the air is thin, she is anxious, and chaos theory won't do. Like most kids, she has been taught that education and life occur in predictable, controlled ways, and she is a master at operating within this system.[8] Many students have the sense that they are entitled to this predictability, life owes it to them. We keep noticing back at our school how Millennial generation teachers and teacher applicants have a sense of purpose which is mainly attached to getting the feedback they want from supervisors, rather than having a goal of patiently initiating or producing work which allows them to prosper. I keep wondering if feedback has replaced real results or achievements for millions of "dialed in" students.

I don't blame the Millennials: it must be discouraging to think you will be judged by what you produce rather than by who you are or who you are becoming. But this is the system many of our teachers experienced when attending high school, this is the way they were able to get into college, and these are the paths they were convinced they needed to pursue for success in college. Success and failure are often tied to compliance with teacher guidelines. Our students are taught to value feedback more than worthiness, or to equate the two. Once class size reaches around fifteen or more, we can no longer engage each of our students in a true conversation. Because it becomes difficult to assess students on a personal level at this size, teacher guidelines are selected largely for their ability to be reliably quantified rather than for their larger worth. How strange that this completely reverses when college is over, especially in any professional or creative endeavor.

Something we must treasure about being young is the opportunity to try out pathways and pastimes where we might get lost, and to still have plenty of time to find a truer calling—to develop our core. This is a part of childhood now being "left behind." My nieces Sarah and Emily are products of a fine East Coast school and the contemporary, prevalent objectives in education: the information download, G.P.A., class rank, and all the strategies students use to replace real, messy values development with a "college resume." Millennial students learn to avoid risks, take classes to please others rather than to honor their curiosity, and to write formulaic essays that follow the same format, nation-wide—the same ones admissions officers and paid readers of standardized essay tests are trained to recognize as acceptable.[9] The same ones that can be computer graded. Writing becomes a closed system. In learning all of this, students pay a price: diminishment of right-brain values like respect for nature, oral traditions, and spiritual education. What's left is a narrow trail for the imagination to adhere to. Straying is defined as a mistake.

We reach a wide stream, it must be the Lyell Fork, and we realize: crisis! We are two miles off the trail. After an hour and a half of hiking, we're barely closer to the top than when we started. And it's my fault. My leadership is such that people have followed blindly. I should have warned them that they'd need their own minds and maps. Now I am imagining a school where the final exam for graduating high school seniors would be the Milgram experiment. Imagine!

For much of my career as a teacher, I tried carefully to carry students along with me like a comedian working an audience and to eliminate risk like most teachers and parents do. Here at the Lyell Fork, I realize that no matter how far we carry our students, when we put them down again they are not a step farther along than when we first picked them up. "You cannot teach a man anything; you can only help him find it within himself," Galileo mentioned four hundred years ago. Socrates was given hemlock for saying almost the same thing.[10] Galileo, of course, was brought before the Inquisition. Still today it is clear that our educational institutions are deeply threatened by the same notions, although now our institutions claim it is for financial reasons—how can they accommodate open inquiry in classes of thirty-five?

Creating leaders means students, parents, and teachers all must stay continually responsive to new and ongoing challenges. It means approaching life so that a roadmap never replaces intuition. It means honoring students who espouse or demonstrate non-curricular, off-trail skills that will endure: meta-values that remain true in changing conditions. What are those values? What is ending up in the spiritual backpack of our kids? How does it get there? Keeping these questions alive is more important than answering them.

Emily's ticked off. "We're lost, but we're making good progress," I suggest, from the famous Yogi Berra quote. Not funny. Staying on the trail was supposed to be a given, and Emily was expecting to be led. I was the guru! Now, doubling back, taking stock in our slow progress, I watch her go through stages from ignoring the reality of our helplessness, to frustration and blame at being lost, to anger at having wasted time and energy. Why should she have to do this extra hiking! She's an honors, advanced placement student. She has been shown only straight-line challenges, taught that anything off that set path is a waste.

But she sucks it up. About an hour later, at last, we can see Emily's new-found resolution and strength. She'll be damned before staying off-trail. Any sign of her earlier high altitude symptoms are long gone. The non-system works. Emily looks focused now, more fully aware, broader shouldered, and it's obvious that her twenty-five pound pack is nothing as she takes the lead bounding up to the higher ground. By mile eleven she's practically running up the trail, leading the way. I start shooting photos to cover for the fact that I am falling behind. And, as the now proverbial Gandhi saying goes, "There go my people. I must follow them, for I am their leader."

I received a letter recently from a high school alumnus of mine on the occasion of her graduation from college after ten long years. She told me this story:

> I've always wanted to work in the veterinary field and was always told I couldn't. Why? Because math was too difficult and I had trouble focusing and learning. For many of my college professors, if you couldn't keep up, give up. If it seemed impossible it must be.
>
> Life in academics is still difficult and will always be more of a struggle for me than for other people. That's fine. I will not be defined by those things that come easily to me. My strengths come from struggle and hardship. I am not an A student, but I have the qualities that come only from fighting in the face of failure. I will stand where A-students fail.

Isak Dinesen (*Out of Africa*) is quoted as saying, "To be a person is to have a story to tell." Today, school heads worry for students and parents who feel they must not struggle or experience failure, people who think false summits and changing circumstances are "unfair" and that school ought to be a standard thing. Dealing with complexity, such as our country will be seeing a lot more of, will require a way of leading that keeps us continually responsive to rising challenges and less control over situations.

In a case only existentialists could love, my buddy Dave, a retired cop, was once sued for failing to stop a man from jumping off the Coronado Bridge and into the infinite. Like *The Catcher in the Rye*, the idea is that we are bound to catch children before they fall, something we all want to do, but which we know all along makes no sense. Kids have to fall, and the world is filled with bridges and cliffs. And they must get lost, even though it can be terrifying. A great many families feel they cannot afford to risk allowing real life experiences. Instead, they over-program. They have to build a course straight to that college resume—no veering. We've all seen these resumes: nine after-school clubs, a dozen APs, and zero open space. And many feel that their children never deserve to fail, or they fear that their children can't handle it.[11] Could it be that Dave did not have the fearfulness required of a policeman?

On average, successful people have had many more failures than unsuccessful people. These failures form the well that makes victory taste so sweet. We now know that perseverance can be taught, but it rarely is. Natural talent is a wonderful gift, but determination, willpower, and desire far transcend this in the making of a successful path through life, or the catching of a brook trout at Vogelsang Lake—something I have failed to do. Success is also when you take the wrong fork in the road and remain open to that experience and consider it to be a bonus discovery. America!

A Transformational Teacher

Climbing higher, we observe a large, dead lodgepole pine. Rather than growing straight up, the grain of this tree spirals around and around all the way to the top to give it strength. Ahead, a gigantic half-dome is reflected perfectly in a high mountain lake so that you can hardly tell which is real. This is arts education!

A field of purple fire grass runs in lanes that curve and crisscross in hypnotic patterns, moving purposefully, beyond the realm of chance. These patterns in nature are the basis of all human arts and they spiral into human interactions that have fascinated people forever. We seek out such patterns because we can rest our minds on the idea of serendipity: things collaborating beyond reason or human intervention. Peace is a natural state. Beauty is "the smile of God," John Muir said. The arts teach a full spectrum of skills covered haphazardly at best in the rest of the curriculum (e.g., visual-spatial abilities, reflection, self-criticism, and the willingness to experiment and learn from mistakes). Even as art is cut from many school budgets, we must make a place for it in every class, in every grade, and in every school.

In nature, young people get lost in patterns of laughter and group formation—they may find the self which lies beyond structure and rules, the self that connects to something larger. Every successful teacher knows that when they sense this happening, it is the best day they can possibly have. Muir said: "Presently you lose consciousness of your own existence: you blend with the landscape and become part and parcel of nature . . ." It can be in a great conversation in English class or a math challenge that stimulates everyone, but it transcends the individuals in the room and engages them in a sense of the whole.

Our successes come when we are able to create coherent connections among diverse life events—our lives form patterns of meaning and make sense across all disciplines, across groups. "When we try to pick out anything by itself, we find it hitched to everything else in the universe." I wish I had said that, but John Muir did. Making this shift, from results to process, has been the advice of many leaders. And still we can go further, beyond process, beyond the journey, to the source of our lives, the core—something beyond all learning and rules, some essential underlying unity.

This is the part of the work where educators become educational artists if we let them, the work of transformation. Elliot Eisner argues "that the distinctive forms of thinking needed to create artistically crafted work are relevant not only to what students do, they are relevant to virtually all aspects of what we do, from the design of curricula, to the practice of teaching, to the features of the environment in which students and teachers live."[12] Can we teach students to make and to trust these connections, to draw from this source? Can we teach our teachers to give that an A? Can we get Sarah a teacher like that? Down the trail or off the map, things could get rough; students might need a core like this.

Fearless Listening

As an emotion, fear can only occur if accompanied by a larger sense of isolation. United States Department of Education goals in the early part of the millennium stressed hanging on to a national supremacy while events like ongoing wars, homeland security, and the depletion of our national treasury introduced fear and isolation into the spirit of many families trying to stay ahead and provide opportunity for their children. Fear has become an unspoken shadow in my community as in our nation. Fear leads us to narrow our vision and to tighten our grip on those things we feel we can bank on: class rankings, prestige "name" colleges, inflexibility in a hurried curriculum, efforts to control life, and outcomes that look good on paper. Well-meaning students feel pressured to tailor their passions in accordance with what clubs and services will look good on applications while college admissions officers at once decry and reward this all. Lives become resumes.

We hike to a path around a lake to a series of two waterfalls where Sarah and Emily rest. Audrey and I scramble up some boulders to some brush. We detect an animal track. Bushwhacking through the brush off the trail, we cross a shallow stream, then begin following a curved path at the foot of a rock cliff. Following the bend, an astonishing, hidden, three-waterfall canyon is before us, completely off the trail map.

Looking up above these falls, we know that yet another mountain lake lies above them, and we smile: we have left the John Muir Trail again, but this time we are not lost: we have chosen to leave.

Leaving the trail means courage and faith in our connection to larger things (the opposite of fear and isolation). Off-trail is where the discoveries lie. Fearlessness in educational programming is no trivial challenge in our nation today. In Latin, heart and courage are the same. Going forward, fearlessness will mean parents and counselors encouraging their students to choose courses from the heart, not their preconceptions, and not out of their concept of the fastest, safest way to get their schooling over with. Fearlessness on the student's part will mean acceptance that authentic education has no prescribed path, that it doesn't necessarily even have any end. This is a future we will have to discover or invent. Even if you do reach the top of your mountain, you can't stay there, and why would you want to? At some point, you have to come down.

A fearless schooling and college preparation is more like a wilderness trip than the fifty-yard dash students often expect it to be. The fearless teacher is one who seizes the time to engage and understand the minds of his students at the risk of taking up other mandates, including competing job duties, one who insists on creating a learning environment where this is possible again. In *Courage: Its Nature and Development* Nelson Goud makes the case for fearlessness as catalyst for growth. Goud asserts "courage allows one to effectively act under conditions of danger, fear, and risk. Without courage, the individual or group remains stuck in existing patterns or immobilized in fear."[13]

Teachers and administrators grasping this are willing to make room for curiosity and openness to discovery over the course of a year, to quit the great textbook race. The great homework race every night is squeezing out time to explore and to relate to one another, and we can reclaim this time, too. Educational fears come when we feel attached to what used to be, or what we believe it must be, regardless of our students, and we can let go of these attachments—without falling off the edge. We can do better. Openness to deep dialog and the formation of authentic relationships between teachers and students has been the way of the great teachers before us, the teachers who have modeled courage and patience.[14] We can call it the John Muir path of education.

We all hear frustrated principals saying, "There are so many problems. We need to change everything, now!" And school critics agree. They are hanging off the edge of Cathedral Peak, and prayer is not allowed. Perhaps there is a way for each of us, on our own, to leave the trail a bit, leave the rhetoric and the research findings, leave the curricular mandates, leave the "prestige" college selections, leave the race, even though there is never really time in the day, and just listen to a student as though that were all the radical-structural paradigm shift we need. Just really listen to a student as though he or she were a force of nature, the only force of nature we ever need to harness.

We are at last in our van, traveling down the mountain, losing elevation fast, heading home nearly speechless as we watch the magnificence of the week slip away like a dream. We understand how this wilderness is at risk now. What once was permanent is now changing, and what was changeable and progressive about our American education now seems entrenched. The girls plug in a DVD where a family is winding through the western United States in a van. Emily muses, "Isn't this ironic, I'm leaving for NYU in three weeks and now I've fallen in love with the mountains." Sarah and Audrey are lost in the video, people clowning it up on a road trip, and I'm looking down the road at eight hours of driving and re-entry, the hardest part. Back on the coast, school starts Monday.

Yosemite, California; Encinitas, California

4

⁓

Hostile Indians Attack Schoolhouse

"Tribal" Education, in Twelve Parts

Finding a Teacher

The cell phone text message displayed: "Spearfish, South Dakota." At first, I had no idea, but it sounded like an unlikely place for spearfish. It had to be a harbinger. "Are you coming?"

As usual, the trip started out alone. But this one grew from a journey alone into one with larger confederacies, then larger and larger as smaller things connected to bigger things, in the end devolving back into a solitary journey. There is a heritage of learning alone everywhere, but for sure up there in South Dakota. In the old days among the Lakota (outdated name: "Sioux Indians"), the people would sit alone in nature for three or four days with no food or water and await a vision. Some still do this.

There was always wind and it was both cool and warm. First there was foreign noise, then it went away or ceased to matter along with all hint or threat of disturbance. Maybe animals. Horses' hooves. Maybe wind shushing the aspen leaves. Water trickling. The unlimited sky a source of opening, the earth for grounding, the four directions. There was time, and then it meant nothing. Slow or fast, like two different colors, but eventually there was no longer even a metaphor, and then a person could be what the revered teacher and warrior Crazy Horse called "a real person."

Now we are ready. Here is a story about a "real teacher."

I had met Roger White Eyes on the Pine Ridge Indian Reservation. Our students were there on exchange and it soon became evident that here was a teacher who warranted further study. It was at the Red Cloud Indian School, which opened in 1888 with a hundred kids, some stripped from their families. The Red Cloud High School is private and tribe-sized (220 students), now charging $100 a year in tuition to attend, although some students receive full scholarships. Roger was one of those rare ones whose spirituality converges genuinely with their life path, and so I came to recognize and trust him as a teacher.

Shortly after we arrived at Red Cloud, he gathered us all together by the school lodge along with his students. We formed a group of about fourteen, a good-sized group. Around the lodge was a cottonwood grove, leaves rustling and rattling a gentle song. (Right around here a couple months earlier, for Healthy Choices Week, the high school students had taken part in the butchering of a buffalo as their ancestors had, including prayers of sacrifice.) The sweat lodge ceremony is centuries old and, like the vision quest, one of seven sacred rites the Lakota pass along through the generations, even through generations where it has been illegal.[1] Roger's version of the ceremony was assisted by some of his students, along with a Jesuit missionary teacher, who had tended hot rocks over coals all afternoon. We moved through the west-facing door of the lodge, which consisted of a low dome of red willow branches covered with many canvasses. Each of us was anxious to a different extent. I was in the moderate range. Now Roger's helpers, tending the fire with shovels and pitchforks, began carrying the white-hot stones into the tent-like *inipi*, dropping them into the center pit with a rasping thud. "We sweat to become pure," Roger explained, along with some Lakota language prayer, pouring water onto the rocks, unwrapping the long, wood-stemmed pipe, placing the sacred, sweet-scented tobacco into the red-stone bowl, and then flicking the lighter. "For thirty-seven years every sacred man I have known lights the pipe with a Bic." Always this blend of old and new, sacred and facetious. And, with prayer sung in the native Lakota language, we learned of *"Mitakuye Oyasin."*

*"Mitakuye Oyasin! You are part of everything! . . . and you are related
to everything . . . Everything is sacred and, therefore, you are sacred too.
That's what we mean when we say 'Mitakuye Oyasin.'"*

—*Wallace Black Elk, Lakota Spiritual Elder*

We passed the pipe around. I had not smoked with students before. I had
no sacred rites to pass along to my students, either, although we had recently
come up with some shared values in a strategic plan. I tried not to assume I
understood this outlook, at least the depth of it, so that I could learn. I knew
some of the history already: the loss of land rights and language, the mass
murder. I had almost been embarrassed to travel there, to face them all coming from our affluence; Pine Ridge is the very poorest part of our nation.

Roger focused on *Mitakuye Oyasin* (pronounced: *Me-talk-coo-ya Oy-ya-
see*, but the best I could ever come up with was more like *Mitoc-we ossin*): "We
are all related." I thought, if this were the only credo of every school in the
nation, or the world, we would need no strategic plans.

The lodge was almost unbelievably hot. Our role was to persevere, which
I did by taking long, slow breaths, longer and slower, and believing it would
all be over if I kept doing that. I trusted he would not risk killing me; I could
barely breathe. Breath. Short. Relax. I knew many people had done this, and
the locals were reluctant to even leave the "embracing womb." I started conjuring excuses to leave, but successfully overcame each one with the next,
slow breath. When each in the fire circle had said the final *Mitakuye Oyasin*,
I was relieved. "This ends our mass, go in peace," Roger announced at last,
nuancing the long-merged Lakota and Catholic faiths with a little slab of
irreverence—you could see why the students trusted him, as I did. I tend to
seek out humor that can pose for serious truth, and so I sensed an unexpected
connection with this man, Roger White Eyes, a seven-eighths blood Lakota
high school teacher, who was about to send thunder into my life—a power
any teacher would want.

An Invitation

My students had not traveled to Pine Ridge in order to visit a broken people
(as, to some extent, I may have), they were there to meet people of a long and
noble heritage who had endured the unthinkable. This heritage was, for me,

Roger's credential, along with his humor; presently, I realized that he was the real teacher I would be studying with.

We exited the lodge, purified and quiet. The sweat lodge ceremony normally concludes with a group evening meal where, since olden times, the ancient legends have been shared. And so we convened in the community hall. There was Roger, a cup of bug juice in hand and a mixed grin. I was careful. The traditions, the loss of traditions, genocide, forced schooling, disease, ethnic cleansing, humiliation and hatred, and now the delicate balance of reviving traditions. I had to wonder what Roger would see in me, coming up here from Southern California. How and why could he conceivably trust me? Could a sweat lodge bring us answers?

Just the night before departing I had attended an art opening. I was having a glass of wine when a well-intentioned school parent approached me, showing interest in our Pine Ridge trip, and noted: "I have heard that Native people actually still exist."

"I will find out for you," I had responded, not knowing where to begin introducing this wounded world so removed from the minds of most Americans.

"What should I tell her," I asked Roger. This time the grin was pure. He talked of the courses he taught in Native song and drum, of Lakota language and spirituality classes coming back into the schools, and about his daughter who had just received a Gates Foundation full tuition and expenses paid scholarship to Dartmouth. I asked him if I could interview him a little more as part of my study of real teachers, and his grin said, "Where do I even begin?" I knew it could never be a traditional interview.

Roger's tee shirt featured a huge dream catcher logo that said, "Wounded Knee Memorial Motorcycle Ride." Every August, he and the Lakota tribal riders, along with riders from the other Sioux reservations (mostly Rosebud, Cheyenne, and Standing Rock), rode nearly a thousand miles through three reservations up to Fort Yates, North Dakota, and back down to the memorial at the Wounded Knee burial site, the site of that terrible, terrible massacre. There they honored the dead and the heritage of their ancestors. As we were leaving that night, Roger said, "If you want to learn more, go on the ride with us this August." It was, of course, a preposterous offer, but it would be fun to joke about.

Next, I met the esteemed Ben, a tall, straight-backed emeritus teacher with gray hair and eyes, leathery, chestnut skin, and wide cheekbones. When

I am on the road meeting new people, I normally get quickly to the topic of education, and before long Ben was detailing to me how, in his parents' generation, the kids were taken from their homes and brought to boarding schools; how they were whipped if they spoke native language instead of English. I left feeling anxious .that perhaps he had disclosed too much and might regret it later.

The next day we convened for our student forum. Lakota and Southern California kids together in a circle—kids from the lowest income zip code in the nation, and kids from one of the wealthiest. We did not have a clear vision of how the kids would mix, or even why. Rod, our trail guide the day before, had warned us that the new generation of Indian kids was no good. Drugs, alcohol, violence, truancy, and hostility. The older generation was discouraged by them. They were communing with bad spirits and disconnected from the sacred teachings. "A bunch of war hoops," he called them. I thought Rod was a jerk. I would find great teachers and a way to honor them, and I would find some light and hope. "Roger, I want our kids to meet and share something deep. I want the questions to be big enough to mean something to all of them." I had been thinking about questions for this forum for a couple months by then and was still feeling insecure. "I don't want to have another superficial forum where everyone goes around in a circle and states their two-sentence, meaningless bio and their favorite rock band." It was tough. Many of our kids were defining themselves by the products they bought or by their tee shirts. Was that true "on the rez?"

I proposed some possible "big questions" to Roger and his colleagues: "What do you want to learn from your grandparents?" Or, "If you got a college education, would you leave your hometown?" "Who are your heroes?" Not even a half-smile. The assistant principal and student council advisor looked at each other and said nothing. I was in left field. At last Roger said, "Ask them why they keep killing themselves."

I looked into Roger's eyes and could not even begin to read them. We had our student forum and it was pleasant. We left. A few months passed and I remained overwhelmed by Roger's comment. Fourteen Pine Ridge kids had taken their own lives over that past year. I had almost no prior, first-hand access to matters like this. The deepest human emotions were hidden from my life, but up on the reservation they were a part of the daily routine and had been for generations.

Tribal Ways

It was a time when our country's secondary schools could have used a little thunder in them, and during my first trip to Pine Ridge, I got the idea that tribal formations could be a source of special understanding in schools, in the way communities work, the way groups and classes form. The concept of tribes. Like most educators, I was looking for ways to understand how to make life in school and in the classroom authentic and connected.

The ideas I was seeing in research journals and conferences taught more about how we needed a culture change in the schools as organizations, much of it recycled and relabeled, while almost no real change was going on. The things policy makers and researchers were calling change were not change, and everyone knew it, or at least knew the shadow of stagnancy was there. To be honest, reading education journals started to feel like buying toothpaste—everything was a new and improved version of the same thing. Less homework—different homework. Less technology—different technology. More critical thinking—different critical thinking. More standards—even more standards. More like Asian schools—more like Northern European. Class sizes too big—class size reductions that still leave classes too big for great conversations. Even the small schools were big and getting bigger.

In article after article, for those who might care to check, these journals and educational researchers, almost across the board, were treating the schools and the whole of education as machines where passion, longing, and spirit played, but only as discursive afterthoughts. Uniformity seemed to be taken for granted as a core purpose of life. And the machines kept getting bigger and bigger. Nationwide standardized testing companies were having record financial years while across the nation school districts were getting deeper in debt. Brilliant and esteemed professors and scholars capable of sophisticated research and analysis seemed to have no concern for how deeply ensconced they were in the system they were claiming to change, and real long-term change might have been the last thing many really wanted. It could put them out of business, the very business they claimed was tanking anyway.

System change did not mean system change at all; it meant making the current system larger, harder, and more efficient. Where could we have a look at something different, an anthropological look through a wider lens? A random cut of text slashed out of one of the many journals I was following read: "Nothing builds trust better than seeing student improvement after data discussions." So this is what had become of trust! I wondered about replacing "data discussions" with "sweat lodges." I could slash out a thousand of these statements that were predominating in the educational literature. With due respect, I wanted out, I did not want to join this nation I felt we were headed for. People talked a lot about their out-of-the-box thinking—in those new millennial days, it seemed like people thought that talking about out-of-the-box thinking was the same as taking real out-of-the-box action. Well, here was a chance for some action, live from Spearfish.

Back home, a few of us who were troubled by the one hundred years of increasingly large school bureaucracies and class sizes had founded a new professional association to research and advance the understanding of small schools, a "small schools movement," but there was not a lot of research to go off of yet. Nor was there much optimism to be found. Native American and minority communities had spent decades dealing with, or shrugging their shoulders about, overcrowding, conditions of chronically underfunded educational programs, and a lack of adequate school facilities, not to mention school violence, high drop-out rates, unplanned teen pregnancy, and a whole lot more. They had not had it easy but I trusted, sans *data discussion*, that the Lakota had wisdom to share within their own culture about how they had sustained themselves all those years, how they persevered against impossible odds.

And there was strange new intelligence coming in: suddenly, in this new millennium, across our land, it seemed like people from more than just minorities were seeking a larger wisdom, and that a shift was underway in the country, both economically and socially. The predominance and wealth of Main Street America and its leaders no longer seemed so assured, and trust in our largest institutions and mega-schools was disintegrating. Problems no longer seemed so confined to inner cities and reservations. Everywhere I travelled, people wanted to talk about their dread over the state of the nation and its schools. The things I was hearing from people on airplanes and in the surf, from teachers in classrooms, and parents at the dinner table not only espoused different values than what I was reading about in the journals, it was incongruous. The reason for this incongruity was simple: the systems which educators were espousing had nothing to do with the formation of genuine student-teacher relationships—they came from people "outside." Systems are no substitute for relationships and they can even prevent them. A tribe may have its customs and "laws"—codes for spirit, survival, and respect for chief and family—but codes like these have evolved around the way people lived. This code heritage is alive in Native American culture; it is not an instantiation of external state demands.[2] Up in Pine Ridge, the Red Cloud School was advancing, refining its almost-lost cultural practices. Likewise, small schools were quietly advancing.

I had read *Tribal Leadership: Leveraging Natural Groups to Build a Thriving Organization*, the best seller backed by massive organizational research, which states, "Every company, indeed, every organization, is a *tribe*, or if it's large enough, a network of tribes." It was a wonderful book, part of a proliferation of the term and concept "tribal," which was sweeping the country's think tanks and infusing corporate leadership development. But the Lakota are descended from a tribal heritage deeper than we could find in any organization in the country. I made an assumption that the Lakota elders had not consulted that book. To me, the study of tribe formation and tribal leadership made much less sense without some understanding of American Indians, their bond with the land, and their sense of place. It matched up with the hints of the farm-to-table movement just showing up in a smattering of schools. Didn't Native Americans practically invent the modern concept of the tribe in America? For comparison's sake, let us ask whether we could legitimately study Christian values while disregarding their origins in the life of Jesus and his twelve Apostles. For learning about *tribal leadership*, Pine Ridge could be command central.

The Indian tribal ways and spirit have been harshly tested through what their tee shirts call "500 years of genocide." Punishment can make the spirit of a culture grow stronger, though. Sometimes spirit is almost all that is left to survive. Tales and allegories told by the Lakota elders enabled their culture to persevere through hard times because the culture was carried within them.[3] It is true, the replacement and merging of tribal values and traditions with Western and Christian ones is a complex and evolved story. But even during several generations of total Indian subjugation, the tribal way of life lived tenaciously underground and even strengthened in some respects, in spirit. Then, in 1978, the U.S. government at last officially acknowledged in coded law that the Native Americans could openly practice their own spirituality again, and the Bureau of Indian Affairs school indoctrination program ended. The survival of the traditional values my students and I engaged with on the reservation is a testament to one of the greatest stories of human perseverance I know. And while people in my generation find 1978 to be shockingly recent, too little time to completely re-form a heritage, from the perspective of my 2011 Millennial students, the Lakota tribal culture was the norm.

Surely the Lakota knew things about bravery, sacrifice, fortitude, and respect for elders that we could learn from, that we would need in schools, and that we would finally be thankful to them for—there hadn't been many thanks since the Pilgrims received the gift of corn on the first Thanksgiving. It would turn out that they did. I had to go to some extremes to access it, though.

Metal Horse Rider

Our own small schools research trudged along that winter and had not yet advanced much. We made a bleak study of how two major funding groups had abandoned small schools research in favor of working with larger, sometimes even global systems. We thought: that's not how the world changes. The world changes when local communities take action, when regular people take the future into their own hands. The world changes when real people share real, common experiences. Fear, loss, a sense of "no way out"—these deepest emotions only deepen when people lose control of their schools and communities. These were the conditions with which the Lakota had a profound history, and which they were now rejoining. I thought the Lakota return to community—to local experience and shared values—would pay off and that even our public schools could learn from it. Across the country, as the young millennium began to unfold, there was no denying the spread of this longing to reconnect schools with local communities.

When the text message came in, lighting up "Spearfish," I could not ignore it: I had to ride with Roger. I gave myself permission to cast off fears and to trust in intuition. I did not know what I would learn about small schools, had no hypothesis, and I had a feeling our research would be received as marginal, a poor target for research funders. Somehow, for me, this all added to the draw. We were like the Indians of the educational research world, *indie educators*. It was decided: our next research study for our small schools association would be on real tribal ways. I would head back to the Pine Ridge Indian Reservation, home of the Lakota and legendary site of Wounded Knee.

No matter that the idea was preposterous; it was one of those rare windows into learning and insight which an educator must look into. Once committed to the ride, the realities came rolling in. I had not ridden for four decades and even then rather quietly. My own mother, reading this detail, will now learn of it for the first time—I never drove it home. It was a Triumph 650. Classic. *Bad.* But the new generation of bikes was gigantic by comparison. Virtually all the Wounded Knee riders would be on Harleys, full-on hogs, twice the power of the bike of my college days. And these were serious riders. Who was I kidding? This, from an email:

> *Stuart, when I was about eleven years old my dad bought me my first motorcycle but I was riding horses before that. When I was a teenager I used to ride bulls in the rodeo. I can remember when we would use our motorcycles to chase the horses into the corral to round them up.—Roger*

Plains Indians were spirit partners of wild ponies and they became legendary horsemen. Wild horses had been taken from the range as it was divided up with barbed wire and roads and Indian reservations but, at least from a spiritual sense, the Indians had managed to replace it with something as American as mustangs: the Harley Davidson motorcycle. In Roger's case, the *Electra Glide* model. In a later email from Roger:

> *Maza Shunka Wakan was a name given by some elders in Eagle Butte when they referred to the Motorcycle . . . Translated = Iron Horse . . . that is one Lakota name I heard given for our bikes.*

The Lakota riders could ride the plains like rolling thunder on metal horses, and they rode hard. When I applied for a motorcycle license, various people close to me wanted to know why I was killing myself. I told everyone the truth: it was a good time for me to find myself a new teacher.

Solitude

Sometimes, as Wordsworth noted, "The world is too much with us." It is time to go solo. Arriving at Black Hills Harley, the agent showed me my ride, a 1,200 cubic centimeter engine Harley Softail model, a formidable, powerful machine. It looked gigantic. I weighed only 150 pounds—what if it fell on me? My uncle had needed skin grafts. Any mishap could be a financial disaster. What have I done? The reality—the gravity—of the situation was creeping up on me as I pressed the ignition and heard the first rumble, and I made a vow that if I completed the trip, if the bike and I returned safely in one piece, I would kiss the ground here, back at Black Hills Harley. And yet, this metal horse was beautiful and elegant, a wonder of nature. Before long, I had stuffed the saddlebags, pulled on my riding leathers, and was headed down the highway, slowly, eyes darting everywhere at once, pulling into side roads to test out my figure eights. I was hesitant, but the response to the throttle, the rising pitch of the engine accelerating, the power of third gear, then fourth, did not take long to start working its spell on me.

As a teacher and school evaluator, I have made many trips alone, and it is a learning mode easily overlooked in an overcrowded, standardized world. Such trips can range from the most terrifying to the most meditative. Solo riding is, of course, covered in enormous depth in *Zen and the Art of Motorcycle Maintenance* (although Pirsig actually had his son with him). Meditating, walking, writing, dreaming—these are all one person schools. Getting help when none seems possible or available has prompted many of my own, most-valued and hard-won discoveries. Being up the creek. Facing fear and uncertainty. These are undeniable parts of being alone. Fighting that pit inside, which always seems buried somewhere you can't really reach it, trying again and again to reach it and overcome it. Like an enemy, you befriend fear so it will no longer have the same power over you.

If school could have given me the time or technique to do this, if I could then give that to my students, if teachers and schools could employ this profound learning configuration . . . I have learned to be grateful for those times when I can come in direct contact with fear, even when it is terrifying, because of its ability to provide a rare instance of mental and physical convergence: we can no longer tell our mind from our body, and there seems to be some essence beneath it all. The teacher who could show us how to reach and really engage this essence, this source of fear, this profound call to live—this invitation to a place of real transformation—would be a real teacher. This could be the greatest challenge of all for teachers, as schools do their best to remove any possibility for fear or risk from daily life.

There are barriers of entry when soloing to reach anywhere significant. This seems especially true whenever you are heading somewhere extraordinary.

Some cultures have rite of passage ceremonies that even celebrate and honor these challenges which we can only pass through alone, such as the vision quest. But more often, we cannot predict or fathom what those barriers will be, what nature will throw out in our path. For those who no longer have such passages left in their lives, they will still have death. For the meantime, I preferred to challenge myself with possibility. So, there are always these barriers and sometimes you, too, want to turn around and just be home or be mediocre or avoid dealing with it all. If you are lucky, this will not be a realistic option. Often at the threshold of these barriers, you think things are terrible or lost; you may want to panic, and the truth is impossible to see at first. And at those points, when you get into another terrible jam, you may have to stop, step back, breathe, and recognize this passage point—even embrace the situation—to allow some time for acceptance. Sometimes you may even need to start all over; but you cannot expect to see that in the first moment.

*   *   *

After an hour and a half, I arrived in Pine Ridge to meet the riders. The opening sweat lodge ceremony for the Lakota riders, conducted by Roger, was the convening of the Memorial Ride, the tribe. We approached the grove of the lodge, muggy drizzle now lapping the cottonwoods, and the sky was turning steely as the Lakota riders stripped down for the sweat. Once again it was unbearably hot for a suburban Californian. I cannot say I persevered since I sat out the last round, choosing to breathe actual air over the choking heat inside the lodge. Afterwards, at the meal, a Lakota elder sat at the head of the table—it was Ben. I joined him sitting to his right. "Go sit over there," he softly ordered, pointing to the opposite side of the table. It took a while, but I came to understand that there would be many unwritten rules on the road, and that it would be a foreign road where trust might not be a given, but that it would be real when it came. Especially for a white guy in this part of the world.

The fry bread was about all gone, and distant rumbling came from the northern sky as the August heat rose. We set off for our respective quarters for the night, set to convene for our long ride early the next morning.

I headed up Route 17 from Pine Ridge late that evening, moving down the darkening, shiny, two-lane blacktop towards Spearfish, towards the Black Hills, the heart of the Lakota people, looking for my hotel. The lightning, which had softly illuminated the night horizon when I first set out, was now sending down bolts and, as I headed for them, into them, they headed for me, growing larger and louder every mile—then they were no longer the abrupt, pounding terror-thuds, they became the great, rolling thunder-beings of Lakota legend, the wakinyan. When the sky lit up, the earth's atmosphere expanded and it was like moving into an abyss to a north I had lost faith in. And after, when someone sent me a Ruth Stone poem, I mused that she must have made this ride, known lightening like this:

When you turn out the light,

you are blind in the dark

as perhaps the ants are blind,

with the same abstract leap out of this limiting dimension.

So that the very curve of light,

as it is pulled in the dimple of space,

is relative to your own blind pathway across the abyss.

It may sound romantic being at the mercy of vast elements, but the drone of the Harley engine was no longer clean and calming, it was just more noise, and my alternative to being terrified and confused was to pull onto the side of the road, and to stop. I watched the white cracks and hazy, long, white flashes in complete wonder, and it all seemed to be happening in slow motion then. It was too much. And I turned around. Heading back into Pine Ridge, now approaching midnight, I pulled into Roger's driveway, got out my cell phone and, shouting through the storm, said, "I'm here, Roger, right outside the house, but I will sleep in the shed. Don't get up. I'm scared, Roger, it's too crazy!" and I was laughing at my cowardice. "I cannot ride that road, Roger. The lightening, the hotel is right in that crazy lightening. I'm good in the shed."

"I thought you were coming," Roger said in full calm. "Wait a minute." Three minutes later he came out, saying, "Go to my mother's house, the one at the end of the block. She has room. You can stay there. She is waiting for you." Solo experiences get us in touch with our fears and inspirations and our own private ways, but going through a storm alone can also have the opposite effect: sometimes you become ready for a teacher. I was, and I was ready to be in the larger, safer collective—ready to be a part of the tribe.

Triads

I awoke in Roger's mother's house, had some coffee, and wandered back to Roger's place to pack up. Roger was inside in a black leather vest with nothing under it, healing up a couple large chest scars from last summer's Sun Dance ceremony (not the film festival). I had on full leathers. We set out. Roger's riding partner from up at the Cheyenne Reservation, Glenn Gunville, joined in.

Many experts like riding alone and there is nothing like this for total freedom. As good as solo discovery is, the triad could easily be the most powerful group formation, when labors are divided up and specialties emerge. Roger, Glenn, and I set out for Wounded Knee where we were to meet the rest of our riders. According to the authors of *Tribal Leadership*, the formation of the triad is the most stable and productive grouping of people, an engine behind the healthy, high-performance execution of a given task.[4] Association in triads can change your life and career. Although few schools have classes of three, many teachers use class study and project groups of this size with varying effectiveness. If done right, the triad is the ultimate power formation. Groups of two, like tutorials or buddy groups, are, of course, popular and powerful, but they can become exclusive and, as a result, unaccountable. If you see more dyads than triads around your campus or organization, be careful. Dyads can become conspiratorial and exclusivist quickly, and they often work in whispers. Triad relationships tend to focus on the accountable relationships that are forming rather than on the individuals, and synthesis can occur—an optimal learning situation.

Riding in threes is creative and connecting, allowing for interchange and maximum play. Roger led on the inside of the lane. I tried desperately to keep up with him on the outside of the lane, and Glenn tailed on the back inside. I could tell I was always lagging a little farther behind Roger than he wanted; he never said so, but the triad did. In a triad, the responses of each member are tightly interwoven, immediate, and intuitive. In threes, there is no conspiring—all partners are up front—so you might call it the power circle.

Leaving Pine Ridge, almost everything is salient, filled with subtexts. We pass the Treaty School, founded by Russell Means, longtime Indian activist. Means helped found the American Indian Movement, wrote books, served his share of prison time, and staged protests globally. In the end, after all this, his foundation of a school with native language immersion and an emphasis on living off the land might be considered his ultimate form of activism. A school.

We pass porcupine roadkill, then the high school, "Home of the Porcupines." (As an aside, there are Native American schools in South Dakota called Indians, Chieftains, Fighting Sioux, and Braves, to name a few, but none called "The White Settlers" or even "The Cavalry.") We pass the Crazy Horse School. If I were alone I could have stopped off at each school, and I would have.

The triad was not instantly stable. I was the least confident and rode on high alert, as though I had a pail of water on my head and must not spill a drop. Glenn rode behind me for as long as he could stand it, but eventually, with a hungrier throttle than I had, blasted ahead like he had afterburners and took the lead. Whereas Roger rode with steadiness and power, Glenn was a stylish rider, a halfback, with a full playbook of moves and three Harleys in his garage to suit his moods.

The pace quickened by a few miles per hour for a while, and eventually I adapted to the new dynamic, noticing things on the road surface I had spent a lifetime ignoring. Increasingly I was becoming less of a liability to the triad. It was time to join the others. I said it might be nice to ride in segments, keep some triads going, but Roger was clear that it was time to become a part of the larger group, the Lakota Riders, and to move together. A great teacher, Roger never seemed to move my questions into the yes/no, do/don't world—he only presented opportunities. For the rest of the ride, the special connection between Roger, Glenn, and myself was probably the most valuable thing I had. I could sense the invisible lines forming our triangle at any time, as though we were a part of a Ken Wilbur thought exercise, and it remained a bond I trusted, especially further along when things got harder.

Perfect Class Size

I had come to treasure groups of twelve throughout the years, sought out opportunities to create them, and, on occasion, been stirred by the results. Outside of Wounded Knee we met up with the rest of the Lakota Riders, becoming a sub-tribe of twelve plus two guides, and I got a chance to study this dozen in a new way. It was time to begin the memorial ride. With everyone gathered in a circle, Roger led a Lakota language prayer. He prayed: that there would be no snares in our plans, that we would be in balance with all life, that we would all be grateful, and that God would watch over us; that we are all allowed into the tribe; that we are bound to all others through a source of life, and so are moved to serve all those around us. He prayed that we are all relations.

We saddled up, clicked into gear, and rolled on the throttle. "I hope they go the speed limit," I told Roger, feeling challenged on the machine that still felt massive. Roger grinned. I was about to learn that speed limits on the reservation are a relative thing. Passing Wounded Knee Memorial is always humbling; we may have slowed down just a little in unity, and I noted the house next door flying the American flag upside down, the international distress signal—and so we were on our way north.

Native Americans sometimes say that the first animal seen in the day can herald what is to come.

> *Heading onwards, seven wild horses on some prairie land see the bikes, and they are the first animals we see this day. They come dancing, looking celebratory. We know wild horses to be frightened of the metal horse and its sound, and they normally race off in the opposite direction when bikers come into their range; but these horses are coming towards us. As we approach, one horse, the lead horse, veers into a tight, counterclockwise circle while four others back-circle the other way, one at a time, peeling away from the formation like water off a spinning ball. Then the rest fall in from behind, now running along with our bikes, and we all share the same, warm breeze off the plains.*

I had a sense that our group, like the small group circled around the fire pit back at the sweat lodge, was able to experience this as a whole. The throttle seemed strong then, and we sped up in collective inspiration.

For something so important to school design, it was becoming hard to ignore how very little research had been done on small class sizes. Surely the Harley Davidson Corporation did more R and D on their smallest bike, the Sportster, than all the school agencies and researchers combined had done on small classes or, for that matter, small schools.

Even before Jesus, many have found twelve, also referred to as a *duodecuple*, to be the optimal group size. The biblical Jacob had twelve sons, who were the progenitors of the Twelve Tribes of Israel. In ancient Greek religion, the Twelve Olympians were the principal gods of the pantheon. The chief Norse god, Odin, had twelve sons. Sacred circles typically include twelve plus the leader. Psychologists refer to a twelve person "sympathy group."

Malcolm Gladwell taught this concept: "Make a list of all the people you know whose death would leave you truly devastated. Chances are you will come up with around twelve names. That, at least, is the average answer most people give to that question . . . At a certain point, at somewhere between ten to fifteen people, if the group is to be focused we begin to overload." For nearly a century, classes of eight to twelve students have sat around the legendary Phillips Exeter Academy *Harkness Tables*. Those of us who do extensive work in circles recognize the invisible barrier we pass when group size moves from twelve to fifteen and the circle begins to run out of space for individuals.

In New York City schools, if you become unmanageable as a student, you are put in a resource class. Containing? You guessed it: twelve students.

In twelve, you become a part of a whole, and yet you are never anonymous as larger groups allow—your voice or lack thereof is significant and will not go unnoticed. I had a couple challenges with this lack of anonymity. First off, I was not a Native. Secondly, I felt a bit alien in the biking world. From the way I felt in my hulking suit of leathers, I may just as well have been dressed in a full buffalo skin, and a greasy layer of sweat was to accompany me wherever I went all week. My complexion was all wrong, and I even wore a helmet, rare for riders in the north where riding is just about the purest form of freedom. The experience got me thinking about how Lakota kids feel leaving the reservation and living in the white world.

The Lakota people traditionally say, and Joseph Marshall III has rendered this warmly in his Native stories, if you are not sure about your own courage, find someone who has the courage you want and follow them. If you follow long enough, the courage in you will begin to come out and it may not be long before you hear something behind you and realize someone is now following you. I soon found this to be sage advice both as a rider and a teacher, and I will never forget it, as Roger and Glenn, master riders both, eased me into the group.

Dave Janis, an Oglala Sioux, was our leader. This was both appointed ahead of time and obvious as he established his leadership and leadership style. The twelve followers not only witnessed a tour de force in his riding, power, and presence, but remained within one degree of connection to it because of our group size. He was thick and tough, spoke with a gravel voice and had a long, thick, braided ponytail. Dave dwarfed his Harley Dyna Super Glide in size and power. Like many people who look scary, he was quite warm.

I do not know how many people can form an intimate group or at what point people can hide in rows. It obviously depends upon the environment and the people. Nor do I expect the educational research community to take the phenomenological intuitions of an Indian biker group as hard data, though I will suggest that our nation's schools are in enough trouble to consider looking outside of the box some, maybe even far outside of the box. At any rate, back home, my small schools research group had been able to compile controlled, empirical research data through various sources. In a prominent nationwide review, for instance, two of the top five top-ranked schools in the nation (and eight of the top twenty) featured classes with fewer than fifteen students, a statistical wake-up call.[5] Few teachers in the America of today have ever had a class of twelve for a sustained amount of time, and so they may not realize why it is so empowering and connected for participants, and why it is a number of such heritage and even reverence. And if one member experiences weakness or pain, it is relatively easy for the rest of the group to share it while it is absolved.

We headed north. I did not know the names of all twelve riders, but learned quickly to recognize them from tribal emblems sewn across the backs of their black leather vests. Roger, from the rear, was my teacher, and I definitely knew and appreciated that he had my back, literally. The idea of a sub-tribe or class of twelve had become captivating by this point—it was turning a situation that could have been alienating into one of belonging and collective experience.

On this particular day, the first formal day of the memorial ride, our goal was to move through three Indian reservations starting with the Oglala Lakota, stopping at the tribal halls of the next two along the way, and then heading on to North Dakota. We stopped for lunch at the first reservation hall. There, our tribe was obviously enthused as five plentiful trays of food were laid out before us. I would not want for the world to offend the good people who created those generous offerings, and I had my share of them. However, coming from a foreign background, I may have been less enthused than the rest of my mates. Because what I saw was not five different types of food, but rather one type of food: high-fat, high-salt *fast food*—all of it, of course, finger lickin' good. I could find nothing that appeared to have recently grown out of the ground. The only choices were the catchy designs on the to-go boxes. Hence, where my good-natured hosts saw five entrees, I saw one choice with no real alternative. It amounted to a socio-political condition with one of the more appealing and folky sounding names served up in academia, a Hobson's choice: when your alternative choice makes no real difference.

This observation is not without useful application to our topic: teachers have had to accept larger classes and they've had to accept smaller classes, both with about the same social dynamics. Twenty-one students? Thirty students? The research was showing them to be about the same. Between group sizes of around twenty and thirty (and in most cases even between fifteen and thirty), researchers had not been able to find much difference in the efficacy of class size—the change amounted to no change. And yet, all the class size reductions and additions we could find in journals had been made within those limits, all the changes were just rearrangements inside the Happy Meal box. I could easily surmise already, still fresh in the saddle, that changing the biking group from twenty-five to thirty riders or vice versa would make no difference to my experience on the road. Do you want that with fries?

We now understood why small class research had been practically abandoned. This was a whack on the side of the head. The more we researched and found twelve to be an extraordinary number, the more we also had to consider that a recommendation for classes of twelve would be considered a disturbance and a frustration to standard theorists and practitioners, but the theoretical challenge remained: should we identify and study ideal design features of great education and great group formation, or only the most practical and convenient? As small schools researchers and advocates, we were not suggesting revolution, we were not suggesting that every school could do this, but we had to ask: could classes of twelve ever be practical, even sometimes? Maybe certain classes? Maybe once a week? Maybe in private and charter schools? Maybe as a special funding target? Should we not seek to learn the best practices? Should we not be open to radical yet unexplored avenues? What if the country's educational systems were widely perceived to be in decline, even by its leaders? Wouldn't that be cause to look for something different?

*   *   *

Dave easily could have commanded a much larger group, and he would, but with twelve you had a personal line of site link to him that you could never have had in a larger group. He was holding a conversation among bikes, conducting a master class, and every one of us was in the front row. On the other hand, riding with someone that advanced could be too much responsibility, and it was a little frightening, too: you knew that he would immediately sense your vulnerabilities as a rider and the drag this could be on the whole. I'm not all that social to begin with. And I'm used to sitting at the front of the class, not usually a follower. And this leather jacket, it must have been designed for bombardiers and I knew it stood out. For such weak reasons, I actually welcomed the larger group we were about to join, where I could be a bit more anonymous. But that turned into a mixed blessing.

Standard Class Size: Followers and Leaders

Heading north through the rolling grasslands we reached Eagle Butte and picked up the rest of our northward moving riders, all headed for North Dakota and the historically laden Fort Yates. Now with around thirty-five riders, a standard U.S. public secondary school class size in the early 2000s, individuals from all points instantly formed a unified collective, riding into a small prairie town, waving to the tribal people who were lining the streets to acknowledge our Wounded Knee Riders in a remembrance, a beautiful kind of healing from the historical horror. Ample blood had been spilled here, on this soil. People smiled from shops and street corners, thanking us for honoring the land and the people. Then, heading for the edge of town and reaching a rise, we rolled on the throttle, disappearing into the prairies like a dream.

Once again, I had to adjust to a new group dynamic. In this new group of riders, suddenly there was no room for any jockeying or play such as there had been with twelve—efforts to be an individual did occur, but they stood out and were rare. As an analogy for visual learners, imagine swapping stories and song inside the tipi (maybe a little fire in the middle), then shift that same conversation to five rows of seven all facing forward in a rectangle. (Better put the fire out now.) And yet, the large group offered an organic sense of collusion that was welcoming, as it had a focusing effect, a way of forcing all riders to focus on sameness: the preservation of the tight formation was paramount.

You hold your position, no slipping. Not easy. The ancients said that the spirit blows through you with the wind, but it did not feel that way to me. It was August and hot, and the wind blustered like cannons. There is no such thing as really going straight; you must countersteer into a wind as though you were in a curve, roll on some throttle to make the bike purchase into it, and hold a line. Not easy at seventy miles per hour. But honestly I had spent the previous four decades feeling like this as a teacher and educational researcher. I like a little countervailing force to lean into. I believe that any number of the small school heads and superintendents I had come to know and admire over those decades also felt this way, even those of national renown.

The geometry of hay bales rolled quietly along the fields; hot wind came drumming across the sage and amber prairie. The deep sound of the engine made it seem like flying. There was nothing which was not in patterns and alpha waves. Being a follower was comforting, as I became a pure observer rather than an actor. I laid low. Keeping up and keeping in the flow took up most of my focus. Of course, as a greenhorn, I also knew I was using 99 percent of my bandwidth while the rest were probably using around 50. It reminded me of advanced calculus in college, where 100 percent of my energy was used to hang on (in a way more than 100 percent, because sometimes I was faking it), while the rest of the class seemed like geniuses to me. My comfort zone slid up steadily until speeds were up around seventy or even seventy-two; beyond that I surrendered to the road vibrations and the wind. The advanced riders seemed to have an inexplicable power source that transcended these elements.

Glenn was at the back of the pack. Then, for some reason, he downshifted and blasted past three of us at once, creating a sub-tribe for the next twenty miles, but it finally dissolved as we closed the gap. I considered this to be a harmless disturbance to group unity, and it happened again and again: we would be holding steady in staggered double line formation, when someone would gun it for a small gap that opened up ahead. This would invariably throw off the alternating rows, so the line-up would adjust like ants in a march, like choreographed activity. There was less personal connection than we had with twelve, but more self-organizing; in fact, a constant energy went into self-organizing. There are always a few who will distinguish themselves positively or negatively in a group like this; however, we cannot have a real conversation with thirty or forty people. A group of thirty-five seems unstable; it is regularly shifting around as if it seeks either to be a fuller tribe and community, or else a smaller, tight-knit team. The number wants to double or halve. This instability became extreme after a short time.

The driving force in our pack was, of course, Dave, a Lakota, who dominated and was making his big Harley look like a toy. He was the clear source of leadership, and this was not a collaborative leadership. Dave wove, powered ahead, hovered alongside to check in with each warrior—um, rider—then blasted ahead. Back at the front, Dave was in his element, king of the world, and there was no mistaking it. At seventy miles per hour, he began a perfect weave, slaloming in and out of the center white passing stripes with one hand on the bars (not recommended), then increasing the group speed to seventy-five. Clasping on both hand grips and focused on simply holding a straight line, I was in awe. This was domination; it was the teacher firmly at the front of the class, and you did not want to fall behind or show weakness in any way. These were advanced placement riders, so I demanded absolute discipline of myself, knowing that the slightest deviation from the pack would not only stand out like a sore thumb and cause others to see me as a weak outsider, but that it could be a genuine hazard and threat. Of course, peer pressure to conform is almost always a mixed blessing. We seek to belong but also to never violate our own nature or needs. This is really the classic adolescent dilemma, and I was recalling it now.

I hung on as the group speed increased, hawk-eyed and hyperaware: my eyes scanned furiously ahead to everything from my nose to twelve seconds ahead and beyond on the road, everything on the side and off to the side of the road, anything that moved or might move, every road surface object, and any upcoming change in road surface. If I caught myself mentally drifting for a second, I thought angry punishing thoughts and demanded more of my renegade consciousness in a way I would do to no student. When it lapsed again, I tried appeals to logic, laughing at it, bargaining, polite requests—but, with such forces, who am I to bargain!—and eventually (many miles yet down the road) working my way to acceptance and even gratitude for the great mystery, as though I were working my way through a taxonomic hierarchy.

Miles clicked away. A long, gradual drop-off lay ahead running down to a wash, then leading gradually back up for a mile or two to the next rise. It was a gentle, amber farming valley. Heading northward through it was a hay truck, moving just a little too slowly for Dave, who determined to move the tribe past it so long as the opposite, southbound lane was clear for passing. On the descent, about half the pack managed to pass the truck. The second half would then need to pass him on the rise in order to stay tight in formation. Being in the back of the pack, by the time my bike was in position to pass the trucker, the end of the rise was approaching a little too fast. I needed to get around that truck, and I definitely did not want to be on the wrong side of a two-lane blacktop going over a blind rise—the most dangerous possible biking move.

With Roger out in front of me, I started to overtake the truck, but the crest was coming up fast so all I could do was roll on more throttle, then more, and the crest was imminent as I came even with the hay truck's cab. I goosed it and held on tight as I curved back in front of him, glancing down quickly at the needle of my speedometer which was now pointed at ninety-five. The wind was drumming into me, and I was thinking, "How can I be in this situation?" pulling up ahead of the truck's front fender and thanking my tires on the hot August asphalt and the engine that sounded clean, warm, and untroubled by all this. I moved in safely in front of the truck, back into the pack, letting off throttle as smoothly as I could, remembering my promise to kiss the ground back in Rapid.

Next thing I knew, the last two riders made it around and pulled up the rear behind me as we blasted up over the crest. I was not sure if Roger had positioned those two behind me just to make sure I did not get killed and, of course, I will never know. I do not know if this was bravery or foolish follower behavior, either, but I do understand that, as much as we do not want our children to be blind followers, to learn bravery they often must follow someone who is courageous. At the next stop, Roger said, "Did you get around that truck okay?" I did not need to answer more than a couple exclamations. He understood and we had a laugh—and I have to admit, adolescent as it must sound, I felt more included then than ever. I was ready to sing a little louder at the powwow.

Trance

Looking ahead and straight up the road was a swarm of black hornets. Us. Roger said, "That's the thing about riding in the pack: you all have to move as one." Now as a part of a larger group, I found a safe space towards the back and I, with some automaticity I think, began to let go of my role as an individual and to experience things increasingly as a small part of something larger, a part of the herd.

Since I chronically process everything in terms of education, it naturally struck me that having classes with over thirty students actually made sense for schools wanting more "standardized" results. Traditionally, in Western countries, class sizes of thirty had been considered large and in need of reduction, but the number of such classes, even larger classes, and the desire to standardize their content and outcomes, was on the increase.[6] Strange, I thought. Two generations before, outcomes like that in schools would have been viewed with skepticism by those fearing the loss of individuality and local autonomy—an affront to the free world, a loss of the Western, liberal arts heritage that made our nation great.

The minutes ticked away like seconds, the world flying under my wheels, and within another hundred miles I was able to move my way up to mid-pack. My mind had undergone a shift, and I could feel it clearly. In adapting to the larger group, which was ultimately comforting, my brain had created a trance that blocked out discursiveness. Today's expert, successful high school teachers, faced with overcrowded rooms of diverse learners, are able to lull their students into a similar meditative state when need be, so that their needs and egos melt away. They have become masters in trance, no small skill. Some dim the lights and show overheads as they talk calmly. Some entertain and captivate that way. Cognitive function is slightly limited across the room, but functional, as if you have been watching television for too long—or listening to the pure drone of the Harley engine. There are specific types of thinking and learning well-suited to this particular band of brain activity. For example, some homogeneously grouped Korean math classes with nearly sixty students thrive famously. When students enter the room already highly motivated and conforming and the subject is highly quantifiable, some class size considerations become less important. But try teaching history to sixty ninth graders in a heterogeneous group. War hoops! Expert teachers habitually appeal to the parasympathetic nervous system and those teachers who are lucky enough to discover this early through trial and error, providence, or research, are treasured by their principals.

A fascinating and, we believe, unexamined side of class size research is that the calming strategies many teachers develop for coping and avoiding upsets in large classes are not at all the same as the strategies for increasing the neural excitation which facilitates learning such as we much more readily risk in an intimate class setting of twelve or less. Different mind-sets work for different sized groups. We checked this idea out with neuropsychologist Rick Hanson, author of the incredible *Buddha's Brain: The Practical Neuroscience of Happiness, Love and Wisdom.* He commented: "Your neurologically-referenced statements are accurate . . . experiences of reward and moderate arousal/passion/enthusiasm, sounds like a small class to me!"[7] It's common sense that we cannot cope long with forty or even twenty aroused people in a collective, be they Indian bikers or adolescents in a room. A few might be in this state, but the risk of "overheating" the group becomes high. In a group of twelve, this might just be a good day's brainstorming session. To address this whole issue in the future, teachers will study techniques that promote or inhibit the release of dopamine and norepinephrine, so that they can tailor their class arousal levels to the activity, task, and grouping sizes.

*   *   *

It is hot. I think my chocolate is melting in the black leather saddlebag. I must rid myself of all these self-preoccupations, sink into the scene. We gas up on low test fuel, all they have up here, and set out for the final leg of the day. People are being pulled along as if in a giant vacuum. I seem to cling to this strange body position and dare not move. I can hardly move anyway. The engine sound is captivating. A seven-foot man with a leather do-rag and black tee shirt saying "Big Indian" passes me. The world is theater, and I am an observer. Gradually a grin is growing on my face, along with a sense of belonging. I look at the odometer which reads 250 miles and think, "I can do this three more times this week." Miles unspool under my wheels.

By sunset we had white knuckled and rattled 320 miles, locked tightly into a fairly rigid formation requiring a tight focus over many hours, a good way to achieve a state of hyperaware trance. At last we were over the North Dakota line, and then we were pulling into the Prairie Knights Casino and Resort, checking in.

> . . . moving through the casino and up to the rooms in an altered state, the engine still running. Laying my head down on the pillow at last, mind purring, I close my eyes and am quickly met with terror—what if I am still riding? I must not lose intense focus on the road for even a split second. My eyes bolt open, it's okay, it's time to rest, and I try closing them again. To no avail: the road is coming at me, now slipping beneath me once more, and I dare not submit to this terror of missing a road curve or surface change or loose gravel, moving riders leaning into the shifting winds, then falling off into the wind. I get up, pad my unbearable awareness down to the casino for a beer where I can break the trance while watching addicted old ladies involuntarily chain smoke, feeding two slot machines at once, everything, everyone in altered awareness: coming off the ride like an anthropologist arriving in a new civilization, everything that moves is amazing. There is Roger, and I only grin because I know he is in this same buzz. He is the master of this grin. Class dismissed.

Being in a Tribe

I awoke and, sure enough, outside the window was North Dakota. At last we convened with our full group, seventy-five strong, at the Sitting Bull Memorial, ready for a long day's journey south, for our memorial at Wounded Knee Cemetery. I had no experience motorcycling with a full tribe, and nothing comparable in my background came to mind.

We formed a large circle in the parking lot and Roger sent a Lakota prayer up to the heavens as a helper walked around the circle smudging everyone with burning sage. Of course, a tribe needs a chief. Dave stepped up, outlined the full route for the day for everyone to anticipate, then said: "Yesterday there was a gap in the middle of the line. Today there are more of us and we can't do that. Keep the formation tight. No gap." Dave, of course, understood that today's riding situation was not about creative biking, banking hard on the curves, or pairing off: it was about unity. A shared trip. Maybe he was just saying *Mitakuye Oyasin*. He straddled the Dyna Super King and took off; we circled by the Missouri River, the Big Muddy, then headed south.

"What's the vision for today, Roger?" I asked at a fuel stop, pointing out that the grasshopper was the first animal of the day we saw. What did that mean? Someone piped in, "North Dakota state bird."

"It's going to be hot," Roger interpreted. I hung towards the back of the pack. Roger did, too, tailing us all as a good teacher might. Again, I was grateful to have him around, but did not express this; he was a mentor to me, and I felt he was depending on me to ride with autonomy and competence.

There up north, along the winding way, we stopped to be fed, powwow, and revive a spirit of Wounded Knee in places I could not find on the map: small pocket villages and creek-side valleys where everyone spoke the Native tongue and hatred of the United States government was open, and I heard haunting chants and always the muffled pounding of the big drum, and always enough fry bread for everyone.

As an aside, it seems worth noting that Native resentment does not seem to focus on the massacred people of Wounded Knee, whom they seem to accept as returned to earth. Instead it seems based on the lies the American press and government officials attributed to them regarding that battle: hostilities of mythological proportion, stinging, humiliating lies, and never a way to even respond. It is a history written by the victors. Indians are not Indian. White men are not without color. Or are they? The verification of reality is made by the one who circulates the writing or film—the one who is in power. Radically different points of view characterize some Indian and "white man" points of view, anyway. So what history had done now, as if by fate, had been to remove almost the entire history of our native peoples from American history classes. And now, headed towards some kind of full circle, people and even high-performance organizations across America were longing for ways to be tribal.

*   *   *

We rolled on, and on, until by midday the Badlands opened up to us with their winding roads, through strange, other-worldly rock and mineral formations, and then back out to the big prairies. "The prairie land is not great for growing much but hay, but it's beautiful," one rider explained. Later on I listened as he thought out loud, "They moved us onto the most rugged land in the Dakotas and they expect us to plant here—you can't plant nothing here. It is bottomless after a rain. Prairie gumbo. But we are slowly healing now, a hundred years after Wounded Knee." Native American culture and even their crops were in revival up there, despite history and geography. Almost every youth was studying Native language and culture at every former Bureau of Indian Affairs school across the Lakota reservations, just as we were finding in many Native schools, nationwide. As for the students, they are sometimes confused, jockeying between embracing a deep heritage and committing to an insecure future, between two worlds. Even some elders are telling them that success will mean moving and assimilating into white culture. It can be a huge conflict for teens preparing for adulthood: is the tribe something they are born to and must embrace, or is it just something they can choose to be in? According to Roger, this is the long road where the tribal kids and teachers need unlimited, openhearted encouragement. I was leaving at the end of the week. No one else was.

With this group size, it was taking a full ten minutes to get the tribe back on the road again after any break. We set out from Eagle Butte west towards Faith, another bright, windy day, the fields piled with rolls of hay across the prairie and along a little, treed hill this is what I saw: twelve wild horses, maybe spooked at first by the wind and noise of our line of iron horses, running in all directions, bucking and running but still moving forward until, gradually, as our line moved by, like moving into a slipstream they came into a line of their own and began loping along with us. I have read in Native American lore, and observed from watching the right people interact with wild horses out on those plains, that it is not unusual to see a horse communicate so deeply with a trainer that, if we watch them carefully, they seem to be teaching each other.[8] Here is a way of understanding perhaps the most basic thing there is to know about real teaching: you cannot teach anyone who is not teaching you. Without an empathic and collaborative component, teaching is not teaching—the kind of learning that can be achieved from this type of instruction will not be of long-range service, at least not from a humanitarian or ecological standpoint.

We headed for Faith. After a while, if the leadership is strong and clear, a tribe takes on the life of a complex but integrated organism. In this way, the trail of bikes gradually formed a union and became, as a whole, sensitive to both the internal and external environment. Someone taps on a brake pedal for fear of an obstacle, real or imagined, and it creates a shift in the whole formation down the line, and you can see the circuit of red brake lights pulse its way down in a pattern. It is a beautiful thing when the leadership is strong and everyone is going at a steady pace—harmony—but this is not always easy to sustain. If the leadership is missing, the signals from the front do not translate well and the group begins to splinter, and you see brake lights coming on at random, disturbing times.

Over time, riding south through the prairies and Badlands for a couple hundred miles in the full tribe formation, my vision shifted. I no longer darted my eyes from road surface to mirror to far in the distance, and so forth. Now I seemed to have a wide perspective, as though I could see everything at once. At times I did not really even need to look at the road—riding around the tail end of seventy-four tailgated bikes, I had no choice but to resign myself to the full mercy of the judgment of those up ahead. I needed to stay tight in formation, and where that formation led me was not my concern. It started to feel like a good time to lean back a little more, maybe use the cruising footpegs. We had leadership, and we were a force, a swarm of black hornets. A rider, the great-great-grandson of the great Chief Red Cloud, described it as "Riding with one heart and mind." Overconfident, I started moving up and took a spot near the middle of the pack. The pressure there in the middle was different: feeling this pressure from ahead and behind, you needed to hold your space, which was intense. I kept the pressure on myself.

As my identity blended with the pack, I began to feel, more or less, invincible. You surrender the self to the larger movement and to the identity and culture of the group. This is what tribes do and, by virtue of mastery over these magnificent iron horses, we were powerful. The bikes sounded alive and infinite, like the ocean. I was goin' Injun. Schoolhouse warrior. A part of me realized how comic-tragic this was, but I did not care. With Roger and Glenn I had *cred*. And yet, it must have been intimidating to the outsider, as tribes can often seem. Outsiders can easily view even well-intentioned "tribes" (of all kinds) as primitive, erratic, exclusionary, and even hostile. I recalled the behaviors of the varsity lacrosse team in my high school in the 60s, the Manhasset *Indians* (playing a Native American game), their insensitivity and pride in their own seditious swaggering, their macho disregard for people who did not belong to the tribe—a male pathology, perhaps, but still a real example of tribal ways. I recalled once asking a bright and well-functioning student at our large, local public school, "What is special about high school in our town, what makes it different than other schools in other communities?" He answered, "I dunno, we have a lacrosse team." I know how badly our kids seek tribes, like-minded groups, and belonging, sometimes intensely or blindly. Most of us seek tribes.

What I was experiencing in our riding group turned out to be well documented. A social circle or network with shared identity naturally goes up to around one or two hundred before it tends to divide into sub-tribes. The great, British anthropologist Robin Dunbar has called this the rule of 150. Up to somewhere in the area between 100 and 230, he found, communities can act as a single voice, and they grasp shared values clearly in ways groups of four or five hundred never could. The average number of friends on Facebook is 120 to 130, just short of the size of a typical community in ancient hunter-gatherer societies.[9] Gladwell's breakthrough research in *The Tipping Point* set the number at 150, and the authors of *Tribal Leadership* provided a deepening understanding of the power of "tribes" of 150 people or less.[10] But most revealing of all was this finding: year after year, against all odds, small schools with around two hundred or fewer students are among the top high schools in the nation, vastly disproportionate to their numbers.[11] What makes them so laudable? This: they are tribes. For my part, on the road, I found the tribal grouping liberating and manageable, even as a relative rookie. I knew I owed it to the tribe to be reliable and to represent the tribal culture. I had made the transition from *me* to *we*.

Of course, we all have to find a place in the tribe. After giving it a go, I had less tolerance for being in the middle of the pack—it is not in my nature— and so I moved up close to the front, something I would not have dreamed of three days and six hundred miles ago. Up there, I found that my pacing was set directly by the leader and there were not too many bikes to drag and draw out the line—no gaps between me and the leader. I liked having that access again. I loved the first part of the pack. My conclusions: the front and the back are both great; the middle is where the less reliable conditions reside. Cars turn left into the middle of the group, speeds mix up, people jockey for position, and the analogies were all wrong for me. Nevertheless, from all positions, we developed a beautiful, powerful, tribal association in a constant state of self-organization as we sensed our final destination approaching.

The sky was piling up with lead and we could see the rolling thunder moving high up, but no one seemed to hurry or bother about it. We were invincible. A damp chill was coming, and Roger gave me the newly minted tee shirt—the ultimate American banner—which I immediately pulled on. It was a long-sleeved tee with the emblem: "Lakota Riders." I laugh at thunder!

Future Tribe

There is a lure that comes out from the Wounded Knee Cemetery. If you drove by blindfolded, you would still feel it. We were moving within range. The bikes slowed slightly to a steady sixty-five miles per hour as we made the final approach—a long, gradual descent. The site looks barren, just a wrought iron archway into the gravesite and a modest stone monument, having none of the theater of nearby Mount Rushmore. But a whole lot more happened here. The story of Wounded Knee is told differently depending on which side of the battle you fought, but the Lakota, and really all Native Americans, lost worlds here. Telling my own story from the politically powerless, small schools camp had given me an appreciation for the frustration powerlessness can cause, although I had lost little by comparison.

But we were outsiders, buttressed mainly by faith and patience. In our work, we had found *small schools* to exist in an absence of violence, not to mention metal detectors. Typically upwards of 90 percent of small schools' students, parents, and teachers were claiming they actually liked school and felt a sense of connectedness and caring (something we might call a *tribal* sense), figures that were incomprehensible from the large school standpoint. For small privates, the typical cost per student is around $18,000. Was that too much? Classes of twelve. Scholarship programs. Unheard of graduation rates. No violence. And almost no credibility with the public systems in their locales, where small meant marginal. Powerless. I understood that.

Although the empirical research in support of smaller schools, tribal-style schools, was clear, the trend towards increasingly larger schools was continuing. Over the prior decade, the number of high schools with more than fifteen hundred students had doubled. Forty percent of the nation's secondary schools enrolled more than a thousand students.[12] While no known study found achievement or safety at large schools superior to that at small schools policy makers across the country continued to seek an economy of scale that did not exist.[13] In public schools the ratio of teachers to other employees had reached one to one, while small schools had closer to three teachers per one other school employee. So much for economy of scale.

We could risk the wrath of many here and compare the large, comprehensive American school to the Indian reservation, a place to reliably contain large populations in prescribed boundaries and support their own bureaucracies. A place where teachers and students are treated as secondary citizens. Compared to the tribal perspective, we had been wasting billions on one-size-fits-all educational requirements, and it was time to recognize this waste. Our nation's large, comprehensive schools were so far overdeveloped, so closely tied to government stipends, that innovation could hardly occur in a meaningful way. Exceptions were possible, and we celebrated them, but innovation in small, tribe-like schools is something which is almost indisputably efficient and, to those in them, manifest. A decade into the new second millennium, satisfaction nationwide was low and yet, as on the Indian reservations of the past century, few leaders or experts seriously expected much more transformation within the existing system. As districts lost money on each student, finance officers in large urban school districts were quietly obliged to its dropouts, each one stemming more losses.

I knew that efforts to circumvent the secondary level, large public school status quo or to implement audacious, small class size plans would be met with disparagement and marginalization at this time of diminished budgets and job insecurity; and yet the educational, financial, and political state of education in most states of the nation was already widely known to be unsustainable. American schools were clearly in a very tough economic bind. But it was the kids who were held hostage while the cycle of bureaucracy and gridlock was repeating, and it was projected to do so indefinitely. Couldn't we just "let a few out early," into some tribe-like schools?

Everywhere people wanted to talk about disenfranchisement. In our banking and real estate industries people nationwide had already joined together in outrage. I began to take this as good news, as a window of opportunity for creative alternatives. What are outrage and disenfranchisement if not an opportunity for creative disruption in the educational marketplace? There was a great, unspoken dilemma in the nation. On one hand, the public school system was a sacred cow, a modern community cathedral, an institution people dared not upend. At the same time, the large high school complex was in the early stages of being rejected by those who did not want schools to be guided by political interest groups, billion dollar corporate government contractors, jumbo-sized school district bureaucracies, and legislatures at the expense of students and teachers—in other words, at the expense of the next generation.

There were hints of a shift on blogs and websites. A few people were talking about what it would be like for their children to go to school in a schoolhouse developed largely by their own community, where they would be an accepted part of a tribe. This early-stage shift would need a generation to develop, if we were lucky. As it stood, on average, high school teachers were beginning to seek quality, long-term positions outside of education. The flight from the profession would have to stop before American education could begin to recover its entrepreneurial leadership roots.

As American Indian novelist Sherman Alexie wrote, "Imagination is the only weapon on the reservation."[14] After a long thaw, we were starting to see imaginative local communities generating new ideas for self-determination in small schools and local gardens and crops, innovative programs the Lakota were restoring, too, programs we could already see at work back in Southern California communities, little pockets not on the map. One reporter filed this observation on national television after her visit to Pine Ridge: she had come to the reservation "to report on poverty . . . and what we found was this impossible, radiant hope."[15] I thought: as long as a community is able to discover that their fate is in their own hands, we will always have this kind of hope. In the coming generations, we will see a revival of the impossible occurring in community-based schools, local charter schools, small schools, and home schools across the country.

We had arrived. Gathering around Wounded Knee for the ceremony, we were joined by many from around the community, including descendants of the massacre. For them, it is a site of horror, a site of a marginalized people who sinned by not wanting to be governed by the United States but were forced to be, a site which is covered essentially as a footnote (or less) in almost any American textbook. The people of that massacre are of course long gone, but the Lakota still see this land as their relative. Each tribe got together to march their flag into the gravesite, united. I insecurely asked Roger if I should go with the Lakota and he said, "Yea, sure, or else you could just stay with that group," pointing to the people who were on the other side of the gathering. Hadn't Ben warned me of this? I had gone about as far as a tee shirt could take me.

Now, today, many people I talk to in our country express an emerging sense of longing, this deepest of human emotions that I now recognize from my time with the Lakota riders. It is a longing for a civil political arena, for a sense of control over our communities, for the efficacy of hard work, and for long-valued traditions. The Lakota, the people of the Pine Ridge Indian Reservation, and many native groups across the country have experienced all these longings for generations, and now at the end of our trail, the grief of the riders gathered together here is bringing some healing. There will be no end to loss for any of us or, for that matter, to the chance for renewal. Gathering together at the end of our ride, it was easy to remember, as Roger said later, "The problems are enormous, but when we bring our community together, the answers are right there." And with this, I knew all I would ever need to know about what it meant to be a tribe.

Conclusions (A Harley Davidson in Every Driveway)

Roger brought our new "tribe" together one last time, in preparation for the final sweat lodge. His emphasis not only on the mechanics of the ride, but the continuing spiritual components of it—its true, intended purpose—was, in the end, supported by calling the group together at the end to process all they had been through. The significant closure of a class, lesson, or expedition, to me, has always been the mark of great teaching.

I am not sure where great teachers come from, as they all seem to have unique histories, and they put a lot more on the table than just their credentialing programs. Great teachers have all surely undergone transformation in at least one stage of life. When Roger White Eyes was a schoolboy, the teachers did not know what to do with him. Outrageous beyond his years, they had him skip a grade. High school was a rocky, renegade time, but somehow they let him be, and kept him in the tribal school. It turned out, like the whole Native American world, Roger did not need the government to civilize him. He naturally transformed from a troubled outlier into a constructive one and, on native intelligence more than scholastic efforts, Roger ended up at Black Hills State University (BHSU). It was up there, in Spearfish, where he took up Lakota Studies, and where a former teacher well remembers the "contrary rebel clown in my classroom," the one with a "special gift."[16] The status quo was never enough. He went renegade again: a bust, a vision quest, an awakening while studying Lakota Studies, and at last graduation from BHSU with a secondary teaching degree. A story and a transformation reminiscent of many great activists were underway.

Roger's college mentor had started a Lakota studies department at the Red Cloud Indian School. Roger took his teaching license and found work there. Later, when they were building the church at the school, some of Roger's students asked him, "Why can't we have our own 'church'?" A sweat lodge. So they built this together, and they invited a medicine man out to bless it, and while he was there he told Roger he had had a vision: that Roger would lead the sweat lodge, that he would pour the water. On his own vision quest, Roger saw that this would be true. In his vision, he and his students would bend the red willow saplings into a lodge; school could be a place of insight and connection, a place where tribal values are alive despite the historical sense of imprisonment and powerlessness on the reservation and in its schools.

Roger was now in his third year of leading sweat lodges at school, the tribal values were in revival, college entry rates were climbing, and this was all a lot of work in an area where problems were enormous, encouragement was thin, and empirical results could take decades to emerge. If we believe in something big enough, some fundamental change, there may not be empirical evidence to support our belief in our lifetime. In the long run, no matter what we do in research, it is persistent faith that supports our vision and our pursuit, not proof. No great turn of events in the history of civilization show any differently.

Are small classes really impossible? Schools that function like tribes? What if American education was analogous to the food situation in India? With millions at near starvation levels, we also know there is enough food in that country to feed everyone, if only we could distribute it properly. In the public schools of America around those early post-millennial years, there were approximately fifty million students being taught by around six million teachers. That's a nine to one student to teacher ratio. As a nation, we have somehow worked this into a situation where thirty and forty students is the norm in most secondary school classes. New York State now spends around $18,000 per pupil. The national average is closer to $15,000, but this does not factor in the $50 billion spent by the U.S. Department of Education or private fundraising. Private schools with income like that feature classes with less than half those student numbers, well into the range where dramatic impacts occur in student and teacher safety, connectedness, and performance.[37]

We don't need motorcycles. Real teachers are all on the "road by discovery." Among the educational leaders I have met are poets, surfers, equestrians, mountain climbers, Zen masters, wine connoisseurs, and tennis champions seeking access to synchronicity, moments of invitation to explore, connect, and ultimately form "inter-tribal nations" and cultures. One conclusion, for people who will never consider small schools, is that even if you are a leader at a large federal agency, a school superintendent, or a university dean, there will never be a replacement for connecting with the educators and parents in real communities based on great listening—not just in town halls, but up close in triads. This is the primary source data we need. The very existence of the high level of disenfranchisement in schools means that we have a window of opportunity for creative alternatives, that the educational marketplace is ripe.

Right there, in communities and small "tribal" schools, conversation is real and we can access the aspirations and fears that people share daily before trying to "fix" them with sweeping, external, big-money systems. We can access their creativity and energy and honor their desire to be self-determining. Without self-determination in our local communities, we are all on the reservation.

It is inspirational to imagine what tribe-size schools of, say, 150 or even anything less than 400 students could do with $18,000 per student. For that amount, we could get each student a brand new Harley Softail, every year. But if we didn't, consider how many more kinds of learners could function and get acknowledgement in small schools and classes, how many less special services would be needed, how many fewer advocacy lawsuits, how much safer and connected our children and teachers could be. If you don't believe it, consider this: you could take a bookish, late middle-aged teacher from a completely foreign culture and almost no local or technical background, give him great and skilled mentoring, small classes, and then integration into a small, caring tribe with a skilled leader and, in five days, turn him into a spiritually-focused, full-blooded tribal warrior capable of riding the great prairies with some of the most proficient, courageous metal horse riders of the American Northwest, grinning ear to ear.

Saying good-bye to Roger and Glenn was tough after what we'd been through. I said, "Roger, that day last winter when you sent me that text message to come up here, it took me a minute to figure out who it was, but I always meant to thank you. I was really on the fence about this crazy ride. What were you doing up there in Spearfish, anyway?"

"I haven't been in Spearfish all year," he replied, half smiling.

I said, "Roger you should be chief," but he saw no difference between a chief and a teacher. To him, teacher was a title of equal reverence. In traveling around, I have found that to be generally true in most traditional cultures.

But secretly, an equally emotional part of the good-byes was returning my bike, a metallic blue twin cam, Heritage Softtail Classic with leather trim, a machine whose responsiveness and character made it seem alive, and for which I will be forever grateful to Harley Davidson, U.S.A. It was time for my drop-off at Black Hills Harley. Among the Lakota, I had learned from teachers of the nation's most persevering values and now, alone as I had started out, I felt different, and more real as a teacher. I left with the sense that a tribe is not just a group of people, it's a way of being and connecting, and this new sense was a source of personal inspiration and cultural empowerment such as any great school must foster. I stuffed all my leathers away into the saddlebags, took off my helmet and strapped it onto the tail rack, turned onto the final highway, and rolled on a little throttle. *Mitakuye Oyasin.*

South Dakota (Lakota Sioux Reservations: Pine Ridge, Rosebud, Cheyenne River, Standing Rock); San Juanico, Baja California Sur, Mexico.

*Aristotle with a Bust of Homer, Rembrandt van Rijn, 1653
(Metropolitan Museum of Art)*

Grauer School students help a local boy install a high efficiency stove in Central America

Promontory, John Muir Trail, Yosemite

Grauer School bus drives through South Dakota Wild Horse Sanctuary on trip to the Red Cloud School in Pine Ridge Indian Reservation

Grauer School tenth grader Savanah at the Wild Horse Sanctuary

Grauer with Rosie the Labrador, born at the Newkirk farm in Lindsay, California

High school teacher and medicine man Roger White Eyes and Stuart Grauer traversing the Badlands by motorcycle during the annual Wounded Knee Memorial Motorcycle Run

The riders reach Wounded Knee and approach the grave site with tribal flags

Thunder moves in during a Wounded Knee Memorial Ride pow wow

5

∾

The Seventh Generation

If you think in terms of a year, plant a seed; if in terms of ten years,
plant trees; if in terms of one hundred years, teach the people.

Confucius, BC 551-BC 479

When we imagine the "traditional school," many of us automatically think
of the public schools in our neighborhoods and districts. But to the Newkirks,
now raising their seventh generation of purebred Labradors on the farm, tradition meant something else.

*   *   *

We had taken the back road to get home from five days hiking in the
Southern Yosemite and Ansel Adams Wilderness, in no race to leave, meandering down. Reaching the foot of the mountain, we were drawn to a paper
sign tacked onto a telephone pole and pulled over. We had walked many steps
renewing our connection to the land. We were rested and calm and fulfilled
from the mountains, the mountain air, and we wanted to hang on to all that,
even for just a few days. We were taking our time for a change. The sign
read, "Labrador puppies for sale." We scribbled down the information and
headed south, then turned eastwards and into the valley, into the farm town
of Lindsay, California, driving fast down the long, straight lanes of citrus and
almond orchards and cattle fields. We pulled into the Newkirk farm, parked
on the dirt. There, off to the left, was a portable wire fence containing seven,
yellow-tan, eight-week-old slugs all cuddled up together.

It was sunny and hot and quiet. A tall, stern man in boots ambled out across the dirt and straw in slow motion. I brushed a horsefly off my head.

"I'm Newkirk. Paul." We did the introductions and bargained on the price for our pick.

"What made you pick that one?" asked Newkirk, reaching down and giving him a little rub.

"Maybe he won't eat as much," I said, being clever. "Anyhow, my wife likes an underdog." He gave a hint of a grin, as though the idea of an underdog meant something to him.

"Well, you ought to live out here, then." We looked at the farmer, puzzled. "C'mon in, it's lunchtime."

Next thing we knew, we were going through the fence gate, through the porch. The aroma was in our noses before the screen door slapped closed behind us. Mrs. Newkirk was closest to the new mother, Old Yeller Sprig. It was her dog, and she told a hunting story as we ladled thick white gravy out of a small wooden bucket. Sprig had fetched plenty of duck, which had ended up on the long, rough-hewn pine table that was all set up for us. We kept quiet and polite, talked a little about schooling like we always do, and dove into the succotash mix, old-time America's effort to make okra palatable by mixing in everything else you could pull in from the farmyard. A metaphor for something or other.

"Where do you go to school?" we asked Newkirk's daughter at the end of the table. She said nothing, but Newkirk opened up like church doors. We did not necessarily want to hear all he had to say, but by the time we could see only the bacon chunks at the bottom of the bowl (left for the hogs), we had learned plenty. Except it was more like remembering than learning. Later on, we recounted some of Newkirk's words to some teachers and one of them said, "What he was saying is what a lot of us are thinking, but might not have put into words yet."

"Schooling kids is a lot like growing crops," Newkirk held forth. "And we can't get the heirlooms* anymore. If we want to sell what we grow, we need to stick to the standard picks of the big chains." A sharp man.

I related that I could hardly hang on to the "heirlooms" in my own classroom, how every year fewer and fewer of my English students had ever even heard of the classics. "Rapunzel." "Pandora's Box." Gone. They knew of

---

* Vegetable varieties that have been around for fifty years or more.

"Snow White," but that was just a Disneyland image. In the generation to come, and throughout our Labrador's life, the situation would escalate as classic literature was steadily replaced by whatever would grind through the interest group debates. "The heirlooms, they're gone from the textbook."

Newkirk looked straight ahead, then down, then scrolled through some thoughts: "In America we get fast food schooling. Fast food . . . fast culture." And he reflected back: "The school keeps getting bigger—it's got nothing to do with our lives out here, or our living, nothing from our area. It's one size fits all. The kids all learn the same thing from one region to the next, just like the local crops getting crowded out."

We nodded. "You mean the state curriculum."

"This is our place. This is our work. But I guess we're not allowed to teach it in the schools."

It took years to mull all this over, but eventually it occurred to me and, I think, quite a few others, that the near-extinction of traditional and heirloom seed varieties on the farm had become controversial and political. Many seeds and crops had been replaced in huge, single-crop fields ready to be transported across the globe, often supported if not monopolized by global corporations or even governments seeking favorable trade balances. But the "aha" that Newkirk's words and attitude eventually brought out was its parallel to large-scale educational programming: the institutionalization of learning and the textbook generation, remote from the community, disconnected from a real heritage, the heritage of the land.

The United States' current massive schools and districts, after the past one hundred years of steady increases in size, have brought with them unintended consequences. The "progressive era" consolidated many rural school districts in order to bring the country folks up to date with modern America.[1] Later on, in the 60s and 70s, came the *school consolidation movement*, resulting in imperfect and often unwanted educational unifications of politically and culturally distinct villages. While large new consolidated districts were established on the assumption that a school's primary purpose lay in providing equal educational opportunity for children everywhere, unintended or uncalculated issues began festering under the surface in these socially engineered communities. The very nature of a community and its boundaries was challenged. The meaning of a school to its community seemed distant. In the small schools of Newkirk's youth, all these questions seem to be answered: a real community is of a size where people know one another.

"When my father got those groves going in 1940, the high school had 127 kids in it," Newkirk recalled, as his wife looked on with a "there Paul goes again" expression; but I was loving it. "The principal knew every family and their dog. Today it has almost seven hundred kids—you think that makes no difference?"

But we understood that the principal had known a whole lot more than that. He knew the land they were raised on, the meaning of the seasons, and the values of their elders. Just this year I looked up Yosemite, great American treasure, in our own high school American history text, a book of 906 pages; but the ultimate jewel of California, the nation's first national park, is nowhere to be found. Nor is there mention of the White River National Forest. As a result, kids in Colorado will rarely (past the fourth grade) study one of the world's great wilderness areas located in their own backyard, any more than the kids in Vermont will understand the impact of their own, historic White River.[2]

I told the Newkirks about my old friend Hanja from Sweden who, back in the early 80s, quipped, as though I were responsible for it, "What's wrong with America! Every part of the country has different curricula, textbooks, and teaching standards." I had thought to tell her that we love our maritime traditions in New England and our cowboys in Texas, how folks from those regions already know all about those orange juice fountains flowing everywhere out in California. Historically, our regional differences make teaching and learning requirements in Florida and the California Central Valley almost as different as they are in Sweden and Spain. The great European treasure is the distinctions among nations and cultures. In the United States, for all our talk of the enormous ethnic and biodiversity in our grandiose land, we somehow end up watching our country race towards uniformity and standardization.

Like a freight train taking on John Henry, Hanja would eventually have it her way: the No Child Left Behind Act, the national teaching standards set by the Race to the Top, and the uniform Common Core standards rolled over local educational practices through the first decade of the new millennium. It would no doubt stun our founding fathers that eventually, in the new millennium, states which adopted national standards would win points in the competition for a share of the billions of dollars to be awarded to the most compliant among them.

In schools and textbooks there had been little mention of farm life since the days of the McGuffy Reader of the 50s. By the 1980s, to farmers like

Newkirk, the American farm tradition of their forebears came across like a quaint and subtly angry fragment of an anachronistic labor movement. We had to wonder: if not our elders, who is in charge of cultural transmission from one generation to the next?[3] What are the politics? Whose agenda is it really?

At the table, I could see Newkirk sitting a little straighter, his face stiffening. Like many farmers and ranchers across the Central Valley and countless other rural areas, it was clear that a powerful sense of place and a deep work ethic attached him to the land. Of course, the land was changing. Traditionally on the farm, heirlooms kept their traits through open pollination, which kept them strong. This preserved genetic diversity, ensuring strength and adaptability. Heirloom and local seed varieties are more resistant to local pests, diseases, and weather extremes. But what Newkirk was conveying to us up in the central farming valley in his apparently simple but deceptively complex detail, was a story of how local and regional heirlooms and intergenerational wisdom were becoming endangered species, both on the farm and, relocated to the edge of town, in the classrooms.

By the new millennium, approximately 70 percent of American high school students would be attending schools enrolling one thousand or more students—the end of the local learning community. Newkirk, not just in his words but in his life, blocked out a vision of a school no longer regional, no longer entrepreneurial, no longer in the hands of teachers as we once defined them: a huge, single crop production. American kids—a monocrop. The spectrum of what you needed to be like in school, of the intelligences that were considered manageable in the classroom, and of the non-medicated behaviors, were narrowing.

"Is she your only one?" we asked.

"She's the one, right Jenny?" he said, winking her way. Old man Newkirk smiled at his daughter at the edge of the table, about eight, corn-silk hair, pure smile—she never said a word—and he showed just a little strain there, he loved her so. We could see abandon in his eyes when he looked down. She tucked in her chin. "We live on farmland as far as the eye can see. Our life is land. Jenny's class has kids who never picked an orange—at school lunch they drink juice canned three thousand miles away or eat produce plastic wrapped in Sacramento. At home a few of them don't even sit down together for supper. Today," Newkirk explained, "the kids' schooling is trucked same as those cans. Yea, anyhow, Jenny's changing teachers this year."

It was August. Though I was only a transient driving through, I could see the Newkirk's tenacious sense of place and devotion to their inherited work—traits that are more likely to be seen as encumbrances in the city and suburbs. And although I deny having any of those encumbrances, what I learned from the Newkirks disturbed me for some years before I was able to work it all out. It took me twenty years. By 2011 there wouldn't be a locally made rhubarb pie within one hundred miles of any school in the nation. In fact, by 2011, in school cafeterias, for lunch and often breakfast, kids would typically be eating products that were once food, processed into high fat and salt, low fiber and nutrient meals. These foods made kids fat and sick while lining the pockets of a small handful of industrial food giants made efficient by virtue of cutting out local farmers and cooks. By 2011 there would also be a handful of powerful textbook manufacturers comprising the national oligopoly. In a striking parallel with the departure of local growers and cooks from schools, in our textbooks actual authors have been replaced by a long list of contributors, censors, and powerful national special interests airing and venting to their concerns.

"We've been on this land for a hundred years and we don't know how we can continue. My father and his farmed what they needed and put everything they had back into our land. But I don't know how much of this new crop our fields can take. It's a lot of seedless hybrids coming in now if we want to sell. We can't grow what makes sense around here, for our land."

I looked at his wife, then to him. "Who really wants standardized crops, anyway?"

He glanced at Jenny, then fixed his eyes on the table and said, "Who wants standardized kids?"

*   *   *

A lot more was to happen in the next twenty years that Newkirk may have intimated but never imagined. Farms and schools would both undergo steady consolidation, and the widening gap between our convictions and our actual lives would strike many of us in the new millennium. American students would become the most obese, depression-medicated people on Earth. Online we'd go to FarmVille, a farming simulation social network game developed by Zynga in 2009 that grew to around forty million active users within a year of launching. This would become their surreal slogan: "Everything grows in FarmVille."[4] By 2010 or 2011 over 10 percent of Americans, very few of whom would ever actually eat any whole foods from real, local "villages," were planting and harvesting crops and turning cyber-plots of land into idyllic little cyber-farms. Online, in FarmVille.

For many kids, FarmVille had become the most accessible means of controlling the environment they lived in, their way out of powerlessness and institutionalization. And, by the millions, they would be taking vacations, throwing touchdowns or hitting holes in one, and making friends "virtually," online, largely incognito and with no eye contact or tone of voice—all this, and no physical movement. Ironically, digital social networking software, even as it was increasingly understood as an enemy of empathic human communication, was marketed by technology firms to districts across America and brought into overcrowded classrooms in a spiritless effort to restore cost effective social interactivity.

Back when we met Newkirk, most American families still sat down together for dinner but, by 2010 only 20 percent claimed to do so.[5] Education was proudly referred to by our wildly growing federal Department of Education as a national race. As of 2010 a child dropped out of that race every nine seconds. If those dropouts, who are mainly boys, wanted an environment that was active or wanted a say in what happened to them (versus passive environments where they had little to no control), they could easily spend several hours a day "wired" into a digital, online environment where a glass screen replaces the open sky. And that is what was occurring.

Kids and other free-range critters naturally seek out environments where they can exert some control, hence the epidemic of online addiction. (Research data substantiating this online preoccupation is ubiquitous.) The fastest growing movement in education was online homeschooling, where students accessed the majority of their classes digitally. This provided them with an apparently limitless school, or virtual school, devoid of the restrictions, fears, and bureaucracies present in the ever-growing public schools; kids will always seek freedom wherever they can find it. Meanwhile, studies started turning up documenting the degeneration of empathy among the young. Of course they felt less empathic: their access to actual relationships with teachers or offline forms of teaching had grown relatively unreliable. Community service was, for many students, something you logged rather than something you offered. And by the second decade of the young millennium, when the whole thing was about ready to implode, the most creative cry from the policy makers and pundits was primarily this: even bigger classes.

In the traditional symbology of America, each animal has its own wisdom. For instance, the crow has no sense of time; he sees past, present, and future simultaneously. At schools, future orientation was almost completely replacing the past and present orientations. It made increasingly less sense to refer to schools as institutions of cultural transmission or preservation when it was a lot easier to see schools as instruments of political agendas and social change. By the time our dog was in her second decade, we began imagining the crow flying back to a whole new movement called *slow education*. School gardens and locally made food. Local history and elders on campus. Smaller schools with less institutionalization and influence from outside interest groups. More self-determination coming from within the communities.

Lunch at the Newkirk's was slow, but we finished up with local oranges and almonds and a lazy smile. It was hot outside, and we strolled out to the dirt courtyard. There, along the edge of the fencing, were the seven puppies, mewling and wiggling all over each other in the shade of the oak tree, and there was our runt of the litter.

When we got home, our daughter knew right away to name her Rosie. She could tell. For the whole first two dog years—fourteen people years—Rosie was incorrigible and high-maintenance; she even chewed up the sprinkler system a major donor had put in the school. We had to throw the ball for her probably thirty times to work off some of her teen energy before we could even think about teaching her. We added a middle school to our school around this time and learned that students that age were, in an important sense, no different from Rosie. To this day we never let them spend a day at school without exercise, even if it's only a few laps around the green before English class. We support free-range kids.

Suddenly, at age two, like a kid finishing eighth grade, almost all the wildness was gone out of Rosie and she was ready to start coming to school regularly. Eventually, Rosie became something of a mascot at our school. In fact, once when we were interviewing teachers, an applicant showed up and, when he saw Rosie out front, asked me, "Does the Board of Health know you have a dog at school?" That interview ended quickly enough.

She loved to graze and lie around our grassy field near the garden—it must have been her farm roots. Rosie grew up strong, calm, and beautiful. We even developed "The Rosie Policy" for all students: if you felt like it, you could leave class any time, no questions asked, by merely asking the teacher, "Can I take Rosie for a walk?" Teens get into some deep stuff, and Rosie handled it all with grace. She came to school with us every day for the next eleven years and received about a hundred thousand hugs until, one day, our old farm dog couldn't jump into the back seat of the car anymore. Most likely the Newkirks are on their eighth generation of Labradors now. I hope so. In my opinion, we will have a tad less ADD and a whole lot more comfort and friendship in a school where there is a beautiful creature like Rosie on campus.

Ansel Adams Wilderness, CA; Encinitas, CA

6

～⚬～

Chief Tayuk, Guy the Bear Hunter, and Me

How Elder Wisdom is Rebalancing School

*Long ago in Nanwalek, long winter nights, the aurora borealis, and life
on the edge of the vast natural world led to a mythology-filled consciousness.
The last century, the petroleum century, eroded this life, and we ventured
north to learn if it could still be brought back.*

Long ago

This is a story of elders, and how we can use their wisdom in our schools.
This is also the true story of how I joined the Nanwalek Band of tribal rock n'
rollers in a far outpost of Alaska, where the salmon are running again.

When we arrived in Nanwalek, Irene Tanape met us on the beach. We
had read of her in back issues of the *Homer Tribune*.[1] She was a grandmother
of many in the village. She recalled speaking only Sugt'stun (the native
Sugpiaq language) while she was growing up in Nanwalek in the 40s, the
decade before it almost disappeared from the schools forever.[2] Irene had to
wait three generations to see signs of a revival, and to get rid of the strange
name, "English Bay," for her village. Now, it was like the Nanwalek people
were awakening from a long hibernation.

In the first of those three generations, Bureau of Indian Affairs (BIA) programs sought to remove all traces of Native American language and culture
across the nation. Students were relocated to boarding schools where they

could "assimilate" into mainstream American culture. All the other ethnic and racial groups had assimilated—why not the indigenous Americans?

By the time the BIA assimilation program had shut its doors and the kids could stay home with their families and tribes and be taught locally again, the native language and customs had eroded; that was the first lost generation. Materials to teach native language and traditions in school were scarce and people had forgotten how to be grateful for them. The young had become shadow Americans and shadow Indians with little clear heritage or pride. There in Nanwalek, the state curriculum was shipped in like fast-food, and the population of the village thinned out while some of those who stayed became obese. A second generation was lost.

Then things got bad. In March of 1989 the Exxon Valdez ran aground in the nearby Prince William Sound and crude oil came spilling out. Eventually, half a million barrels of it. That past summer, the salmon had wriggled their way upstream to Third Lake in Nanwalek and then set out on their ancient migration. But most of those salmon would never return, and much of the seal meat would be gone along with them. By day eleven of the spill, as the elders sat in the tribal hall passing around the salmon jerky, they could see the black slick gliding onto their beach.

The jerky tasted savory and rich, and from then on, when they reached into the bowl for more, they would have to do so more deliberately. The little bit of "black meat" they had in home stores would become the rarest of delicacies because on a seal's fur, oil destroys the insulation, leaving the seal to freeze to death. The local education was already gone, but now the age-old ways and rituals of subsistence—of eating—were about to degenerate, too. Through the years it took to "clean up" the 1989 oil spill and restore local education, the U.S. government (using Exxon's damage payments) shipped in every standard, high-processed, high-fructose corn syrup, high-salt fast-food they could.* Less than half a percent of the food consisted of fruits and vegetables.[3] There would be no fresh meat.

Through those same years, government officials and even a number of locals somehow fell under a spell that made them believe shipped-in, mass-produced food was better than living off the land. Living off the land, *subsistence living*, came to be viewed as the lowest form of human existence.

---

* Government subsidies for meat, dairy, sugar, oil, and alcohol are 85.5 percent versus the 0.4 percent for vegetables and fruits.

As we visited, the Nanwalek were waking up from this spell, subsistence living was now in revival as a core value of the tribe, and we were given the gift of a new world view.

Sugpiaq natives, coastal people from whom the Nanwalek are descended, have fished the Alaskan waters for 7,500 years.[4] From time immemorial, the first salmon caught was met with ceremony. The beaded and ribboned shirts and bright wing dresses came out, and the people formed a circle. Then, as the drums played, dancers leapt and swung their eagle feathers.[5] In the kitchen, women prepared roots and berries to serve along with salmon and any meats. Education took on another dimension as, what traditional minds had not studied scientifically, hearts and spirits interpreted.

But during this strange time, around the time of our visit to see their school and meet their students, the tribe had almost lost their taste for salmon. Subsistence cultures manufacturing basic goods by hand had long been in decline. The past generation could easily have been subjects for a controlled experiment in the development of diabetes. "The oil spill kinda took away our unity in our village—the government was coming in and try-ing to give everyone a quick job," an elder, John Tabasnikoff, told us. The bear rarely visited any more, for there was so little salmon to eat. The young had developed a refined taste for Coke and packaged food. But the bear didn't have options like that. They went the way of the salmon. And of course the hunters of bear and seal went that way, too. This hurt more than the people's diet; it hurt their identity, for who could be more esteemed in Nanwalek than the bear hunter and the seal hunter?

Then, like an awakening, families began repairing their old salmon smok-ers and seaweed dryers. How that reawakening came about was an extraordi-nary thing that any school could benefit from studying and, up in Alaska, we were walking right into it.

Long ago in Nanwalek

There is an old Jewish folk tale where the little girl asks, "God, is it okay to love strangers?"

God replies, "I don't make strangers, you make them."

God does, however, make us into elders. And although it is hard to assign a precise time when we made strangers out of our elders, it is easy to see the trend of isolating our elders accelerating over the past century, nationwide.

Elder wisdom has always been presumed to be a big part of any culture's educational process. Historically, most cultures have used their elders as a fundamental part of education and often the term "elder" implied a teaching role. For instance, the word *küpuna* in native Hawaiian means "wise elders," a word which has no counterpart in English. The French language has *doyen*. A "sage" is historically someone wise and, usually, older. The storytellers of many cultures have been the elders, as well, and education is normally viewed as fundamentally intergenerational: a passing along of traditions and wisdom. Elders were traditionally viewed as those who had the experience and perspective needed by the rising generation, hence, a normal part of education. However, this tradition appears to have silently disappeared in American schools, changing a subtle, age-old balance. In the village of Nanwalek, we were able to observe a rebalancing first-hand, as a national harbinger.

Three generations ago in Nanwalek, traditional subsistence life required everyone to be involved in education. "We cleaned the smokehouse and gardened—putting up food and picking berries," Tanape's sister Kathy Brewster said. "There was always something to do."[6] Kids in local schools had to learn these intergenerational skills, passed down from their elders.

Two generations ago, when the Bureau of Indian Affairs schools changed all that, a generation came through with a new kind of education and all new words were passed down. Irene and Kathy's parents taught at the BIA School. What did they pass down?

The BIA displacement of indigenous kids, mostly in the 1950s and '60s, must seem like legend to the Nanwalek, because it sure isn't covered in the high school history books. As Indian kids across America were moved to boarding schools, their native language and customs were "cleansed." Tribal schools were disbanded. The campaign ultimately foundered and ended and now, with some sense of victory, the Nanwalek were calling themselves Sugpiaq, meaning "real people," once again. They were proclaiming on their website that their culture "has steadfastly survived the Russian and later American impact on traditional lifestyles": one more testament to the astonishing tenacity of ethnicity through the ages.[7] How did they do it?

Here is an association that has not turned up in any educational journals we can find. During this same lost generation, call it *the BIA/Valdez time*, American elders were moved to a *reservation* of another kind. "Up to the

1950s, about 2 percent of the country's senior citizens were in institutions of some kind. Between 1960 and 1976, nursing-home beds increased by 302 percent, and the revenues received by the industry rose 2,000 percent." By the year 2000, nursing homes in the United States had become a $100 billion industry.[8] The proportion of those over eighty-five years in age increased to 25 percent, largely supported by social security, Medicaid, and Medicare. Notwithstanding Congress's method of entitling the disadvantaged, the parallel between old age and Indian treatment could have come right out of a Russell Means speech: "The United States is one big reservation, and we are all in it."

When an environmental disaster strikes a remote, traditional culture, the toxicity creeps into their spirit and their schools as much as into their land and wildlife. What the Nanwalek feared losing after the spill, and still feared losing later on, was not much different than what any community in the country was concerned about losing: unity. Unity of the family, the community, and the ecosystem. But risk, loss, and fear can also be calls to arms. And while a more detailed history might be a greater draw for the scholarly, this brief but hopefully substantial background was our canvas as we journeyed north. Essentially, the old ways were being recalled to life, and we were about to learn this from the least likely source for elder wisdom: the kids.

Revival

Nanwalek is located at the farthest point of the Kenai Peninsula. To reach this place, one must head by car west and south out to the bitter end of the Kenai Peninsula. And so we set out. Along the highway, out on the peninsula, we passed a sign stating how many moose and caribou had been struck by cars this year, so far. 180. Just past this sign, along a river bend, a grizzly bear sat in a shallow cove of the Kenai River, pawing three red salmon he'd freshly killed. Of course we pulled over. As if called by the wild, our students were lured too far down the embankment and we had to call them back.

Continuing on towards the edge of civilization we passed bald eagles and beachfronts with no footprints, eventually reaching the end of the road: the Homer spit. To continue, we boarded a single-engine Cessna 207 at Homer Air, piloted by a twenty-one-year-old bush pilot named Ricky. We headed south towards the end of the peninsula, passing bay after bay along the Cook

Inlet. Then, just before leaving Alaskan airspace entirely, our pilot bore full speed upon the last mountain on Kenai, the last landmass between us and the open, North Pacific Ocean, and just as we became certain that the only possible course would be to crash straight into that mountain, Ricky banked hard into a hairpin turn and caromed straight into a perfect, one-wheeled, sandy beachfront landing onto a crescent beach, the smoothest landing you'd ever see.

We wobbled out of the plane onto the damp sand and pebbles of Nanwalek Bay and found the tribal youth coordinator, Darryl Kreun, and the former tribal chief, none other than Irene Tanape, sister of the current tribal chief, Wally.

Irene and Darryl hiked us straight up to the Nanwalek School for our introductory tour. As we peeked into the classrooms, we got a glimpse of something that we had always wished to see down in the lower 49 states. Like the salmon, the local language, traditions, and customs were in revival, right there in the classrooms. In one class the question on the whiteboard was: "Why is it important that we know the names of our berries?" (Local bushes hold the blueberry, mountain berry, salmonberry, high-bush cranberry, and more.) Why this is not on every standardized achievement test in the nation, I will never understand. We heard the elders were making their way into the classes and were teaching how they used to make bread from back when it still had whole grains in it.

In mainstream America, grandparents are no longer really a part of our schooling, and a diminishing part of our cultural transmission occurs from the eldest generation to the youngest. We are searching for an equivalent to the salmon run or the bear hunt. But in Nanwalek, we had a unique experimental group to study: a microcosmic, multigenerational culture relatively disconnected from mainstream America. You can't even drive here. You needed permission from the tribal chief to even visit.

For the record, none of the Alaskan students we met were "Eskimos" (depending on where you are, some find it rude to call these indigenous Yupik and Inupiat people in Alaska this name) and none were living in igloos. In Nanwalek, about a third of the people we met were of Native American or "Indian" blood, from the ancient indigenous peoples of the area, and about a third have Russian blood (from migrants crossing the Bering Strait); the other third are of European descent. For illustration, the tribal chief's name was: Tayuk Wally Kvasnikoff: Native/Western European/Russian.

I surely wanted to meet this tribal chief. I wanted not only to thank him, but to learn why, after three months of trying, he finally accepted our request to visit, to learn what he, as a leader and a grandparent, had to share with a group of affluent Southern Californians. What could he want from us?

Leaving the school with hints of revival, a few of us walked down to the Nanwalek grocery store. A young, powerful-looking villager with a Mohawk haircut motored the whole two blocks of the village on his off-road Honda four-wheeler, rifle strapped to the back of the vehicle, before pulling in to the store. In the mudroom, a three-year-old was downing a clear plastic bottle of Coke while his mom sat on the bench, pulling in long and slow on a Marlborough.

Inside the store were four twenty-foot aisles, most with colorful plastic packaging. No fresh food, everything in cans. Of the four rows, one full row was of Kool-Aid and similar fake, sugary drinks and snacks. Another row was all canned drinks, mainly soda. The baked goods and breads were all made of bleached, sugared white flour. Leaving the store in a few minutes time, the same man was loading two boxes onto his four-wheeler: two cases of Coke and, under his arm, a case of cigarettes. Later that day, in a different kind of world, we were to meet this man. We would know him, and revere him, as *Guy, the Bear Hunter*. But here at the store, as his post-millennial self, he was one among the diabetes generation, the Valdez generation.

I missed much of our culture of the 80s by living in Europe at that time, so I am still puzzled by the *hair bands* that captivated our youth culture during that time. I also missed the entire Reagan revolution, though I've been briefed. But missing the second half of the twentieth century would have been a whole lot more puzzling—no Baby Boomers, no Gen X-ers—imagine jumping from the Greatest Generation straight to the "Millennials."

If the American public school system is efficient at a single thing, it is this: testing groups so that they can provide them with labels. In Nanwalek, with little real change, what had been a *traditional school* a half-century ago was now being described as a public school with 72 percent of all students labeled Economically Disadvantaged, 78 percent Alaska Native/American Indian, and a 50 percent graduation rate.[9] All new labels for the same old Nanwalek. Today's Nanwalek "natives" are more ethnically mixed and seem to test better in reading, but that's about it.

It was as if most of their educational values and traditions had lain in hibernation for at least a couple generations, and they were now awakening.

Even the bears were coming around again. This was a startling anthropological situation for the Nanwalek in particular, because a generation ago all the signs were threatening the death of their traditional culture. But the elders in this remote Kenai Peninsula village had not yet been marginalized from the community in the same way that they had in the lower 49. Why? Because they were now essential.

The elder John Tabasnikoff, who would later become chief, said, "The spill took away the resources like fish, seal and sea lion, seaweed, and it took away our unity. They are still trying to recover, and we've made progress, but I personally don't think they are all the way there yet."[10]

A few years into the new millennium, as the summer work of harvesting gardens and putting up fish restarted after the long sleep, Tanape and other elders started passing on the old stories of how things were done in the old days. We found these stories drifting into the school, and even into the curriculum. The Sugpiaq language was required again (as a second language), although this remains a part of an ongoing fight with the district office that keeps wanting to cut it back. All the same, every Thursday when the elders would meet to talk *Sugt'stun* and have their community meal, the kids were wandering down to listen to them, to learn the language. The students were building a traditional smokehouse. The self-reliance of growing gardens and putting up winter food was taking on new significance in this age of high electrical and fuel costs. "We didn't have refrigerators, so we salted, smoked, or dried our fish . . . and gathered up goose tongue (grasses)," Tanape recounted with the pride of tradition. "We ate bear, moose and seal."[11] And now they were eating this again.

A few local teens met us upon our arrival at the school. They didn't look like Alaskans, or sound like them. They looked like kids, although our kids looked preppier. As I followed two of them into the school I overheard one student whispering to her friend: "We could intimidate them." Just a few hours earlier, while encountering a bear, we had had to order our non-intimidated students back up the hill; now they huddled together at the school doors, eyes widened—a separate pack.

All generations are defined by their stories but, in our Southern California community and probably also in the rest of the nation, the old stories are rarely being told. Back at our school earlier that same year, we had attempted an elder "story recapture" and observed the difficulty of warming up different generations to one another. In one such project, each of our students was assigned an elder community member from our town. One seventh-grade girl was paired up with a ninety-two-year-old gentleman from a neighboring assisted living facility. She began her interview with him:

"Can you tell me about your family?"

"I can't. My family all died in the gas chambers, in Nazi Germany."

The seventh grader jotted down a word, scanned her interview script, and continued, "Have you suffered any hardships or misfortunes in your life?"

The gentleman processed this information, silently for a while, as the young student studied her paper some more, mystified by the silence that it often seems only elders are wise enough to allow. Then, shyly, she risked this:

"What's a . . . gas chamber?"

The gentleman took a big, deep breath, recognizing with the compassion that only a man that old might have, that he was not only needed as an elder, but as a teacher. He told her the story of Nazi Germany, a much bigger story than his own.

There in Nanwalek, the struggle never leaves Tabasnikoff's voice: "Now the families tend to buy all the stuff money can buy, like satellite dishes; it takes away people getting together—they go home and watch TV, and they could be visiting and have human contact, have a cup of tea. We're trying to work that back, but it's hard to grasp it back; the elders practice it, and they tell the stories, but the kids are plugged into headphones." He then said thoughtfully, "Some are starting to understand how much we lost."

*   *   *

We had not known that we were flying into a revival in self-reliance and subsistence, but we were quick to embrace it. Public art featuring traditional scenes and nature adorned the buildings. Berry picking and gathering was once more feeding the community, and elders were showing the young how their grandparents had made jams. When a fisherman donated fish, an elder had given notice that she would be there in the community hall kitchen to teach anyone who was willing how to can it.

Six different types of salmon had been back in their inlets this year, along with halibut, cod, octopus, and razor clams. In learning and observing all this, we began to draw some parallels between sustainability, salmon, and the role of elders—we began to discern their cultural ecology, much different from our own.

At some point on any great trip, we become aware that something larger than the trip is happening, that a shift is occurring—a new set of eyes—and we begin to observe different things in a different way. Walking around, we start to see things, see beauty that we completely missed when first passing through. Maybe new colors or sounds start to pop out in our awareness. We *see*.

Walking through the village again at the end of the day, we now noticed that the salmon driers had been newly mended, and at mealtime we listened as people recalled the natural seasonings that their grandparents had prepared for cooking. People brought up old debates about the texture and flavor of the Coho versus the Chinook salmon. They had restored the seaweed dryers last spring: four types of kelp. As all this came back, something else was being recalled to life such as I had not seen elsewhere: the elders.

I had yet to meet Chief Wally, and did not know if I would, but I had read a quote in the local newspaper from him: "Our elders are very important and we want to take good care of them. This ties young people back to the stories of the old days. It keeps them busy and wakes them up to the real world."[12]

The community garden was being harvested, the first-picked going to the elders. That was the tradition. And at the school they were passing around CD-ROM disks of the Sugpiaq language songs and rhymes. The social and educational cultures were shifting.

The Oxford anthropologist Robin Dunbar has famously suggested that, culturally, around 150 is the "cognitive limit to the number of individuals with whom any one person can maintain stable relationships." The rule is based upon cross-cultural studies of villages ("ecovillages") of various sizes.[13] In large schools boasting of diversity, five, ten or even twenty times the size of such villages, culture is hard to define and harder to shift. The standard public high school is an easy place to observe students retreating into groups, confining most of their interactions to those who seem most like them in attitude, attainment, and background: cliques.[14] Schools of over two hundred students, and certainly those of over four hundred, routinely spawn clique formation in such a natural way that few ever become aware that it need not be this way. In our region, Southern California, schools normally have over eight hundred students, if not over three thousand. For sociology buffs, you might recall this as Max Weber's old *gesellschaft*.

Nanwalek is tribe-size (population of a little over two hundred) with a school of eighty students in kindergarten through grade twelve (ninth grade class size = one student). Here we can observe theory in action.

The people talk and interact freely across groups. They feel connected, even with their teachers, their grandparents, and their village elders.[15] They are *tribal* in a way which management gurus incite schools and organizations to be for high performance. The very old and very young, the nerds, bear hunters, and singers—all mix and share the same core values. *Gemeinschaft.*

Guy the Bear Hunter

It was time to retire to the cabins for the night. According to the local kids, the cabins were right around the corner at Second Lake. We pulled on our muck boots and marched into cultural relativity and chilling air. "Right around the corner" was a slog longer than we'd had in a month, through ruts and mud, up and down hills, across the stream beds, and brushing against stinging "devil's club" nettles. Guy followed us on his four-wheeler, cradling a loaded rifle, just in case. If Guy were in our home community, he would be the fullback on the football team—he'd probably be too busy with the team and cheer squad to pay much attention to us. For our students, it was a revelation to spend time with someone fulfilling the role of popular high school athlete, yet doing something real. It is hard to prove that there is a true difference, but we sensed one, joked and sang about it, and Guy became its personification. In an age where the distinction between reality and virtual reality is blurring rapidly for students, where student value and worth are assessed with "validity and reliability" after they pencil in bubbles on a paper score sheet, it can be hard to find any schooling we can call, with certainty, *real.*

Walking across the last streambed before the lake, we heard crackling. Looking down, blended into the mud, we saw an embankment of dead salmon—stacks of them. Last year the *humpy* salmon (more widely known as pink salmon) came in so thick that when they spawned and died you could literally walk across the stream on their dead backs. Two days earlier we would have thought this many dead fish was an eco-disaster rather than something to celebrate: the salmon were back!

At last we arrived. Second Lake is a pristine, two-mile lake surrounded by virgin forests and mountains so high we could see glaciers. In our town, this property would be worth billions. In the lake, five-pound salmon were swimming so thick we could snag them with a treble hook, Guy always on hand to unsnag us. Across the lake, two bald eagles sat perched in a cottonwood tree.

It was the third week of September. We looked up at the mountain at the season's first snow. A rich life, but a tough life, closer to survival than we'd ever seen; life lived with a loaded gun. September and we all had three layers on, waterproofed. Guy, in a tee shirt, twenty-one at the time with two children, had six kills this past season. Bears. He said he was looking for number seven.

Guy was possibly the toughest man we'd ever seen, but he stood in the balance of some tough forces. The Nanwalek dependence on the satellite dishes which the federal government had made so cheap during the dark days after the oil spill did not make for a hearty tribe with a deep connection to the natural surroundings. From Southern California, we naturally love the image of people up there living off the land, savoring folky traditions. But when we call up there and ask them what they'd like us to send, they often say: warm blankets. Tabasnikoff said, "You know, not everyone can be doctors and lawyers, and that's true up here, too. But not everyone can be a bear hunter, either." Guy was hoping to get a little posse of kids to learn the ancient skill, continue the tradition and the connection to the land; but there aren't too many people out there as tough as Guy, the bear hunter.

How I Joined the Nanwalek Band

It was our last night in Nanwalek, and we prepared to gather for a village feast in our honor: a feast and a dance. What we got now seems surreal.

We moved over to the tribal hall. There we were to meet the elders, commune with them, and to thank the tribal chief, Wally Kvasnikoff, whom we had still to meet.

We arrived on time to the minute, but tribal time doesn't work like that and hardly a soul was there yet, except in the kitchen. In a far corner of the tribal center was a full rock band set-up: drums, guitars on stands, amps, etc., and it drew me right in. Presently, a man ambled over and started warming up on an acoustic guitar. I said, "Show me a song." He opened up a guitar case and handed me a vintage Fender Telecaster, showed me a rock standard, and we started playing around some. Just noodling. (I'm a hack, but he was good.) After a couple songs like this, a villager sat down behind the drums and joined in, and soon enough another guitar player. In the most natural way, an actual song started up, a blues progression with a minor chord, an easy one, and the song developed with our new combo. Probably what makes classic rock classic is the connective power it has, pretty much worldwide. It's like *unity*. I won't be giving up my day job as a headmaster for a music career, but in this situation it suddenly meant the world to me to keep up with this impromptu rock 'n' roll combo. Magic.

The elders had mostly arrived at the tribal hall by that time, and the real ceremony began. The youth emerged from the kitchen, dancing in a line to a boom box, forming a circle around the hall. They then presented our students with traditional ribbon gowns they had made themselves: a blend of indigenous and Russian trimmings. Next, drawing our student group into the circle, the two groups combined as the Alaskan high schoolers led their California counterparts around the floor, dancing the old dances of the elders. Later, Olivia, grade eleven, said, as only a teen could, "It amazed me that they were able to keep the dance alive through all the years and still not be embarrassed to perform it to a group of outsiders they just met." The tribal gathering was finally under way.

We set up encounter groups of four to five mixed Nanwalek/California high schoolers. Using *World Café* methodology, these high schoolers from remote cultures dialoged in small groups and, after a while, their stories, aspirations, and fears came out. "Waking up, seeing the same people every day, every day. I gotta get out of here, man." Big issues.

"What are you afraid of in life?" we asked the mixed groups. A nineteen-year-old who graduated last year picked it up from there: "I wanna leave but I don't wanna leave." Another disclosed, "I'm scared to go out to the outside world because I don't think I could do it on my own."*

Elders here had somehow engaged the youth in a forgotten perigee to prompt not just a rediscovery of knowledge, but a renewal of the rituals people have always relied on to survive in the sometimes forbidding and incomprehensible world of adolescence. The Nanwalek were attempting to rebalance their rational and spiritual worlds, the practical and the ceremonial, the light and the dark, the old and the young, which contrast so harshly in this part of the world. Forming a circle with their California counterparts, the students from both worlds began another traditional tribal dance, the fish, as the elders watched on.

---

* Overall, American Indians have the lowest rate of eligibility for college among ethnic groups in the nation, and yet tribal colleges which provide general education as they preserve tribal wisdom are growing rapidly.

Villagers were using furs again, and our teachers were presented with pillows of sea otter and fox to take home. The Russian Orthodox minister said a blessing. Then it was time to eat.

In Nanwalek, the first catch always goes to the elders. The first cut of bear meat goes to the elders. Students served their elders, while our kids acted like that was normal, then all the students and other villagers began moving down the food line. While we ate bear and seal meat, salmon roe, and locally smoked tamuuq and balik salmon, the likes of which Russian czars killed for, the elders told stories about hunting and cold times. We heard of times when the salmon spawned in the millions. The women are still not allowed to hunt, but they described processing and preparing the food brought home by the men. Smoking, drying, and canning. Stocking up for the dark, six-month winter.

Hunters I have met have always told me that bear meat is too hard to cook and hardly worth eating, but this bear was tender and tasted like lamb. Our student Kelianne, grade eleven, added: "We couldn't get enough of the bear and the salmon jerky."

As dinner and the ceremony wound down, a new situation unfolded such as, while pondering a teaching career over three decades earlier, I could never have predicted in my wildest dreams, and it is recorded in my journal in this way:

The Nanwalek guitar player gives me the nod, and points to the Fender. A new band member, one of the elders, comes up next to me and straps on the bass. A teenage lead guitarist leans over and gives me the chords and we crank up. These guys can play! The new kid is tearing it up on the guitar, and the new elder is pulsing away on the bass, rockin'. This is the full band, formerly called the English Bay Band. The lead singer is a round, smiling, rich-voiced elder woman, former chief Larissa Jimmy, and she knows every lyric from the classics: Stones, Eagles, Zeppelin.

The grown-ups are out on the floor, rock dancing. Next, our students and the Nanwalek teens move onto the floor, except they are not doing California or rock 'n' roll dances. As long ago, drums to the west, all the kids form a dance circle, moving counterclockwise. They are dancing the seal dance and the bear dance, dances the Nanwalek elders made up long ago to mimic the movements of the animals that gave them sustenance, moving bodies with a bend of their knees, swinging cupped hands to their hearts, recapturing the spirit and heart of education that the state syllabus cannot address.

What we witnessed must have defied anthropological wisdom: the elders rockin' out, the kids dancing the traditional dances of long ago. It had been nearly a thousand moons since Native Americans had first started refusing to become integrated into the United States. Could this be happening?

> *Pulsing through the community hall, the song is more than just a Rolling Stones classic, it's a cultural universal. The bass player, a bearded, seasoned looking elder man and I are riffing off one another. I lean towards him, synching our two, stringed sounds as the song comes to an end with a sense of triumph, and I can only grin at this man, who reaches out his hand and says:*
>
> *"Hi, I am Wally Kvasnikoff, The Tribal Chief."*

At last, proof: everything in the universe is connected to everything else.

The Way Back Home

So that was the story of how I was in the Nanwalek Tribal Band. It may not be the world's greatest story, but it's not bad. More importantly, it is the story of how the most historical and natural source of educational wisdom and tradition since the dawn of civilization has been almost completely removed from schooling—and how there are some signs of a revival up in the North Country.

Things change and all enduring cultures embrace that change while simultaneously resisting things which disturb their delicate equilibrium too much. The Nanwalek model suggests the great power our elders can retain by watching over that equilibrium with kindness and patience.

We cannot identify much in the way of trends because the topic of elder wisdom in schools is not seriously studied, nor is it covered in research journals or current schools of education.

All the same, I recommend communing with them. Trying their bear meat. Because up there in the once but no longer forsaken outpost of Nanwalek, they were happy to show us the frontier, and the salmon returning two or three years after they had spawned, coming back home to sustain their village. They showed us that devil's club, boiled to a condensed mixture and taken only in small doses, can hold pain-healing properties and help with arthritis, that wild rhubarb and parsley taste great (although not all the native dishes did). And that it's hard to get vitamin C way up there, hard to find enough muktuk! I cannot prove that elder wisdom is a necessity for schools— it's all a matter of values—but this much I know: *without our elders we can advance, but only with them can we sustain.* It's harsh up there, and not a place to take wisdom for granted. Back in California, what do we care about that resembles this? *What sustains us?*

A posting from a student journal: "Friday, September 25. This morning we woke up and it was so cold and windy that we weren't sure if we were going to be able to fly back to Homer. Luckily I had my 'Cat's Meow' sleeping bag to keep me warm." But the planes arrived and we were gone.

We had brought them fruits, nuts, and vegetables from San Diego. In exchange, they gave us furs, bear meat, salmon, and many of the things that come from their land. Somehow, as almost always happens when we set out in the world to serve others, we left feeling we'd gotten the better end of the deal. We brought home a message we shouldn't have to travel to the edge of civilization to find: land and our forebears are sacred because they mean survival. Our student, Olivia, commented, "While in Nanwalek, I found how sacred the land, culture, and traditions were to them."

In an age of educational metrics, there is still no pop-quiz to assess this knowledge to the satisfaction of the Board of Education or even the local Nanwalek board. Even they, like everyone in the lower 49, tend to see subsistence living as relatively primitive and uncivilized. This year, every Nanwalek teacher had to sign a new contract agreeing to acknowledge the traditional values of the village but, as Wanda Kvasnikoff (she married into the family) explained, "We had to fight tooth and nail to have our school acknowledge our traditions and, luckily, we now have a great principal." Most of the principals I know would kill a bear for a strategic plan as clear and as good as that new contract demands. Now the teachers will need the elders. It is hard to prove that there is a difference between the book learning the teachers could do on their own and elder wisdom but, for our students, time with the Nanwalek elders opened up different ways of seeing the world. And now, in an act of courageous leadership, the principal is bringing Guy into the school for a semester to teach students bear hunting and outdoor skills.

The news of movements like this worldwide do not guarantee that elders teach better or that students will learn better from them—culture is not like that. What matters here is simpler than that, and being acted out on the U.S. national stage regularly. A culture can develop with intentionality, can choose the values it aspires to, can preserve and focus on what its people find valuable—can do all this, unless it stops revering its past. Intelligence is, of course, culture- and values-based, it is not an external standard someone sets in an office of education somewhere afar (!), and we forget that in the lower 49. It's not that Nanwalek kids will test higher now that the elders are involved in the schools; it's that the Nanwalek will fight to change what's on the test. In the past couple decades, in addition to a growing body of research on the subject, we have witnessed, first-hand, ancient, endangered native languages being re-introduced in schools far and wide across the globe: Ireland, French Polynesia and Hawaii, Guatemala, and the Pine Ridge Indian Reservation—enough to make us wonder about a rebalancing of schooling on a larger scale.

From the courageous Nanwalek elders, we were given a living laboratory detailing how to rebalance our rational, sacred, and spiritual selves, on our land. In return, we send them fruits, nuts, or blankets. That much cold and dampness really can give you the chill and feel of death, a reminder such as we all need now and then of the power of the human will to survive, and of how much we all need one another. On the way home, waiting on the beach landing strip for that crazy bush pilot from Homer Air, our lead teacher, Christy Goodson, said: "What I observed during my stay with them was how close everyone was." Unity.

Why do United States schools distance themselves from elders, their wisdom, and their concept of a shared sense of community wisdom and self-reliance? (We never talked about that in graduate school.) "Unity is what . . . what we lost . . ." said Tabasnikoff, his voice filled with mixed feelings.

Alaska, translated, is *the final frontier*, an apt metaphor for our elders' place in life. In many cultures, this frontier is honored. In many cultures, "the Teaching of the Elders" is the most revered teaching. We saw why: in Nanwalek, a whole culture had been lost—not just in the schools but in every institution—and only the elders could show them the way back home.

That week we were eye to eye with salmon, bear and bear hunters, bald eagles, and traditional wise men (and women), but not with a moose. Back in downtown Anchorage on the way to the airport, magic was delivered. Stopped at a mid-city red light nibbling grass was a three-year-old, four-point bull moose. The crosswalk light turned green, and our moose ambled across the street while cars waited, the most natural thing in the world. Just a few moments later we boarded the 747 headed south for Encinitas, Southern California, where week-old *Sugpiaq* salmon is called "sockeye" and gets fifteen bucks a pound, signs on four-lane roads caution drivers about surfers crossing, and elders living largely in remote, institutional tribes rarely set foot in a school. "Unity is what we lost . . . but we can get some back," said the wise elder, but it now seemed more of a challenge for us than for the Nanwalek. A universe of old and new, natural and technological forces, inside and outside influences on education could almost seem overwhelming, and it seemed to me that the tribe's school was culturally approaching a place of balance.

Later on, I had a good laugh with Chief Wally about how all he really had anticipated from our visit was just to jam a little.

Nanwalek, Alaska; Teahupoo, Tahiti

Grizzly bear on the side of the road, Kenai River, Kenai Peninsula, Alaska

Boy in the mud room entryway to the Nanwalek, Alaska grocery store in the early morning

Encinitas students are shown native dances by their Nanwalek counterparts

Grauer with Guy the Bear Hunter and a freshly caught salmon

Boy in Superman shirt with homemade chocolate drink for breakfast in Monte Albán, Mexico

Grauer with an original Herrshoff in Penobscot, Maine—one of the finest small wooden vessels ever built

A student in the market in Oaxaca, Mexico looking for native healing herbs converses with a basket weaver

The water prison in Monte Albán, unlocked for one hour every Tuesday morning to allow the community to take what water was collected from the gorge

7

The Awakeners

"I am not a teacher, but an awakener."

Robert Frost, *American Poet*

Oaxaca's best-known curandera, a native shaman and healer, was Maria Sabina, who died in 1985 at the age of 91. Maria had visions of "little saints" who would finally take the ancient shamanic traditions to the world after 500 years of keeping their secrecy under Spanish rule. After revealing her visions to outsiders, her son was murdered and Maria's house burned to the ground. Towards the end of her life, she lamented: "The power of the sacrament had been lost in the clouds."

Lost in the Clouds

Lost mysteries. The power to reveal the greatest mysteries of the world is held by the very few teachers who can access them. The enlightened. The shamans. The curanderos. The teachers. Cultures erode, but their great teachings are somehow rediscovered through the generations.

These few who are "called" to shelter and carefully pass along the world's mysteries and secrets of life may have started out as ordinary people, but they usually have undergone some transformation. In some cases, the power and presence of their own, contemporary culture is no longer their prevalent guide. They seek larger, older, or more unified worldviews. It is as if these great teachers all share a single, eternal source of wisdom, as if they sense an interrelatedness of all human and natural phenomena.

119

In the airport waiting room, looking out over the tarmac, my daughter Audrey, a fifteen-year-old California high school student, and I are mapping out our trip on paper placemats. The Tijuana airport coffee, a blend of Kona Hawaiian and Kenya African, is strong and good. With one sip, we are at the top of a geographical isosceles triangle, a power point, but we will be *offline* for the next week. Without Google categorizing the world, our ability to communicate effectively about geography will be broken down in the coming days. We (or rather, I) chose this trip over spending spring break on the island of Oahu, a blue-green heaven of balmy breezes and palm trees.

We are traveling to the state of Oaxaca, Mexico, to a tiny village perched on a hillside below the ancient ruins of the legendary Monte Albán. We carry in tow an oversized duffle bag of school supplies, ready-to-inflate soccer balls, and toothbrushes that we have dragged across the Otay Mesa border. We feel uncommitted, empty, and not sure of why we are doing this instead of flying to Hawaii. We are flying due south. It feels like going back in time. Not long before our trip, across the state of Oaxaca, the teacher's union (among other unions) staged a long strike and the power struggle almost shut the entire state down. During the time of the union strikes there were not only few tourists in the villages, but few teachers. Now, quite tentatively, both are starting to return. The violence has been driven underground for a while. This has presented us with a rare window of time to study a question worth asking: what if, in a community, the teachers have gone away? Where we were going, there were virtually none, and there may not have been real teachers there for centuries.

The once-sacred village of Monte Albán was the center of the Zapotec culture for close to a thousand years before it was devastated and abandoned. Today there was only scant public schooling, and the people were not involved in conceiving of something more substantial. Creating a new school was entirely the idea and plan of the DIJO (Desarrollo Integral de la Juventud Oaxaquena), an Italian humanitarian and religious mission.

Ximena greets us at the airport. She is from the DIJO mission. They are hiring me as their consultant. They wish to found a school. Much like the Peace Corps volunteer and the foreign aid worker, the educational consultant and evaluator can easily become a neo-missionary, with presumptions of his own healing power that may be incongruent with the barely known subject group.

Ximena has long dark hair and appears youthful, though middle-aged, with an expression which is both curious and hopeful. It dawns on me that she has sincere faith that I will do something powerful down here. She manages the *comidor,* a free kitchen for the village children. There, their plan is to develop a school of their own in the village so the children could get to it easily.

My plan is a little different. In Oaxaca, I hoped to access knowledge about Monte Albán culture and traditions that will contribute to the establishment of their school, and I did not know where to find this. Where would I find the teachers? Would there be wise elders?

"I just want the mothers to know the world is more than Monte Albán and their children," Ximena says. She has a heart like the moon and a business sense to balance it. "I want them to believe in themselves. The fathers go north to the United States. They don't send back money."

No. They don't. Rather than transform into community leaders, spirit seekers, or even bread winners who nourish their own homes here in the village, these same fathers transform into *coyotes,* the name for those who travel north across the U.S. border at night, then through the canyons and across the desert, if they don't die of exposure or get caught. The ancients imagined sorcerers capable of transforming themselves into coyotes, then back into men. This, of course, has come true. These sorcerers laid the foundation, did the framing, the drywall, and the roofing for the Grauer School in Encinitas, California, the school I founded in 1991. Many try to forget their former lives south of the border. Time speeds up. They adopt a new spirit. Some have new children there in Southern California and almost half of these new children, first generation Mexican Americans, graduate from high school—great and wonderful odds compared to Monte Albán.

"You have such a big job," Ximena says to me, showing her enormous respect for me, because I am a real teacher, she believes, here to help, and I have just flown down from the clouds—from America.

Research Design

Considerable preparation goes into the design of an authentic and valid educational evaluation or intervention.

Over decades I have done scores of school evaluations and consultations and created hundreds of recommendations and action plans. The ethic is to study the school's documentation carefully, prepare questions and hypotheses, go on the campus for a few days and superimpose an external system of generally accepted controls on the school, and finally see how those controls stand up to the local reality. From these you can make recommendations.

Each school in each part of the world has its own, unique and wondrous characteristics, its own validity. The external controls and "professional standards" evaluators set forth may be devoid of local wisdom, so it is essential that the school consultant or evaluator work closely with the locals and incorporate local perspectives and wisdom. It is equally important that the organization have clear intentions for inviting in evaluators. I recall at least one case where an excellent school chose a rigorous, externally developed evaluation format and failed in their efforts to be accredited, ending up bitter and disenfranchised—they were excellent nonetheless, at what they were excellent at. If only that had been evaluated.

The desire to marry the community or school's organizational goals, idiosyncrasies included, with the standards and skills of outside evaluators has helped advance exciting methodologies in *appreciative inquiry, process-oriented evaluation,* and *action research.* Using these strategies, all parties can engage in a collaboration where the learning is shared. It seems that from sharing perspectives, engaging with true mutuality, and a sense of openness, both parties would have much to gain. For some years I believed this positive effect was a given, that is until far down south in this ancient, some say mystical, Mexican town, everything began to fall apart.

An Evaluation Dilemma

I have provided school consultations with varying degrees of success over the years. One time quite a few years ago, evaluating in a school out in farm country, I stopped into the local bar and had a few brews with the locals, just to see if there was a perspective I needed in helping their school. I knew that neither would the water taste the same nor the grain grow as tall from region to region—that you cannot evaluate every location, every people, with the same checklist. I learned a lot at the bar, although the chairman of that evaluation team grew skeptical about accepting my ethnomethodology. Accrediting organizations generally expect more standard, reliable practices out of their evaluators.

Some educational leaders and evaluators, for instance at the national and state levels, are spending careers standardizing curricula so that they can get reliably measurable outcomes, and the temptation to wish each school into a sterile, "culture-free zone," interchangeable with any other school, with a rigid curriculum simple to develop and simple to evaluate, is strong. When we think about the etymology of the word *education* (essentially, "bringing out" what's in the student), how strange that a culture would make standardized outcomes the goal for its students. Nothing of enduring value has ever been systematized. Especially not people.

First Encounter

So we arrived at Ximena's mission office, dragging and pulling along a giant duffle bag full of cheap school supplies, all manufactured in China to U.S. specs. It felt a little ridiculous. Why should they want our plasticky junk?

I have "a big job"! I wondered if Ximena really knew how big? Only 1 percent of 15-year-old Oaxacan kids can pass a basic math test and literacy is below 75 percent. Why? Surely these one-dimensional metrics had deeper meanings. What was the real issue here?

The job of schools is to pass along the cultural heritage and way of life, moreover, to advance that way of life. In Monte Albán and around the state of Oaxaca, in neglected schools, often with volunteer teachers with little training or understanding of local needs or traditions, I guessed they might be passing down a tiny fraction of their cultural heritage. The fathers did not write the textbooks, few even knew how to write, and few of them had seen a textbook after the age of ten. The fathers of this village were mainly gone. Their forefathers, once considered to be sorcerers or shamans, had been missing for generations now. Today's fathers are up north cutting my lawn.

In history, teachers were sages who sought out and explained the sacred. I resolved to find what was sacred there before telling them how to educate their children, but where to look? Dust-choked traditions etched into some community subconscious somewhere, in a way it might take a curandero to detect? Anyway, they have not called a curandero down here. They called me. They are paying me, a white Southern California educator with a pile of academic degrees, to organize their village school. Could my lifestyle be their hidden aim? If it is, is that okay?

I did not want to believe that the local or ancient consciousness had entirely vanished—the culture here is too rich, too historic. And yet, I could no more easily access those than I could the collective consciousness of the current day. We needed help. And so, Audrey and I set out with Ximena in her car to meet the real people.

Pulque

We drive up from the base of the mountain through winding, dirt streets until we reach the dry, hillside village. Six huts with corrugated aluminum roofs cluttered around a gash in an eroding hillside—here was the legendary Monte Albán.

It was time to meet some potential school parents and students. We walk up the steep, dusty steps which lead to an extended family compound. At the entry, an old woman is sweeping the dirt.

9:00 a.m. Two days after Easter Sunday. In front of the houses, small children huddle underneath a long, wooden table eating candy and drinking warm chocolate or Coke. There are thirteen children, some still in their Easter Sunday best. Right by the entry in the communal family kitchen a giant mole* vat is nearly scraped clean, two wooden spoons the size of shovels sticking out. There are still plenty of frijoles and tortillas. Nobody wants a holiday to end. What would be next? No one is working. (Read: the women are obviously working.) As in many "developing nation" settlements I have visited, there were no males of high school age around.

"I don't know why the people here suffer so much," Ximena said. I looked around at the empty eyes, the dust, and I could see why: for one thing, they suffer because they are running out of water. There is a pervasive sense of dryness. The reservoir is empty.

They are low on fire, too. A man emerges from a one-room hut next to the kitchen and hands out shots of pulque. Around the table, we raise glasses,

---

* From the Aztec word "mōlli" meaning concoction or stew, Mexico's centuries-old, undisputed national sauce, a virtually intoxicating blend of chocolate, chilies, garlic, onions, nuts and thirty-some ingredients that are ground, mixed, and blended by hand.

drinking the agave beer first brewed by Aztec shamans, to toast the holiday, to toast new acquaintances, the emptiness and false hope we share and, in this moment, in the heat, to the fire spirits entering the liver. I no longer feel educated. Like a threat introduced, the questions occur: What could there be in this village in Monte Albán to be passed down? What would it mean to be educated here? Where are the shamans?

It dawns on me strangely now, that I don't even know what it means to be educated back home. I can hardly speak to these people beyond a simple toast and I just sit there smiling as my mind busies itself constructing a typical Southern California town near where I live.

This particular suburb, this population, has few detectable, remaining roots, and is regionally famous as a huge and successful educational bureaucracy noted for reliable production of high test scores and high-dollar grant-writing. People move here for this.

Questions rain out and I wish I could stop them but I don't know how. Are we developing "mall education" in American—a homogenization of American culture? Are we disappearing? What authentic culture could this particular town be "passing along." Is the junk food Arby's, Burger King, Jack in the Box, El Pollo Loco, Hardee's, KFC, Domino, Del Taco lining this town's and virtually every town's Main Street related to a new form of junk education? Where is the cultural wellspring of what we call "education"? Is there some indigenous mall or real estate culture that is handed down in school? How is it different from some other affluent American community? Where are the elders who pass the culture down to the next generation? If I buy one can I get one free?

This we know: few elders in this community are in our homes and fewer still are regarded as a source of wisdom; many are isolated in "senior" communities or residential care facilities; maybe we can visit them if we can break free.

It's morning but already getting hot. We continue to toast our meeting, to the day and to the turning sun—at long last, there is someone who understands how to do evaluations and create school programs from scratch. We toast with the pulque which, according to the ancient shamans, gives access to vision, growth, creativity . . . and anger.

"Salut!" we all grin.

Agua

Not much grows around Monte Albán. We wander around the few homes in the compound, one- or two-room shacks, most without evidence of any fathers present. My daughter Audrey is saying little. How could she relate to the fifteen-year-old mothers in the shadows inside these shacks? How can they look in our eyes and trust and not feel powerless?

We walk up to the very top of the enclave, to the concrete block home perched at the top, and there he is, a smiling and tightly wound fellow, Rigoberto. He had been married two days ago on Easter Sunday. He is twenty-three years old. His *novia,* Annabelle, is twenty-three, too, although it is her second marriage. Still in his black pants and white tank top undershirt, he will not be going to work today. The ice from the wedding is still frozen in a large bucket: he extracts a dripping, icy bottle of Corona beer.

"Agua," he says, half-smiling, and hands it to me.

The morning is warm and quiet, and beer like this is the coldest beer in the world. What could be better than this? Five thousand years ago a shaman stood here overlooking this hillside, presiding over sacred wisdom worth hiding, worth dying for, worth extinction itself. But now, it is only the groom and I, on this dried-out ancient hillside beneath the great, moist clouds. We look out across the jumble of corrugated aluminum roofs, far out into the overexposed whiteness of the day and down into the Valley of Oaxaca. From this perch, perhaps we can tap into our dreams again. "They think you are a god," Ximena says, breaking the spell.

Breakfast of the Gods

Rigoberto leads us into the main room of his hut which just barely circumscribes his new queen bed, his *matrimonia,* his pride. Something moves. Through a side opening in a low-ceilinged nook in smoky darkness, squinting, we can see two of Annabelle and Rigoberto's three children sleeping on a single bed. We duck back out under the front door. Rigoberto emerges smoking a Marlboro—this is pride. It is good to be on this hillside. We survey the gray-brown pollution of the city below. What will become of the Earth's lungs?

We step back down a hundred or so feet to the kitchen to join the others. Annabelle is down there fixing breakfast, smiling. Rigoberto has not struck her in three months, we have heard whispered. Outside the kitchen door stands her little boy in a tight Superman shirt and two, unmatched shoes.

One of Mexico's great gifts to the world is the cacao bean, which is used to make chocolate. According to legend, Quetzalcoatl, the God of Light, brought cacao down to the Toltecan people and taught them how to cultivate it. According to tradition, as it has been for 3,000 years now, chocolate must be made by the hands of a woman only. It was a special offering: "Food of the Gods." Standing by the kitchen wall of corrugated aluminum, Superman is drinking chocolate so thick it is caked across his face.

Somebody emerges with a bottle of mescal, the sacred, smoky gift of the agave, distilled from its fermented leaves. This has been the way of the holy week for two hundred years now. We will not get much done today.

Europeans and Metal

The next day, Ximena picked us up in downtown Oaxaca. My consulting was beginning in earnest. We passed Santo Domingo Cathedral as we made our way through the old city of Oaxaca, punctuated by bronze statues of the elders—mustachioed men with stern, European expressions—then wound our way out of town. Fired metal, the area's most valuable resource, brought some of the first Europeans here. Metal, which the shamans called "father." The gunmetal hues of the statues tended to hide them in shadows along the roadside in contrast to the mud, maize, and mauve wall colors that popped out in the sun as we passed local houses and shops. Father was European.

"How can I help today?" I asked Ximena. We headed to higher ground, to the comidor in Monte Albán, the community kitchen.

As if floating, above the village of Monte Albán stand the ruins of one of the world's greatest historical civilizations, the pre-Columbian archaeological site of Monte Albán. About 2,500 years ago, Zapotec Indians reshaped this 1,500-foot hill overlooking the Valley of Oaxaca, cutting into hillsides that still erode, and constructing hundreds of terraces. Later, the Mayans began blending in and predominated ethnically. On this plateau they set palaces, temples, burial tombs, and homes for the ruling elite. Down below was space for over 20,000 citizens who lived in one-room houses and cultivated corn, beans, squash, avocados, and chilies, in addition to doing a little hunting. This magnificence lasted 1,000 years. Then, around the year 1500, the Spaniards came, bearing crosses.

Missionaries, they called them. Squash, corn, and beans became "the Oaxacan trinity." Spanish Catholics were devout, "more Catholic than the Pope." Catholic spiritualism was rigorous. Virtually every aspect of native life and spirituality was converted into the European and Catholic way of life. To the missionaries moving through South and Central America and then up towards California, even corn was Catholic.

One-third of Oaxacans still speak primarily an indigenous (Amerindian) language, though it is rarely spoken in schools. The question of whether an indigenous group like this can ever regain something like an authentic cultural identity must remain a matter for study and debate. At any rate, it seemed unlikely that I could be of much help in the matter.

The conquistadores, such as Hernán Cortés, delivered the entire Aztec nation to the Church, by force. Back in Spain, Cortés was awarded the title of *Marquesado del Valle de Oaxaca,* and then, like the missionaries who followed him, like so many of today's Oaxacan fathers, and like me in four more days, they went away. Cortes died in Spain at age sixty-two.

DIJO's grant came in the year 2000. The mission was founded by an Italian priest, Luigi Giussani, who expressed the neo-missionary spirit: "Above all, our very nature requires us to be interested in others. To be interested in others, and communicate to others, enables us to fulfill the supreme and, indeed, the only task in life: to become ourselves, to complete ourselves." DIJO located me as a consultant through a mutual friend. For the record, I do not find transforming others to be the ultimate path to personal fulfillment, unless maybe they ask repeatedly. But I am there to listen and to help. And these are clearly missionaries who are not using force or coercion of any kind—they, too, are there to help.

Ximena explains: "Please advise us. You have done so much." It is not the first time I have been asked for bad advice. The lost empire, the foreign geography, the rooted poverty, the sheer size of the educational void that we are seeing—how can I engage them? A set of used American textbooks is not going to do it—they need "everything." I have already learned that the truth concerning a great deal of this culture will always remain hidden from me, lost in the clouds. I lack the courage to present any of this perspective to Ximena, especially having been on the job only two days. I know she will not care, anyway. She just wants a school. I am her mastermind!

A Statue

One of the things that enabled Europeans to take over indigenous cultures and inspired their intention to civilize them was their belief that their mental capacity was superior.

For some two hundred years the notion of "synthesis" has been viewed as the holy grail of Western intelligence and creativity. The concept of synthesis—and the mental faculty for it—has been useful as ideas and traditions have blended and civilizations have evolved, especially in the West. We generally thank Friedrich Hegel and his popularizers for elevating the idea of synthesis as the epitome of Western-style thinking.

Synthesis is the precursor for creations of many kinds. The vision for my own school in California consists of a synthesis of practices ranging out from Socratic Method and reaching all compass points and most historical eras. Like many U.S. schools, our curricular and organizational model incorporates state curricular standards and the way our teachers interpret and spin them, and then blends this with our local (Southern California) resources and the values of the families and elders who live in our community. That is, of course, a lot of synthesis (and the U.S. Department of Education would surely favor something a whole lot more reliable).

Travelling around the Monte Albán community, it was difficult to ascertain the existence of any such synthesis. As far as my consulting was going, what I was finding so far was this: scant remaining traditional identity, little evidence of community pride or aspiration, few experienced teachers or teacher role models, and prevailing values that, if they existed, were unstated and, at least to an outsider, seemed buried. Ethical practice and emerging models of educational consulting—action research and process-oriented evaluation—call for real collaboration with the subject group and the merging of values. How could I create a synthesis of my own educational expertise with the local values?

Where could we even begin? "Maybe we could call on the men," I tell Ximena. Because women are everywhere like mother Earth, but father is gone from this part of the world in several respects, though there remain many metal statues of him.

In Monte Albán all of the aid, education, and food programs are implemented entirely by women. "Get the men involved in nutrition. Get the men bringing decent food into the home again. Get them to stay in the homes.

Hear their storytelling. In my home in California," I explain, "I make breakfast with fresh foods for my family every morning."

It is a terrible suggestion and I am sorry I made it because it is impossible. What's more, the men who left this village could be harvesting my fresh food right now. It is not yet making sense that I am their consultant.

"Here they would make a statue of you for doing that," Ximena assures. She is very kind.

Dried Mushrooms

Aztec ruler Montezuma II, who died in 1520 at the age of fifty-four, may have believed Spanish conquistadores were coming from outer space.

The Zapotec (later Mayan, Mixtec, and Aztec) were the indigenous pre-Cortés people who flourished in the Valley of Oaxaca. In 1519 a comet predicted by their calendars signaled to many an annihilation that would soon eliminate 70 percent of the Mexican native civilizations. History has it that the same day this comet was observed by Montezuma, a ship appeared on the horizon to him alone, a ship that some say remained invisible to indigenous eyes as it approached. It was the ship of conquistador Cortés. I too felt invisible to the indigenous all week, there with my foreign agenda.

The Oaxaca area happens to be the home of two of the world's revered psychoactive plants, *Psilocybe* (a.k.a. "sacred") mushrooms and *Salvia divinorum* ("diviner's sage"), used by a long tradition of shamans, notably Maria Sabina, to facilitate visionary states of consciousness during spiritual healing sessions—a practice replicated by some early twentieth century artists and intellectuals, 1960s college students, and rock stars. Throughout history many people have actually believed that psilocybin arrived on Earth as spores that migrated through outer space—really, look it up. Spanish conquistadores observed psilocybin mushrooms being served at the coronation feast of Montezuma. Psilocybin and chocolate.

To this day, Zapotec shamans are revered for their quest for a universal consciousness. The revered ones would make the ultimate collaboration—beyond the prospects of today's researchers—to provide access to the original spirit world that was the life and educational force of this ancient civilization. What would their school be like?

Corrugated Aluminum

It was a hot and busy day of loose ends—meeting missionaries and seeing settlements, tiny dwellings, and community gathering spots. We were on a mission now, in the data-gathering phase.

Every day about one hundred fifty families who suffered from extreme poverty and related problems we often refer to as "intractable" were getting breakfast in the free comidor. And DIJO had started to provide books for the children. They had even installed a community computer room where villagers of all ages were learning basic programming.

Returning home after a day of touring, we headed over the pass, out from the hillside, and then back towards the downtown. Now up in the high ground, as if presiding over the whole of Oaxaca, we passed the city's most prominent bronze of all, larger than life, the beloved Benito Juarez, Mexico's most revered man and most revered statue. But what went unnoticed from this point was that, looking west in perpetuity, Juarez looked out to the mountainside and heights of Monte Albán. And from that mountainside a Zapotec shaman once stood, looking out across timelessness and the valley to where, five thousand years later, Juarez, a Zapotec, would stand looking straight back into his eyes.

We surveyed the rooftops of houses across the land, noticing the same thing we noticed on our excursions to Central America and Africa: shiny aluminum has taken over. Quaint, traditional thatching is gone. Not just in Mexico and Latin America, but all over the southern hemisphere disadvantaged neighborhoods are being thatched with corrugated aluminum, an ocean of corrugated aluminum roofs—the cheapest form of metal. Aluminum, which is believed by spiritualists to release vibrations of sadness and sorrow (we had to go to Asia for that particular claim). Nobody from Monte Albán could have known. Across continents and here in Monte Albán, universally, men are bragging about where they got their roofs and their baseball caps. "They must be happy to get out of leaky, musty, rat-infested thatching and to just pop on a roof or a wall," I noted to Audrey. But the aluminum is not quaint or pretty and I do not believe it has the same spirit inside. These roofs cut us off from the sky.

In Monte Albán and across the valley, young families had moved into the marginal hillside terrain just as their ancestors had more than 2,500 years ago—but they are no longer living off the land as their ancestors did.

You can't eat agave (although the curanderos still have some uses for it). Once again, just as it occurred over a millennium ago, the outlying farmlands will not be able to produce enough food for the rising population. And, once again, the Europeans were back. But this time they were here to serve the natives, to lift the natives up.

That year, houses across Oaxaca were displaying the latest roof colors: aquamarine and gold, even the color of red clay, exactly like that of the Spanish missions—except here they were made of corrugated aluminum. In Latin America, lung cancer is one of the main results of all this aluminum roofing. Our lungs were choked when we walked into some of these homes, especially while they were cooking. Metal roofs do not breathe like thatch. But Juarez is watching over them. We drop down into the city of Oaxaca for the night.

> *Late that night I am visited by nightmares. The weight of my role as consultant here—the very reasons why they are giving me pulque and mescal and mole—is bearing down: one DIJO patron has taken my hands in hers and looks into my eyes as her own eyes well up.*

Accountability

The next morning at DIJO headquarters we meet Florencia, an American expat of Spanish lineage married to a landed Oaxacan builder. "We make the mothers work in the kitchen once a week or we will not allow their children in the program," she explained. She was tough; she was a donor and worked hard for the children. She would not allow the charity to demotivate the families. To do this, DIJO had set up Western-style accountability systems for tracking local progress in the free preschool/kindergarten, their only school so far, until we establish upper grades. (They would someday have four schools.) Six categories were being tracked. The children, they found, were doing best in the "conduct" category, worst in "perseverance." This sounded fine at first cut, but it could mean that, like the missionaries before them, DIJO was focused on compliance rather than something more intrinsic. After all, what does "good conduct" normally mean but: "You do what I want you to do." It was the age-old domination model, moving the subjects to silence in the name of humanitarian support. What happened to the new, enlightened missionaries?

In Monte Albán, they have been waiting for five hundred years (since Cortés) for the renaissance. In this village, perhaps their spirits had gone to sleep. Could missionary teachers wake them up with good conduct and perseverance? Could shamans wake them up with herbs and chants?

In 1990, in a statement oft quoted by methodologists in the area of *participatory action research,* Paulo Freire wrote, "The silenced are not just incidental to the curiosity of the researcher but are the masters of inquiry into the underlying causes of the events in their world. In this context research becomes a means of moving them beyond silence into a quest to proclaim the world."[1] The silenced are not incidental to the curiosity of the researcher. But these silenced do not seem to have words. What is the role of the *collaborative researcher* if we can see no signs of local interest? This is, of course, another terrible question, since it suggests I should do nothing, which is obviously not true. I must help.

The third of six basic steps to effective participatory action research is, "Do research on what others have done to overcome a similar problem." What was done before was the complete subjugation and loss of a culture. Is there something wrong with me that I am not over this loss?

In past days, Westerners imposed their own, dominant, often foreign values upon the *indigenos.* Now we must find collaborators. And what have others done? In the 1930s through the 50s folk musicians and anthropologists from New York and other urban areas took matters into their own hands. Like little saints, they learned the classics from old Delta blues and Mississippi folk records, then scoured the southern states locating old blues guitarists, many who had not picked up their guitars in a generation, then literally retaught them their old riffs until finally the old legends were ready to go back on the road again.

Where were the legends of Monte Albán? Gone. Who could reteach the old, who remember only fragments?

I met no teachers native to the village of Monte Albán. Surely more Oaxacan shamans are doing the tourist gig in Marin County than practicing down here. Imagine going up there and working with them, paying them to go back to their villages. Could I? If I solicited their advice and put it in my report, what would DIJO say? Downtown in Oaxaca at the central market, the healers sold bagged herbs to tourists—would they know where to find the real teachers? Who would know where to access enough local wisdom to at least start a school on?

Young village mothers are rarely equipped to prepare their children for school. Many haven't chosen to become mothers. Some are afraid of what might happen to them if men thought they used birth control, and they are afraid of many other things, as well. Many are teenagers, alone in the houses and, though they mostly live on earthen floors, they have almost no relationship with nature. Some literally don't even know to feed their child more than once a day.

Where to find teachers? When we say the word "teacher," or train someone to be a teacher, does it have anything at all to do with what it meant to be a *teacher* in the water-rich days of ancient Monte Albán? Today in Monte Albán, teachers might come from anywhere except their local community: a few teachers from the city of Oaxaca, some would be graduate students from the university, and then there were the DIJO missionaries. Is this okay? There is state-run primary education in town, but not much money for it, so the children either go to morning or afternoon school. An elementary student could expect four half-days of school per week. A high school student, none. The teachers' strike was officially ended, but in a continuation of this power play, threatening union bosses were still mandating work slowdowns on Fridays, and teachers could not be sure of security, much less a steady income.

DIJO had concluded from its initial studies that, as a first step in bringing in a school system, the children ages three through five needed a preschool. That was already well underway. There, by the community kitchen, inside an eight-by-sixteen portable, relocatable storage canister with no windows, was a bright and lovely collection of colorful cartoon-like kids' books and primers filling up shelves on two walls. All around the room were yellow, blue, and red molded plastic toys and furniture. This was not much different from an urban preschool in our hometown. Since there was not much access to the elements for local educational wisdom, this synthetic environment was the outcome of the best efforts of a few caring outsiders who sent in whatever they found that could match the category of "things used in kindergartens," or "what foreigners carry in duffle bags." These things could be in kindergartens on any continent. Most of it is manufactured in China, but to me it is more homogenization of global culture.

Next stop was the actual building site for the future elementary school. DIJO owns about five hundred square meters of hillside with a five hundred square foot building in need of restoration, and we walked around the hillside, surveying. This is where we could create an elementary school if we could get the money, and teach all the things the young mothers are not teaching: basic literacy at least, if not their forgotten culture and lost spirit. As the saying goes, if we had some rice, we could have rice and beans. If we had some beans.

Prison

We ambled down below the proposed school site into a dry gorge where this whole contract, this whole journey, became overwhelming. This gorge was a power spot. I wanted to envision a future for this community, but in this location forces came into focus that dwarfed any capacity for redemption that I could imagine. Here in this gorge, this day began filling in with a sense of loss and extinction. In consulting, there is usually a phase like this, and I had moved through it in scores of schools, but these forces, right here, seemed too large. Where were the shamans?

In 500 B.C. the people prayed to the god Tlaloc, and he scoured out this gorge to a depth of ten to fifteen feet deep with water. From above, the hills rise into the sacred Monte Albán from which Tlaloc freely sent down his waters and the required nutrients for life dissolved into the run-off and were carried down through the gorges and into the villages across the Valley of Oaxaca. Monte Albán flourished as the center of the Zapotec high culture. There we stood in the very ditch that once held the liquid of life itself running from one end of the village to the other. And today it is desolate and dry.

Today, almost none of the families of Monte Albán are farmers. Only a few things grow here. Crickets (chapulines) for deep-frying. Maguey, a type of agave used for mescal. No matter. The Mexican government considers the village of Monte Albán to be an illegal invasion of the protected archaeological zone and not a real place to live.[2] I am to conduct best practice, ethical research and consulting in a community that does not technically or legally exist and it matters little if that leaves me at a loss because these people are far beyond loss.

At the highpoint of the gorge, just below the proposed school site, is what could best be described as a small prison. Behind the bars of this prison is a small spigot. The sign posted on the bars reads, "Every Tuesday from 8 to 9 a.m." During this hour, the gate may be unlocked, the spigot twisted on and off, and the water allowed out of the prison. The surrounding families allow whatever water has collected uphill, from the wounded Monte Albán watershed, to bleed out into their five-gallon, yellow plastic buckets. Then the prison is locked up again until the next week.

I had never seen water imprisoned before. It does not take a mystic to see what is and has been true for every civilization: water is the basis of all life, the cleansing needed to sustain all life, the embodiment of life. What it has taken mystics to say, though, is that water is sacred, water is the key to human consciousness, and the key to our linkage to all living things. This has been said in one way or another by sages from virtually every civilization throughout history, too numerous and consistent to even warrant citation.

Globally, in many communities, it is the girls' job to collect water and bring it home, thereby contributing the loss of time for school. No water means a dehydrated community, which means no school.

Today water is scarce in Monte Albán, and coffee is no longer an ethnic ritual but an exported product. In the same way the ancient mysteries of water have run dry, rain comes seldom to wash and replenish the people. Most water is still, unmoving—we can hardly expect healing from this kind of water. Will the water return? Who will pray to Tlaloc the rain god? Will the DIJO do this? Who will teach the words to the prayers and restore the faith? What will become of the earth's kidneys?

The Mayan spirituality that the Europeans discovered reaches back to the beginnings of education, before the Bible. But the water is all gone from this gorge now, and the fire is mostly gone, too, and the men, and the ancient wisdom. I would try to address this at dinner tonight, in one way or another, when we gathered to discuss all of our plans for a school.

Coffee

The next morning, in her one-room home on a dirt floor a mother boils the water and mixes in coffee for her infant's breakfast, holds the aluminum cup up to the infant's lips and brushes the liquid in. Maybe she thinks it is beans.

Like so many small ones in Monte Albán, many students back in Southern California also have only coffee for breakfast. This coffee has seven spoonfuls of South American cane sugar with whipped cream on top and it comes in cardboard stating: "Starbucks."

The last remaining cloud forest in Mexico is home to more than four hundred migratory bird species. That number includes two of the rarest bird species in all of Latin America: the Horned Guan, a large, black-and-white, turkey-like animal, and the Azure-rumped Tanager, known for its beautiful song but shrouded in mystery because fewer than ten thousand of them remain. This forest is also the source of the coffee that Starbucks marketers call "a crisp, nutty brew with a sparkling aftertaste."[3] Magellan and others of his era circumnavigated the globe five hundred years ago for aromas like this.

In semi-arid Southern California where I live, this coffee is on special this week. It's mixed with water that runs from out of the Rocky Mountains into the Colorado River in Arizona, over dams and across hundreds of miles of aqueducts at a rate of about 185 cubic feet per second, then into our coffee, but only after Starbucks runs it through a triple filtered reverse osmosis system.[4] Triple. Surely there can be no more spirit left in it. Interestingly, Starbucks shops run water all day long so that their utensils can be cleaned in what they call a "dipper well." Starbucks dipper wells catch enough water to quench the thirst of almost two million people a day.[5] That's about seven Oaxacas.

God

Easter, most sacred of all days, is over in Monte Albán but Easter week is not. The men lay low. It's hot. We enter one of the huts in the lower part of the village and notice the family altar. On it are the statues of Jesus and Mary, the collection of wooden crosses, an empty beer bottle, some nondescript collectibles and, tucked randomly behind the crosses, a hand-carved ancient Aztec god, Tlaloc, god of rain. The images on the altar can help worshippers remember how to endure. Today's altars appear to combine any available belief systems and symbology like a spice blend.

Down here, Catholic ways handed down from Spain are overlaid onto the ancient spiritualism, like gold plating on wood: after five hundred years the holy spirits of the saints imported by conquistadors still humble the people of Monte Albán into submission. The imperial saints had earlier Mayan names: Kakulja (ray of light), Rax Kakulja (the green ray), and many newer spirits and saints came after them. Religion, like education, like chocolate, is a continual blending, a new synthesis. Can all these saints and plant spirits from East and West serve the same God, the same truth?

According to the calendar set forth in the Popol Vuh, ancient Mayan scripture, we have entered into a period where the world has fallen into a state of neglect, but the sacred text also assures us that the tools of love and higher consciousness can enable us to survive and light up the future. Who will light the way? Who will be its teachers?

South in Guatemala, the traditions and ancient spirituality have managed to stay alive, in the cornfields high up in the Altiplano. The peasants learned to speak in whispers, to reveal their true spirits and even their real language only among the indigenous. They learned this the hard way in the 1980s, though many were killed or tortured first. Then, and in the previous several generations, they learned that when they discussed their spirituality with government and business officials down below by the coast, their beliefs were seen as threatening, and they would be imprisoned or killed. Here in Monte Albán, the people do not study the old spirits much anymore. There is nothing to speak in whispers about. And not much grows.

Back north, in California's Marin County, a Oaxacan curandero examines a migrant worker: "Her spirit has gone to sleep and must be woken up," he concludes. The curanderos, with their herbs and incantations to return the spirit to its equilibrium, are spread out across the American Southwest now, managing exhaustion and toxicity in a very intense, highly populated society.

Meanwhile, today in Monte Albán at the community center, DIJO is teaching the people to sew on metal machines. They don't remember how to weave. In the next rooms are rows of computers and the comidor.

Chocolate Spirits

By around eight o'clock that night we are mostly gathered for "dinner at seven" at Florencia's. At the table, Florencia asks, "How strict must I be in upholding the rules we have established for the DIJO children?" I hold my silence. "I don't want the children to go hungry," she continues, "but if I deprive them of their next meal they will understand they must not be late. There has to be some discipline. How can I make them understand that this is necessary?"

I think, "Do you want them to understand, or to obey?" but hold my tongue.

The question lingers unspoken over dessert as we toast a round of mescal, the chocolaty smooth and smoky plant spirit, but eventually I decide I have to act like a consultant: "What is sacred to the men of Monte Albán?" I ask. "What do they value for teaching? And what is sacred or profound that we must teach in the schools?"

Florencia thinks these are delightful questions, and I can see they might make good dinner talk. Little tradition has been handed down to this generation. Only the chocolate and mescal are still staples here—and of course mole negro (chocolate and chili) sauce.

Chocolate is a legacy of the ancient Americas, mixed in recipes from the north with spices from the east and the ancient winds stirred in. Chocolate, like religion, has been mixed in continually new ways since before the Mayans, stirred in the mole vat for three thousand years. And through the ages chocolate has been widely believed to offer a bond between the earth and the gods. (That works for me.) For this many years few high cultures around the world have failed to mix their own most subtle spices into their version of chocolate. Could some of the deep secrets of Oaxacan education and spirit be alive in the mole vat, or in their chocolate? To taste the spicy, Oaxacan chocolate, one could only believe so.

Even eating chocolate for breakfast, if Superman is to become educated he will face many challenges. The forms of logic and skills he will need to learn in order to address the problems of nutrition, education, and human development must be taught to him in school—it's not going to happen in the family. Given my cultural background, my inclination is of course that he will need to learn about various forms of Euro-centric thinking and intellect, such as the dialectical views developed by Hegel and others in the literary salons and universities around the early 1800s, deeply embedded now in Western education:

Inductive logic: the concept that when things happen, we apply a rule or theory to our understanding as to why these things happen. We can then respond to this by conjuring up various actions or ideas based upon the rule or theory.

Synthesis: the concept that the mind can transcend disparate, disconnected, even oppositional ideas and actions and give birth to a new paradigm, universal vision, or world view.

At Florencia's, I meet the missionaries who were looking to me for wisdom and guidance on schooling. I notice one in particular, Isabella, a Northern

Italian of alluring beauty with eyes like oceans. She was inspired by the words of the great Italian priest Giussani, who wrote, "If we are not able to give, we experience ourselves as incomplete beings." She would have inspired him.

"I don't know if we can make the people understand, but I am trying," she says with difficulty in English. I say, in sound-bite-sized sentences: "Have you talked to the men? Someone must talk to them." A consecrated, young, widowed missionary, she looks down. I think I am blushing. "They must have stories—they are *indigenos,* not Europeans." I want to see if we are on the same page at all. "If we work here alone, will they call us imperialists?"

"In the hills, there are no men," she exaggerates, "or few."

Alone in the world, light brown hair, and worthy of a Donatello sculpture, she is wearing a wedding band made from three shades of gold which she brought from Bologna. She has a doctorate in literature. "What called you here?" I ask. Between us we share probably five hundred words of English, Italian, and Spanish. She cannot answer, and I am imagining that there is an untold story. What makes a missionary, what prompts this expatriate life of sacrifice? Could DIJO be here to remind us how alone we each ultimately are?

It is not so simple to wish for what Giussani offers, or to support the new era "enlightened missions."[6] The ongoing five-hundred-year transformation of indigenous groups across the Americas includes loss of language, loss of lands, loss of spirituality, and disruption in traditional ways of living. Add to that the contamination of resources, politics, ethnic bloodlines, religion, and education. What yearning calls to Isabella? I am the only man at the table, the only man on the mission. I wonder what loss Isabella is living out, and what stories her ring could tell. I sip the mescal, smoky on my mouth and warm as it spreads through my body.

Florencia's seventeen-year-old daughter comes downstairs in short-shorts, tight stretch top, wide studded belt, straightened light brown hair, with a six-inch, shiny aluminum-studded cross hanging from her neck. One cannot ignore this cross or its evolution. What can it mean? Big faith? Submission? Taboo? Anger? Love? Latin punk? Is this something wholly new? An expression of tradition? A clash of traditions? This is a synthesis three thousand years in the making. The symbology is powerful but abstract.

She is going out.

Alas for my consulting! Nothing is unrelated, unconnected. People will not understand. Could this be solipsism? Can something not be a metaphor! I must retire back to my hotel for the evening.

Water Music

We know that listening to music can be transformational, even to the completely untrained ear. DIJO visionary Giussani, in his writings, actually makes a choice of music to play to natives from traditional cultures when educating them.[7] It is music by the German composer, Ludwig van Beethoven. The music "expresses, with great communicative strength, the drama of the *synthesis* [emphasis mine] of the tradition one belongs to and one's uniqueness." Giussani believed that the Concerto in D major for Violin and Orchestra, Op. 61, works for all traditions. The concerto was written in Germany. The year was 1806.

Indigenous peoples have known for thousands of years that sound is a powerful spiritual tool.[8] Could a German classical, romantic composer invoke more indigenous consciousness than the shamans' hypnotic bonfire drumming over animal skins, high on a hillside, five thousand miles west of him? The DIJO leaders have not been using either drums or Beethoven, and I have to wonder if this is a consulting issue.

Various ancient traditions have ways of accessing the deeper psyche in order to bridge the inner and outer worlds. Can we access the ancient mind to reunify or restore the ancient heart and consciousness of a people? Shall we blast Beethoven into the comidor at mealtime?

What of meditation? Trance? Journey? Access to dreams? For five hundred years these forms of consciousness were all considered relatively useless by all but a handful of Western rationalists and their missionaries, and they were bled out of primitive cultures worldwide as Beethoven impassioned them back home. As a backbone of our traditions in the Western world, we still rely upon Hegel, a former prep school headmaster who had a hand in changing education through his belief that only the rational is real. *Hegelianism.* Still today, in education in the United States and Europe, our great achievements seem designed to avoid any perception of non-ordinary or non-surface reality. The Western gift to Monte Albán: the removal of most spiritual traditions—the awakening from the trance started by the ancients and ended by the imposition of Western logic, Western God, and Western control.

Germany's first chocolate factory opened in 1804, three years before the release of Hegel's "The Phenomenology of Spirit," a journey through the evolution of consciousness culminating in intellectual synthesis. When Hegel hosted his famous parlor talks on passion in philosophy, it is well known that only men were included. Less well known is that the ladies prepared their drinks, and one thing they often served up was: hot chocolate.

Magical Imperialism

The pristine Hotel El Camino Real, though a short cab ride away from dusty Monte Albán, is a world away. Audrey and I, on a day off from consulting, walk through the ancient, ornate entryway and feel transformed. We order outdoor lunch so that we can use the pool with some legitimacy—we know that we look like we belong and will not be suspect. I am drifting dreamily on an inflatable pool raft on the crystal, turquoise water reading João Guimarães Rosa's gorgeous "The Third Bank of the River," written in the 1960s, and am transported.

This masterpiece of Brazilian magical realism is the story of a man who decides to float eternally on his beautiful, hand-carved canoe, just beside his family's house. The contrast between the amazing concreteness and beauty of the river and the impossible conflicts in this man's fetid life makes it so the reader loses track of if the man is still a man or just a vision. It is like a nightmare—*an endless, impossible transition. Floating and drifting deeper into the dream of the day, the peace is pure and the light is so white you can breathe it.*

"Perdóneme, señor." A man appears, upside down at first. He is wearing a tan suit and saying, "Señor, that is the raft of my son," and I reorient, a little stunned.

In the story, "The Third Bank of the River," as the father is leaving, the mother forcefully declares, "If you go, don't you ever come back." The illusion is that benevolent, advanced civilizations can take charge in order to educate irrational, primitive natives. I am waking up.

The prospects for a California-style education in the hills of Oaxaca may be an endless transition, trapped in an impossible illusion.

Popol Vuh

In San Diego we have a gardener, a very hardworking man named Alberto Cortez. In San Diego, where a legitimate excuse for not showing up for work is, "I had to meet my girlfriend at the beach," Cortez is one of the hardest working people we know. Cortez arrived here penniless from Oaxaca twelve years ago, now employs a sizeable crew, and he will not be going back. Who did Cortez leave behind?

Is this a repeating history or lurid dreaming, the whole history of the cross dancing across the water, Cortez meeting Montezuma, missionaries marching up the coast of New Spain, leaving a trail of mustard grass, teaching everyone civilized European language and then leaving the *indigenos* behind? "They came together in darkness to think and reflect. Their flesh was made of white and yellow corn. The arms and legs of the four men were made of corn meal" (Popol Vuh, c. 1520). Is that us, is it I of pale skin and hair? Are we back?

Awakening

It is time for us to leave Oaxaca. As an educational consultant and supposed leadership expert, I accept the thanks of my patrons knowing I have done nothing. For this I have been treated with enormous respect and deference. I promise my report is forthcoming, but essential pieces are missing. I can lob a few grammar and math programs at the children, but surely they deserve something more, something authentic.

We sit in the airport waiting, drinking local chocolate from cacao that has been cultivated right here for three thousand years, first attributed to the Aztec god of fertility, and now across the Western world made into eggs and bunnies that symbolize spiritual birth and renewal on Easter.

When the Aztecs found the drink that the Mayans were calling "chocol," here is what they called it: water. Today chocolate is linked to serotonin levels in the brain, levels which, neuroscientists can now show, stimulate the brain to inspire new thought: synthesis.

Synthesis is no longer my god, no longer my unifying field, yet what could take its place remains a mystery to me. Like many, I was enthralled with intellectual synthesis at a young age and now, two generations later, I have a lot invested in the concept: if synthesis is not the highest level of thought, where am I?

I muse with my daughter: Can these dreams of man's harsh dominance ever end? What if we really have been called to heal these people? What if we were true *teachers*?

Authentic Evaluation: A Paradox

I have been to places where cultural relativity has made evaluation difficult, and it is always a factor. But this was different, more basic. From the ancients to today, in the pursuit of both education and spirituality, every culture has produced way-finders and cultural icons. I encountered no such cultural elements in Monte Albán.

DIJO consists of generous humanitarians who come from a place of deep compassion and spirit. Giussani seemed to reject the idea of importing religion, of teaching natives how to attain salvation.[9] Faith, he understands, is "found in the depths of our own being." And human connection ". . . is played out in the early, most subtle dawn of consciousness in its impact with the world." Nevertheless, I have not experienced consciousness like this in Monte Albán. I don't even know whose consciousness I am supposed to consider, the DIJOs or the *indigenos?*

Harvard law professor David Kennedy wrote in *The Dark Sides of Virtue* (2004), "Humanitarianism tempts us to hubris, to an idolatry about our intentions and routines, to the conviction that we know more than we do about what justice can be." As a teacher, I hope to avoid hubris. I believe that, for real teachers, goodness and wisdom must be found inside those whom we wish to teach. Can we divine the wisdom of a dry, indigenous culture before it is gone? Can I get authentic access into dormant spiritual truths silently carried forward by this culture? Is this my role? And what of my final report? Monte Albán seems to lie in a netherworld neither nourished by its historical roots nor lured by a vivid future synthesis. Of course, we could say the same of some Southern California American towns I know.

Back home, I contact a friend who operates a global relief fund to ask for support. "How much are they living on?" he asks. "Two or three dollars a day," I tell him. He apologizes. They do not qualify for help. He only deals with groups living on less than a dollar a day (recently upgraded to a dollar and a quarter). It is true that Monte Albán exists in a strange limbo, detached from our help. Secretly, I believe that only once they realize that we have truly abandoned them will the possibility for real education begin.

The search for natural wisdom and universal truths is perhaps our highest goal as educators. The physicist David Bohm has described an "explicate order" of the world that contains all information, past, present and future. Similarly, Giussani stated that he sought "the most intimate and original position of our conscience." What if the DIJO missionaries and the elders of Monte Albán could seek out such an *explicate order,* a timeless, spiritual well that will be there irrespective of any contrived, Western intellectual synthesis? The answer might be the question, the answer might be the search itself.

Reentry

Back home, I begin to write up my findings, but I am adrift. Whatever research questions or hypotheses I had on entry have been radically challenged. I search the literature on Monte Albán, on educational evaluation and organization consultant ethics. I'm going in all directions. The Monte Albán culture I experienced is not well. The shamans attributed illness to soul loss, to losing our awareness of what is sacred in us and around us. Accessing this awareness is the original job of the teacher.

The day clicks by. It is growing late. I try putting on Beethoven. Violin Concerto in D major, Op. 61. This goes the wrong way. I can't think. It sounds . . . victorious. Commanding. Mozart's "Vorrei spiegarvi, oh Dio!" is better, but I remain distant in my educational insight.

Now I have native drumming playing low in the background. I make lists of educational needs that need documentation and, like a companion to the list, listen more.

I dim the lights, light a candle. After a while, Timothy Leary playing "While Birds Sing," which he composed after meeting Maria Sabina seems to suggest time travel. In this dark music one can at least begin to tap into the mysterious emptiness and isolation of the lost past we all intuitively share, but surely there is more. James Asher's theta wave music . . . sounds like shamanic drumming the Mayans may have used five thousand years ago. But Asher's pulsing music is not being played on ancient instruments at all. Asher is playing an electronic instrument.

It is a synthesizer. Breathing. Slower. Can scholars do this? Deep in the background, someone is speaking as the muted drum rhythm and candle flame move together slowly. I am back in the village, peering into the cinder block hut. A mother of two, alone. Never have I seen eyes so blank. I want to go in there, but I can't. Time evaporates and I can sense that there is only one time in all history. Wisdom kept high in the mountainsides for millennia, secrets lost in the clouds, beyond analysis and synthesis, seem possible now. Where is the lost wisdom? What if there is only one life spirit and all of creation shares it?

I take out stationary, and write to Ximena at the DIJO wishing her luck. At last I can give my conclusion to her:

"Find mystery. Will you make sure the children can study mystery? Then I think they can become teachers some day."

I lick the envelope, think twice . . . add a check for $500, my total consulting fee, and seal it.

Oaxaca/Monte Albán, Mexico; Encinitas, California

8

⌒⌒

Men in Decline

History repeats itself, first as tragedy, second as farce.

—*The 18th Brumaire of Louis Bonaparte*, Karl Marx

(1)

As a young teacher, I read Oscar Handlin's narrative essay, "Living in the Valley," about Handlin's days in the Alps, which fueled my urge to teach in Switzerland. I still have that worn, classic 1977 *American Scholar* issue (the paper was thick and soft back then), and it has been a companion to me through the following history.[1]

Handlin's metaphor, that living in different places means that people legitimately perceive different, even opposing, fundamental truths and that both can be "right"—the concept of multiple perspectives—would become the core theme of my teaching career for the next three decades; although at critical times, I've had to learn it all over again. "My first encounters with the mountains were shocking and disturbing," Handlin recalls, "for they exposed me not only to a novel set of sights, but also to modes of thinking totally different from my own." Many years later, as a teacher adapting and being immersed in the new millennium while confronting the new generation of students it brought, I would feel similar disturbances. While this may sound romantic and natural in theory, it can be exceedingly hard to accept that some of your most fundamental perspectives are limiting and ideological, however romantic your travel journals. As such, this is not a story of how my teaching philosophies formed, or even of how meaningful or useful all these

147

philosophies have been to a generation of students. Rather, it is a story about how they began to unravel.

Before our school's annual *Tolerance Day*, a student progressive forum, three leading students gathered at my desk to promote their agenda: one "punk" type who was tall and thin and brooding, one ivy league-ish and overly respectful, one rosy-cheeked with a perpetual half-smile that blended inspiration and pain. One female, one male, one transgender. They stood before me and the wall of wood-framed graduate photos going back with me twenty years. A hot item that year was gender equality, and I told them they should not have the forum at all if their approach was merely to parrot the popular causes. My back went up a bit at the idea that my students might be trend followers. At the same time, I was hoping they would not realize how very thin the ice I stood on was: gender equality was a cause politically, socially, and mentally risky to deny. But, being a teacher first, I was aware of a parallel to this risk: as difficult as it is to deny, gender equality is still more difficult to grasp. I understood that the issue might end up being perceived like that of many other interest groups in our country, drowning in entitlements and logjamming departments of education with competing agendas.

(Those were the "great recession" days when people began to grow seriously weary over the funding of "somebody else's" social programs.) Personally, I was harboring great uncertainly about the efficacy of equality in our nation. We're supposed to be free, and we'll never be equal. It's America: we earn our stature in accordance with our labors and fortunes—this is life. A jungle! Did these students expect otherwise?

I did not want to approve a program that was unclearly conceived or politically driven. Show me a man—or woman—unscathed by a world of claims, entitlements, and establishments! I will be the first to sign his or her diploma. Or so I reckoned.

"You cannot legitimately protest something if you cannot articulate both sides with conviction," I claimed in an opening gambit.

The nature of adolescence is simultaneously (and impossibly) to be drawn into the pack while being programmed by nature to seek autonomy. The rush of equality slams into the eternal call to freedom. Sweet conflict! I wanted them to understand that as straight and true as the view from the valley floor is the view from the summit is completely different, although at least as clear and far. The former corresponds to the linear lines of equality, the latter to the open, non-linear heights of freedom, and some people will not make the shift. I also understood, as a practical matter, that access to this full range of perspectives is rare among our citizenry, and for me as well, and it is a lot of work to analyze any important issue so dispassionately and rationally. Perspectives keep shifting, too. Formerly treasured regional and personal identities are now considered to be cultural stereotypes, where politically expedient.

I wanted my students to understand the freedom versus equality trade-off that I felt was forever being sued for and tried in our country. I needed them to know that every entitlement, however "fair," might also take a bite out of free enterprise. I wanted them to get the promise of our Founding Fathers, several of whom, in providing for free markets, warned us to the effect, sacrifice a little freedom for a little equality and you will soon have neither. I believed that if you were a teacher and could teach this one profound value, our labors in teaching for America would be worthwhile.

An articulate student said that his cause was gender role equality, total equality, and so there is no other side to this. It is an absolute. He was sure about that, and the passionate resolution of a student is never something to squander or push. "Be careful here," I thought. "Be careful." Receiving total certainty from a sixteen-year-old is an excellent test of our ability to remain Socratic and empathic as teachers, a commitment I had made. I believed this empathy test to be of particular importance in this case; I was well aware that students identifying as lesbian, gay, bisexual, transgender, or those questioning or changing their orientation could be facing grave risk: victimization by peers, truancy, and even attempted suicide.[2]

As a school leader, you can get into serious trouble if you arbitrarily deny students the right to speak out as they like, although I have to admit I was uncomfortable letting go of the status quo of my upbringing in the case of gender and some other things, as well. I had always treated males and females differently, and was puzzled at anyone who wouldn't. So I did what all teachers do as a stall tactic: I assigned homework. I reasoned that the origin of the situation, gender equality, had to be tied to the principals of our democracy, to the Founding Fathers—Mothers, if they would—and, if these three students could research that connection, if they could gain some historical depth and perspective about their issue, their proposal would be accepted. They would have legitimately earned the right to speak out at our annual forum.

The truth is, I had no real idea how I could get them to understand the cost of the freedoms and rights they both demanded and presumed, and I had limited confidence in my own ability to create such a transformation.

But I disliked the presumptive notion that they might be picking a cause that they viewed as indisputable primarily due to its political expediency and apparent righteousness—you weren't really even "allowed" to disagree on an issue like that. Situations like this always made me buck, and these students had so little experience. How could I lift their focus from equality to freedom—could they even tell them apart? Can anybody any more? The revolutionary Founding Fathers and their continuing advocates surely could, and yet I did not believe my students cared a thing about the difference.

Looking at their tender faces, I wondered if young people like this could even fathom freedom. "Is it just fairness you are looking for?" I asked. How could they know the meaning of freedom, like fish knowing water? Illustrating freedom profoundly and unforgettably should surely be my teaching goal here. Or so I thought, as I recounted for them this story, set in the Swiss Alps, the same setting as Handlin used in his great essay. And to you, treasured reader, I can hardly imagine your knowledge of the history of the Swiss, and so I will assert that this is an absolutely true story that, as such, made me, surely alone in the United States, privy to one of the most timeless pivot points in human history, as though I sat on an Alpine peak and could watch all human events of a millennium quantum-shifting before my eyes. A tall claim, for sure, but read on.

It was 1983, in Bern, and I was seeing a Swiss girl, Margrit. She was rightfully named after the gentlest Alpine flower, and she was patiently teaching me to speak Swiss-German. A terrific skier (she taught for the legendary Swiss Ski School), she came from the ancient hamlet of Appenzell along the Swiss-Austrian border. Steady as a chamois, not five feet tall and sturdy as Appenzellers tend to be, she could ski even the steep chutes and deep snow. I can still sing some of the yodels she taught me coming down from the mountain after beautiful days of powder and sky. I thought the world of her, even though she was of a different world than I.

Following a ski trip into the Bernese Oberland around Christmastime, we drove east towards her home in the Alps, an hour south by autobahn from where William Tell supposedly freed the nation from tyranny seven centuries earlier, in 1291 to be exact. We planned to visit her mother, and I longed to ski tour up to the fabled heights of her home mountain—the dark, brooding Santis—to peel off the sealskins, and to ski back down to the valley, our own tracks alone on the mountain. It was the evening before Election Day. I found driving there to be transformative—not just as we purred through mountain passes with their shepherd huts and snowy alpine meadows, snow swirling before us on the perfect Swiss Autobahn—more because it seemed like passing through time. We pulled into town. Passing the graveyard, it looked like a good percentage of stones had the same last name as hers, generations of gravestones, and her father's grave was there, and every name on every man's stone was marked with an army rank.

There was scarcely any food in the house save bread, but there were seven kinds of that. We sat around the huge, ceramic hearth where the bread was baked, Margrit and I, while her mother sat by the window, the sun flooding onto a round sampler she stitched and onto her hands, the largest hands I'd ever seen on a woman. The local Swiss-German dialect was thick, but her mother and I were able to speak in rudimentary terms— we could talk about bread, the barn. We did not mention the election, as that entails a more complex lexicon. Her mother showed us around, mainly the barn that was older than America, how clean that barn was, how Margrit's father had always kept it so until the day he died. They had little money, but they were proud. I was quartered for the night in a neighbor's house, in the room of their son who was off in the army (as were 6 percent of all landsmen at that time).

The next afternoon, Election Day, the town bell rang, and we bid Grüss Gott to Margrit's mother, walked down to the town square with its ancient cobblestones and water troughs. There was some tension gathering with the people today, more than usual, auspicious, and plenty of women in the square. Everyone was preparing for the mayor to read the proposition, "All in favor of public voting rights for the women of Appenzell . . ." Margrit's was an old family, and so, at the square, we were met by friends and relatives. Someone had a second story balcony just overlooking the square—a page from history being written before my eyes. I wish I could find the photograph. People seemed to be whispering everywhere.

And so at precisely the appointed moment, the Bürgermeister read: "All in favor . . ." A few stray men raised their swords in the air. Whispers . . .

Then, "All opposed . . . Die Stimmrechte aller Bundesrätinnen," and the
sky in the town square filled with the swords of men, some of whom may
have meant with that very gesture through the generations, "I am the one
who will die for my family and I am the one who will cast their vote."

The sense that I had witnessed something historic was so strong that I could
not help feeling inspired: the cobblestone square, the traditional outfits, the
gleaming swords all made me feel adrift in time. The dying sense of patriarchy
in the West was rationalized to me by the locals' explanation that really the
men were only voting on behalf of their households. At that time, all Swiss
men were required to serve in the military. I had no experience in evaluating
five-hundred-year-old traditions, but I understood them to be the very source
of freedom and democracy. Besides, politics aside, I loved seeing culture preserved, like fine art, and to this day I am, by nature, charmed if not blinded
by folkways. I now know this to be a sensibility (or lack of it) that normally
increases among humans as they age.

There in my office, I searched the eyes of my three students. Incredu-
lously, as I was prepared for them to be stunned with the charisma of history,
none of the three appeared to be enchanted at all by my time travels. I had
recounted this extraordinary scene to various audiences over the years and
often been met with wide eyes, but this time I was explaining it to sixteen-
year-old students with their own, new millennial agendas. Had my tale lost
its mojo? Had today's sensibility rendered a millennium of human striving
trivial?

The Alps? The mountains? The swords? Apparently even this charming
history had cast little spell over them. Were they so lacking in historical perspective that the story just seemed like stupid men with swords? Did the story
merely serve to make them feel even more victimized as students trapped in
schooling, or trapped in a stagnant culture, can feel? Was this cognitive dis-
sonance?

Perhaps if I just drew a few connections for them.

I pressed on with my case:

Direct democracy, which is still there in the Canton of Appenzell, is a
cumbersome commitment. To reconvene in the square and raise a sword
over everything that comes up is a lot of responsibility. As a matter of

convenience, it made good, practical sense for the father to represent a family, especially if the other family members were doing other important things. In the history of the world, just imagine the right for each family to even have a vote! Who among us could sincerely call this tyranny? How amazing and rare Appenzeller democracy was compared to most places in history! And one final consideration: who would insist upon judging an entire historical development while confining themselves to today's consciousness, as though there is no other consciousness?

And we discussed cultural relativity. Or I did.

Before dismissing them, I asked my students, "How many hearing this story can, with certainty, say you'd have raised the sword in opposition to the proposed law had you grown up in Appenzell?"

They shrugged their shoulders. It was as if they were conscious only of their own generation and took their freedom for granted. Had they never heard how we were shot down at Kent State, how Martin marched all the way to Washington, how they shot JFK? They had probably heard little of Bobby, much less Bobby Seale, the son of a carpenter, or Russell Means or Cesar Chavez; and probably, for all their massive music collections, never really "experienced" how Hendrix played "The Star Spangled Banner." All that feedback. It was as if they had never heard of freedom fighters, the rose in a fisted glove, or how that greatest generation before us took down the Nazis. What about Alice Paul or Lucy Burns? Was freedom a pre-millennial thing? I dismissed them, feeling the press of unchecked emails from people seeking me out; I had a school to run, and they had already sacrificed lunchtime. I had not imagined how hard it would be to imagine a just and compassionate society. We would reconvene again in a few days to discuss our research on the treatment of gender roles.

(2)

Questions. In anticipating that next meeting, many subsequent questions arose. I planned to be Socratic and to pose just the right questions to the students.

In causing a mind shift, normally we must think of the largest questions possible, mull them over until we can toss them out and replace them with even more encompassing ones, and then do that again. We arrive at the biggest possible question, one that somehow goes to the very core of our motivations. This is a methodology known as *appreciative inquiry*, a technique used to heighten shared group understandings. Teachers can err here by focusing so intently on the mind shift of their students that they disregard their own, private needs for such evolution. If I was sincerely Socratic and not just manipulating my students, wouldn't my ultimate question really include an ethical or cognitive challenge to myself, something I had to learn along with them? I couldn't ask a leading question; that would be disingenuous. I thought to ask our students, "If you could meet one of those sword raisers, what would you ask them?" but that was just a setup, just my own agenda. Hell, would they even want to understand my point of view, much less that of ancient, European cheesemakers with swords? As my set of possible questions grew in magnitude, I began to question my own background assumptions and ideology. That time in Appenzell seemed so classic and so pure. Must I cast it out? Could I even separate history from anachronism? Was I becoming an anachronism myself?

I began to wonder if I had failed to consider the different world Millennial students were growing up in, and whether I was capable of understanding it. Having been married for two decades, I knew that gender relations could hardly be judged in terms of some eternal, universal truth, even freedom. Even equality. All culture is relative and all relations are messy, especially the romantic ones youth seeks. Maybe my own stories were just lead weight. Human consciousness evolves, as it should. Legitimate perspectives change from mountain to valley floor and from one generation to the next. Typical of human memory, even my own imagination was at play. Men raising swords! Suddenly I was unsure if I was remembering the real event or just a memory of it—what could my students have been using to construct meaning: mental pictures of men in colorful costumes wielding swords against the universe like rubbery cartoon figures?

The Appenzell election preceded my students by a generation or two. My sense of relevance was disintegrating before my eyes. There were real changes going on. Today. Over the past generation, college attendance had shifted so that most students were female. Gender studies could now be found at virtually every college, with feminist scholars taking a lead role in rewriting America's history texts. What happened, anyway? In grade school, more than twice as many boys were being diagnosed with ADD and hyperactivity, and at least four times as many as girls with autism spectrum disorders.[3]

Did boys change? Would schools have to educate boys and girls using different strategies, as though each had special learning needs?

Or had America become an overcrowded society with an emphasis on standardized academic and scholastic communities that worked poorly for boys? Like a purging of the subconscious, the constraints of political correctness and superego absent, a fantastic reverie ensued:

> *What if boys were like panthers, each needing a full hundred acres to hunt and roam? And now, there was no place left for boys like that. We did not need to hunt any more. We did not even need to build fires to keep us warm or to cook food. The great American cowboys were all stock-yarded outside of Omaha, or else realtors somewhere out on the coast, and the free-range was all fenced up. Of what good was a man? What if, all along, freedom fighting was just a guy thing? . . . and now women had started thinking, alright now, that was exciting for a while, and kinda sexy, and you were so brave, but enough's enough? Now everyone sit down and hold hands. What if roaming was no longer part of the new world order but men, somehow, in their DNA, in their glands, needed it? As men struggled to find their new place, whatever it was, was there no loss whatsoever to mourn, however romantic?*

Early in the new millennium, we were hearing more statements like, "On average, boys could achieve a high standard of self-control and discipline in an environment that allows them significant freedom to be physically active, an environment that, on average, girls do not rely upon."[4] None of these assertions were being made back in the sword raising days, although we now know that boys' eyes track faster, so maybe this accounted for their comfort in moving swords around in crowds.[5] Fast eye tracking? Was that suddenly out of vogue? I didn't recall gender-specific biological programming working against males during the Vietnam War era, either; and certainly not during the Greatest Generation. Was this supposed to be good news, a helpful finding for teachers who might patiently keep the boys at bay while cooperative, calm-eyed girls glided easily through the lessons?

At last, I had to come to terms with another concern I was having in the evolution of gender: I was concerned about the emerging uncertainty of roles for men, another almost inadmissible sentiment. We each have a shadow side, even the most enlightened among us, and mine mused on:

Courageous sword-raisers filled the Appenzell square, afflicted with attention deficit and hyperactivity disorder (ADHD) all along, and what the ancient village really needed to do was to spike Ritalin into the snowmelt as it came bubbling down across the alpine meadows of the Santis Mountain, down through the streams and little brooks and into the ancient stone drinking troughs in the town square. Or ferment the beer in it.

This is, of course, dangerous political turf, but who will deny having a shadow consciousness swimming with untempered notions. Forbidden images occurred as a meditation, and with no implied truth:

I saw men as hapless anachronisms, appearing heroic through the millennium primarily due to their brutishness. Or were the Swiss men I witnessed, now already a generation ago, impassioned insurgents keeping the faith after eight centuries? Could there ever have been a legitimate cause for a paternalistic society?

Questions spooled out as though they masked some deeper truth, some shadowy longing. Where were the questions my students and I needed to face together, authentically? How could I access the wisdom of these students, enter their realm of possibility?

Emerging from man's harsh past, the promise of America, set forth by the Founding Fathers, is not the start but rather a continuation of the people's struggle for democracy, and this struggle will have to be reimagined wherever we organize in an effort to transcend tyranny and fear in whatever form they may take. On this, I felt my students and I would agree, though I struggled with the idea of gender being the tyrant. Wasn't this an issue that pits old versus young far more than it provokes the eternal contest of male versus female? For what does youth compel of the young if not to disturb the systems created by those before them? And what does age compel of our elders if not to protect that system from the intemperate causes of the young and hurried? It was this point, this physiological and God-given generational divide which made me lose confidence in my own stories. It was this point which made me simultaneously ashamed and amused by my own subconscious, as well as driven to reveal it, to hold it like a paper airplane above Appenzell Square, ready to release. It seemed unthinkable that I could let go of my beautiful,

Alpine folk tale. It was so real. It did matter, it had to matter. How could I bear to let it go? And with this, I let go of the paper plane, and I knew I would never tell the story the same way again.

The dilemma was taking shape. Now, here, in a new millennium, our students were to have their own forum, and they needed the confidence to raise up their own swords. Through a lifetime of experience and reflection I had become a master in showing students that they had relatively little or nothing to protest, that if anything they had it too good, that their own efforts and their own histories were little puffs compared to the prevailing winds of history. And I let this go, too.

(3)

We resumed later in the week, back there in my office. Facing three students, each of a different gender identity, I understood it would be easy for them to feel like victims, especially from the confines of student life. Perhaps they would identify with Margrit in the story. Margrit and her family's sense of freedom and fearlessness was surely a world we could all stand in awe of: the swords raised, the enormity of the natural Alpine forces, a culture that had sustained itself with a wisdom five centuries more deeply rooted than our own. For me, the story had been alive and in need of telling. At no point, not even then, had it occurred to me that there was only one reason Magrit was able to take me to the balcony to watch the wonderful spectacle on that day: she could not vote, either. Nor had it ever dawned on me to ask her how she felt about this.

Months later, on my rounds at a student graduation party, one of these students would call to me, "Hey, Stuart, why don't you tell us all some stories of the '70s," and I still wonder if my pure laughter then, if my mere understanding that he was kidding, might have been a crowning achievement of my teaching career. He was joking. Of course he was joking. Louis Feuer once recalled this theory of relativity for teachers: "The greatest tragedy that can befall a teacher, according to Einstein, is when he finds that his language, method, and problems have ceased to be those of the new generation of students, whose presuppositions he may find not only alien but willfully irrational."[6] And there, at that follow-up meeting with my students, I began to feel a shift in my consciousness. There was something missing here. There was a force of gravity, something more basic than even freedom, pulling at them, and now pulling at me. Naturally, every story is two stories: the one observed, and the one experienced on a personal level. I realized that I had been only telling the first half of the story—the part that takes place in the mountains—and that for thirty years I had kept my real story, the story less easy to share, hidden down in that valley, hidden even from myself. It was not much more than an image.

Later that day, Margrit pointed to the darkening sky and peaks to the east and wisely said that we were not to go up there ski touring; it could avalanche in these conditions. I had to get back to Bern, anyway, and so I packed up and drove out towards the valley that very night, alone, and the enormity of the natural forces surrounding me made the aloneness seem strange and eternal. On the way out of the village, the awesome Santis pushed up against Enggenhüttenstrasse like a gothic cathedral and I put behind me what is often, ironically, called the world's only true remaining national democracy, as though it were a story from long ago. And on the radio, the miraculous car radio, the glockenspiel, like a sacred, distant cowbell choir, orchestrated the whole of the ancient world in pure carols. I remember them in slow time, my car headlights spotlighting the thick snowflakes in slow motion, the streetlamps revealing heaven. There was only whiteness, a universe in unison, the white lane leading me out of the mountains. I was stunned at this space beyond dimension, this epiphany, am still stunned to this day, and equally at the people who could be a part of such a cultural ecosystem as this—why would I want to leave this world? Is it possible that it was not real?

Then, during that drive, I first understood that time and space are not bound in a linear fashion, and that there are no absolutes—a discovery that Einstein had made back in Bern, where I was headed. Appenzeller women got the right to vote in 1990, but that time in the square is permanent, it still exists like a capsule somewhere; in the same way, that drive out of the mountains is a permanent image, like a child's carousel dream, a pure time and space to which I never returned and never could, a time of pure freedom. Margrit, flower, was in true love with an Austrian fellow from across the border and I never saw her again. I was leaving the mountains.

And there it was: loss. Loss of youth. Loss of the old times. I could not bear my own losses. I'm glad I never found a way to tell my students this second part of the story, especially at that graduation party. They would figure it out when they were ready.

We are not only disunited by the hills and valleys that separate the generations, we are cut off even from parts of our own lives, trapped as they are in other, distant parts of our being: distant ages, distant genders, distant ethnicities and religions, distant people looking for connection. There it was: loss of love.

Oscar Handlin, great American and teacher, whose essay had enticed me to the Alps to begin with and whose work now inspires three generations of scholars, died a week before his ninety-sixth birthday, which is when I commenced with this story. He had given us, as teachers, plenty of warning: we cannot relive folk tales, trapped as they are in their own time and space: "In the mountains, aphorisms coined on the plains become either irrelevant or false," he wrote. Long after I had first read this, my students showed me what it meant. When our school forum came, one of the students had studied the history of discrimination—good scholarship; one student did not present, and was really there to support the third. The third student had done his own research but none of it concerned any Founding Fathers or songs of freedom; he had done nothing I had suggested, so far as I could tell. Instead, he vigorously and, really, courageously, presented a forum on emerging gender roles. The whole forum derived and unfolded in the full conviction and charge of the students: a success. There they were all over the campus green, like an old-time town square, sorting out their prior generation's failures and aspirations to wipe out inequalities in race, economic status, age, and gender, and raising their swords for postmodern freedom. I observed from my metaphorical balcony, confronting the crazy notion of a genderless generation and marveling at the vibrant students below. As for freedom, they now had it.

I sometimes wonder if students believe their issues to be the only problems that have ever existed, that the millennium started with an empty chalkboard. Somehow, the gender issue drew the empathy out of them. Who knows, maybe my image of Swiss men with swords inflamed them all the more. Maybe I was on their quaint shelf with the Brothers Grimm, making them feel all the more in charge. And now they were walking out of the hall and into the quad in tight pods, in their own time and space, tapped into this issue, feeling a part of something big, like they were all under the same spell. Many have the same wristband, and I'm thinking I could get one of them, or should I? Even the solitary students are walking out to the quad in contemplative postures. The legacy of human democracy must have seemed just a footnote to them compared to now. For them, what is now in the quad, this pumped-up, real thing, is all there is to lose in the history of the world. And I can't say a thing because it is too wonderful to watch, and it feels to me like a distant time, another dimension.

One thing I should mention is that this third student, this rosy-cheeked, entrepreneurial rabble rouser who did his own homework rather than mine, had actually been born and known as a girl up to that point in his life. The very next year, his junior year, he declared his gender to be in transition, and changed his name. We shrugged our shoulders. Not a trace of ADD, we'll take him: we could use a guy like that. And his curriculum that year included American history, starting out with, of course, the Founding Fathers.

You can always tell a generation on the way out; they believe they are indulging youth in their role as freedom fighters when all they are really doing is usurping any potential the young (or the underclass) might have for courageous autonomy. To stay in the game, you eventually have to let it go, even some of your most heartfelt stories. You must somehow access the larger mysteries that lay inside of them. Some would say a real teacher is one who makes his points persuasively, with power and imagery and conviction. But I tried that and would no longer say it's true. Real teachers are fundamentally there to invite and listen to the passions of their students. The more we hear the better we become and the greater the chance that we can ultimately provide them with compassionate service.

Students whose own appetites take them far beyond any feedback we can provide, the academic and intellectual roamers, are the ones who make teachers out of us as we cultivate those appetites with a light heart and a sense of wonder. I would love to know that my lifetime of reading and travel made me a real teacher, and I do know that our generation's stories must be passed on. This is imperative and foundational. But the real teaching is not in the stories, it is in the faith we have in our students. A posse of renegade students taught me to trust that if I lived the lessons imparted in my own stories, they would do the same. The real teachers are our students.

As teachers we know this but often ignore it:

They will not let me off till I go with them, respond to them,

And discorrupt them, and charge them full with the charge of the Soul.

—Walt Whitman, "I Sing the Body Electric"[7]

Freedom isn't lifting the sword, it is letting it go, and I don't know if we can ever do that. We will, of course, never be free—a paradox the Founding Fathers never told us about. Gender roles are only one of a great many paradigms we could use to illustrate the relentless human search for freedom and for the self. Maybe these paradigms are not much more than interchangeable, temporal placeholders in our endless search for universal truths. Maybe we are all men in colors wielding swords against the universe like rubbery cartoon figures. Socrates, too, and Confucius, Magellan, Isaac Newton. Bono. JFK. Joan of Arc. Maybe it is a useless thing we practice as teachers, hanging on to the old, cowardly perspectives centered around grade books and rows of students, only there to give us the right answer. I think these are all important maybes, but maybe we need these practices and all these histories anyway because without them we are left with only loss. We can't hold on to anything.

At last, I have arrived at my true, big question, and I can't ask it: how much of this can we bear?

We are all floating, yet we must never say so. We put up a good show, keep teaching, keep listening. The generation born around the turn of this upstart millennium will never understand freedom in the way twentieth century men did—and I understand it less than I used to—but they will come to understand the freeing of human identity in ways which we still have not arrived at or even imagined, the places passion and heart take them, with us and, in good time, without us.

Bern, Switzerland; Maui, Hawaii; San Juanico, MX; Encinitas, CA

9

~~~~

Single-Handing It in an Age of Fear

People say that what we're seeking is a meaning for life.
I think that what we're seeking is an experience of being alive,
so that we actually feel the rapture of being alive.

Joseph Campbell
American mythologist, writer, and lecturer

Single Handing, Multitasking

Fishers Island trails off the northeast fork of Long Island and stretches north, as though longing to grasp Rhode Island. But it neither truly belongs to Long Island or New England—it is a private place to be lost somewhere in between.

I love single-handed sailing. I spent years on the Long Island Sound, sailing from point to point, mainly alone, on a twenty-five-foot wooden sloop called *Sequoia*, all around the North Fork. Silently getting it rigged and taking off downwind, filling the jib with wind one-handed and hearing it snap into silence, then hoisting and cleating the main halyard with the other hand while steering . . . with the other? I hardly even know how to explain how single-handing is possible, but for those of you who do it, you understand.

I was trying to become a teacher in those years, not at all sure of my "real" path, and single-handing gave me a sense, or the illusion, of independence and control over my destiny. My favorite book became Joshua Slocum's *Sailing Alone around the World*, a book I would give anything for our students to want to read. My weekend retreats from teacher education became

163

beautiful destinations and landings all over the Sound, although I never landed on Fishers Island then. With barely a post office and just nine miles long, Fishers Island always seemed a mystery, with a bit of an Alfred Hitchcock aura about it.

I loved the life. When we sail away, gone are the straight lines and fences, gone are the rules imposed mainly to control and rarely to free, gone is the status quo. There is still fear at sea, but this fear is not of the limits and regulators imposed by education and social life, but of the limitless.

We replace "what" with "what if?" Gone are many questions with answers.

Single-handing through wind, tide, and current, gone is the schooling. But the study and practice of seamanship leaves out no essential facet of education, progressive or traditional; discovery and curiosity are reborn as basic skills. As educators and parents, can we reclaim the courage to pursue these equally timeworn and forward-leaning values? This would be real work for teachers.

Educators from at least as far back as Socrates have speculated about how to engage curiosity and discovery—Socratic inquiry—in the classroom, and how to develop these faculties, faculties which are so akin to entrepreneurship and our country's heritage. Can we commit to a penetrating line of thought rather than be tossed about by the sea of standards and disparate agendas that we face? The "multitasked" life? Coming of age in the new millennium, "Millennial" students and teachers look to technology to enhance the level of classroom inquiry, since today's school sizes make Socratic methods seem impractical, unsustainable, and unusual. Socrates was willing to die for these values. What are we willing to do?

Class size is at a historic high in the United States making it hard to access each student individually. Can we reclaim the time to listen to our students honestly as they find their course? Can we reclaim the courage we'll need to take that kind of time, time for true inquiry?

*   *   *

We were at the Green Inn, in Narragansett, Rhode Island, summer of 1976, and it was getting late. Some still remember the old Victorian-style inn, its huge green turrets and awnings perched over Monahan's Dock on Narragansett Bay, before it went into debt and burned to the ground. ("Kitchen fire.") We were out on the front porch on the wicker rockers, sipping warm cognac in giant snifters, the lights of Newport glimmering across the bay. My friend Rick walked across the deck, concerned. He had a twenty-eight-foot sloop docked out front at Monahan's and his crew had just backed out.

It was August. Rick had agreed to get the ship delivered to the south shore of Long Island, to the Great South Bay, in a day's time. That's well over a hundred miles, mostly in open ocean I was guessing, but mainly in sight of land. If the weather stayed clear, a sailor could do pretty much the whole run using coastal piloting without having to get into too much off-shore navigating. I knew the whole run already, pretty much, except for the final reach from Montauk to the Great South Bay, the last fifty knots of straight, coastal piloting, which sounded like fun. I agreed to single-hand it.

I set out at midnight, fully engaged in learning the new rig, and plotting my entire course in rhumb lines right up to dinner the next night in Bellport, Long Island. Or maybe breakfast. Shoving off, I hoisted the jib and set it loosely, then let go of the land, heading downwind.

Nothing engages the entirety of one's mind and body more than an open-ended problem, like setting out on a new ship, learning a new rig, alone. Single-handing, you'd have to get the sails to manage themselves for a minute using some spare lines or the bitter ends of a sheet or something—you'd have to come up with the craziest knots, quickly.

In the Harbor, and out in "The Real World"

Recently, I asked my friend Matt from Utah, "If you could push a button and your daughter would be admitted to the college of your choice, and then end up with a secure job in a cubicle and live out her life with no prospect of failure or pain—if she could "straight line it"—would you push the button?" Matt thought carefully for a minute, then nodded his resignation: "Yes."

I was stunned, truly. Matt, a button pusher! It would never have occurred to me that someone would feel this way, much less Matt. He skis some of the steepest chutes on the mountain, he even teaches avalanche protection.

I'm not stunned any more. Who among us would stand up and claim we are living in an age of courage? How many of our neighbors or school teachers would *live free or die?* Notwithstanding the romantic imperative for this, do we all really prefer the journey to the destination? (If you've flown and passed through our airport hubs much lately, don't answer that question.)

Tying down the ship's wheel with a slipknot gave me time to raise and set the mainsail, shuffling back to adjust the steering several times. Then, managing both sails while keeping the ship on the right heading and every few minutes adjusting the course along with the chart, I sailed out into Narragansett Bay . . . beautiful night.

Tunnel vision is not only stimulated by the decision to focus the eyes on a book or a road, it is also a physiological response and it can be caused by things like consumption of rum or the bite of a black mamba—or by fear. But as we adapt to the ocean with nothing to block any vista, the peripheral vision expands and breathing naturally slows down, moving lower in the chest. To the extent that one is truly in the peripheral vision state, clear sailing means we block anxiety or stress—we become emotionally and intellectually receptive. At length, we may approach the trance state as our vision spreads out over space and time. We are receptive, perceptions enhanced. Teachers, pressed on by curricular demands, often feel little time to assess the state of their students in these two, physiologically incompatible states of seeing.

As I travel the Southwest visiting schools and talking to parents, teachers, and school leaders, I meet many parents who show low tolerance for *a tough journey,* for an open-ended journey, or for watching their children finding their own way. Millennial parents believe it is their responsibility to keep their children headed on a straight and narrow tunnel, or as I call it, "the race to the cubicle." A growing choir of Ivy League admissions officers complain that the intellectually sensitive and supposed "best and brightest" (i.e., highest scoring) among our children have become masters of compliance and tunnel vision. Parents can seem like the biggest victims, viewed as meddlesome in school, where the gatekeeping has become superb.

The groups and pressures bearing down on our schools seem like high seas, out of control, and I don't know how superintendents can face them all squarely and still keep the focus on great teaching: curricular standards; grant funding requirements; competing national, state, and local testing requirements; violence prevention and safety and health requirements; insidious vendors and interest groups; monopolistic textbook corporations;

insurance companies; teachers union and department of labor regulations; and sprawling, self-sustaining bureaucracy at various levels. Add to these groups: fearful parents.

We have not transcended horrific, millennial-era events like 9/11 and the Columbine school massacre, nor have we removed them from our collective consciousness. Many parents I meet wear the overprotection of their children on their sleeves, as evidence of their responsibility in a world defined by these kinds of events. It's instinct. As we become fearful, our peripheral vision narrows and, with the arousal of the sympathetic nervous system (the part of the "involuntary" or autonomic nervous system associated with activity, adrenalin, and stress), our views are limited. We tend to focus on one object or the next rather than a broad field of vision. One psychologist observed, "Whereas energetic free-play outdoors used to be the typical activity in childhood, such opportunities are rare now, largely because of parental fears about their child's safety."[1] *We leave the open ocean.*

Our own school, as a benign illustration, uses the slogan "Learn by *Discovery*," but the slogan has undergone years of criticism from marketing teams and parents for being too childish for a college prep school. Imagine a world where discovery, the work of Einstein, Magellan, Galileo—of Fossy, Admiral Parry, and NASA—is a quaint, storybook effort dispensed with easily enough in kindergarten or cub scouts—not something you can actually "do." These are subtle enough assumptions, but they rumble beneath American elementary and secondary school education like a distant storm heard by whales, deep down, irrelevant.

Competing world views, and the unwillingness of those with one to recognize the truth of the other, explain why parents and teachers either view Albert Einstein, through tunnel vision, as a theoretical physicist who discovered the theory of general relativity or, in a state of peripheral vision, as a Nobel Prize winner who tried to teach us that "imagination is the highest form of wisdom." Einstein could never have discovered one without the other, so rapt and complete was his curiosity. There is game-changing research on curiosity coming out of the psychology field, but it is not finding its way into educational research (except in articles criticizing its absence). This is not new in the field of education. As Einstein wrote: "It is, in fact, nothing short of a miracle that the modern methods of instruction have not yet entirely strangled the holy curiosity of inquiry; for this delicate little plant, aside from stimulation, stands mainly in need of freedom."[2]

Nevertheless, at his death, Einstein the teacher was to be missed as much as Einstein the physicist. School is treated as a protected, controlled harbor, but we sacrifice when we attempt to turn education into a controlled, closed system. When teachers and students delve into topics in depth, it follows that they will almost certainly be unable to get through the year's prescribed curriculum.[3] Teachers thereby risk their stature and security. Their students risk test preparation. It is a world where a key criterion for college admissions (the SAT) was designed sixty years ago based fundamentally on its breakthrough attribute: it could be scored by machine. It is a world where students get credit for online physical education.

In-harbor, written expression is reduced to strict formulas for writing one, three, or five paragraphs, as though thought and discovery alike were a fill-in activity. In-harbor, every middle schooler must take algebra or be "left behind." Efforts to regulate schools of over five hundred students, often consisting of up to two or three thousand students divided into classes too large to have an open, curiosity-driven conversation, seem sensible. In harbor, this all might look like a reliable formula for life preparation because it is accepted as the practical normalcy, but it does not look that way at all from open ocean. Unless, of course, our wish is for the next generation to spend a lifetime in groups of thirty to forty people forcibly gathered together daily. Or, perhaps, if life could reliably and expeditiously present us with three or four solutions for our most significant problems. Imagine such a life!

Surely we will need fearless parents, teachers, and administrators to hold the largest vision for the larger purposes of schooling. Real teachers will be willing to risk their jobs solely to have a single, great, openhearted conversation.

Over the Edge of the (Virtual) World

"You're weaving all over the Atlantic!" a ship's captain once told me as a drifting boy still learning to handle the helm. I was surely that way in school at that point, too, fuzzily wasting my university education away. There would be a few more years of weaving for me, too. I'm glad I was not online in those years. I'm glad I remained untethered and out in open ocean, even though I often felt lost.

Single-handing at sea begs contrast with a concept now villainized in educational and social circles nationwide: "multitasking." Multitasking is a term now on the "cusp" of paradigm shift, and the confusion is, no doubt, intergenerational: "Baby Boomers," "Generation X-ers," and "Millennials" all see it differently. In general, new millennial definitions seem to share the idea that multitasking entails attempting multiple tasks at once while using digital technology. The acceleration of "interruption technologies" can impede deep concentration and our students' impulse control. Growing scientific research points to a need for digital time-outs.[4] The wonders of digital citizenship are bearing hard upon a growing understanding that we seem to be sacrificing deep focus and a steady course.

Single-handed sailing is not like that at all; every action is focused on a pure, single purpose: moving the ship ahead properly, all skill, creativity, and ingenuity combining for the same, single purpose. Wind and water, sea and sky, all part of the same, unified whole. Although it has the advantage of promising a seemingly unlimited number of collaborators, multitasking in our wired world can force us to stay at the superficial level, always grazing, weaving all over our own, intellectual Atlantic.

To the old-timers, the latter is indicative of distraction and a lack of deep focus. It appears artificial, inauthentic, and time-sucking. However, Millennials, text messaging with one hand and video chatting with the other (or, horrifically, while driving), going about their "connected" day, will say what a seventeen-year-old, plugged-in high school senior told me recently: "Of course I focus on all of this at once—I am just staying in touch. It's not a distraction." Are these students distracted, or merely busy? Are they isolated in a virtual world, or developing collective intelligence?

There is a substantial portion of our student population—those repressed students whose worlds are stifled in school—who find whole worlds right there deep in the harbor: passive, electronic, and often angry or profane worlds far beyond the comprehension of mom and dad. They are spending half of their waking lives with their spirit drawn down into the twilight zone of an electronic screen of some kind.[5] They are not weaving all over the Atlantic; they are just finding another course, naturally: wired. Unfortunately, the addictive nature of a good deal of digital engagement presents many, primarily teens and tweens, with risks to their health and happiness.

Students aren't the only ones who appear distracted and consumed. Teachers in today's large comprehensive schools have incredible time-compression

demands, 150 or 185 students a day, and their students and these students'
parents can often access them 24/7 through the world of electronic messaging. Electronic communications alone intensify the demands on their time,
both increasing their work and decreasing their ability to pay attention to a
single task.[6]

It appears that previous generations, including pre-millennial teachers,
resent multitasking and chronic online social networking. It also appears that
their students do not mind it, often doing it compulsively throughout the
day. They feel it opens up the world to them, while their teachers may feel
this all cuts into their "real time." This generational divide will continue to be
debated while commercial meditation studios (and even school clubs) launch
all over the country, attempting to reclaim slow time and open space. If
enough people presume something for long enough, it becomes real. Hence,
we watch as things the previous generation thought to be contrivances
become real. As generations change, we are spirited away from one collective
consciousness and into another. Socially, we are drawn into a world that feels
compelling even as we sense it as a world apart—since well before Magellan,
well before Socrates, we have been so drawn—and now we are drawn to the
streaming edge of a virtual world.

Full and By: Perseverance

*Sailing out of Monahan's Reef, I headed west on a steady reach out of the
bay for a couple hours, passing the mansions along the shore lit dimly under
long, wispy clouds. A bit icy way up there, I could feel the air, chilling and
dampening, but it was a balmy, clear night and the breeze was lovely and it
would soon be fresh. The Big Dipper overhead, Arcturus my constant friend,
the black ocean straight before me and spreading wider: I loved the simplicity
and persistence required of staying on a single bearing for hours at a time.
Now Point Judith to starboard.*

You practice persistence when you're single-handed sailing, doing one small
action with increasing focus and precision along with decreasing distraction
and discursive influence. Not even a ghost of anyone to rescue you, nor anyone to bail for you. No alternative task to shift to when you feel unexcited
or unsuccessful. If you bump your head hard or find yourself twenty nautical

miles off course, it can feel desperate and terrible. Some of that passes, and you persist, only with more intensity now, and with more focus. The specter of being lost is always on the horizon, but eventually no longer as a fear so much as an aside, a companion ship you merely wave to over and over again if you are lucky, and you keep plotting and checking your course, pressing on single-mindedly.

Some of the greatest challenges in single-handing come from piloting and navigating—finding your way. You set out on a course, trust that a good many wind and water conditions will be as you planned, and arrive at the right point some hours later. Underway, you keep the faith. You adjust, dead reckon, trust and reflect, adjust and dead reckon . . . and trust and reflect. Often for hours.

Perhaps there is nothing quite as valuable as the reflection process as you move along your course towards your imagined destination. Setting an intention and holding fast requires patience and persistence beyond the academic norms on land or in the harbor—the patience and persistence we find in a great teacher or student.

Single-handing is from an era before multitasking was conceptualized. Rarely in elementary or secondary school can we find curriculum or testing where students must hold fast to the same point, the same concept, withstanding every distraction and threat posed against it, for six whole hours. (Learning disabilities specialists might even label this as "perseveration.") After a while, we slip into the timeless.

And the peaceful sea—its alpha wave sounds and its blues and greens—lures us to allow our minds the space to become increasingly trusting and peacefully disciplined. Sometimes it can get rough or endlessly unpredictable and, especially if you have practiced, you may hold your intention through those times, too.

I stay full and by on the warm breeze, not too damp yet—all moves dedicated as close towards a single bearing as the heading wind allows. Five hours on the helm, in open ocean now, I am almost in sight of Block Island Sound. It is near dawn, the wind coming from the southeast, right where I focus, so I make a starboard tack to be closer to the mainland, sailing full and by.

Sailing full and by, we stay as close to the wind as possible, knowing our best course would be to go straight into it, which we cannot do. Full and by, we're just making the best way we can, and it might be said that this means we arrive at our destination at the very perfect time: at the only possible time. As an educator, I'm not sure what is so appealing about sailing full and by, but it makes good speculation. I see parents and guidance counselors and high school students treating the path through school and college as though it were a railroad track, a tunnel, rather than a life sailing full and by, aware and adaptive. Full and by, we are responding to every wind and eddy, every current and opportunity that actually presents itself along our way, and we remain open to each change. Nothing is predetermined, and so we remain lithe and resourceful, inspired by whatever it is the day, the class, or the wind is serving up. The teacher shifts the tone from prescriptive and judgmental to empathic and, to a greater degree, open-ended. The teacher is dealing with the students as they really are, listening, full and by—not always easy to do. What if this were the purpose of schooling? What would that school be like?

A Squall: Awakening Passion in Education

The squalls of late summer on the Long Island Sound are legendary and sudden, they give little warning even to the most experienced sailors, and the path they take is no more predictable than that of a top, spinning.

One sure way to make sure people are focused, learning, and fully present is to engage their passions. This is never a small trick, even for the best teachers. University admissions officers and corporate leaders alike agree about what we need out of our high school grads, out of "educated" students: passion.[8] You can't really assign or teach it, you can only allow it and appreciate that great teachers will somehow tap into it. And you can't do it part way. Passion is full commitment, full presence, and full presence can transcend class bells and school fences. How can we tap into passion among students?

My favorite part of single-handed sailing is when a storm is coming up. We get some kind of small warning, maybe a gust or a dark cloud, and we can feel it inside. A little squirt of dopamine in the brain, not too different at first than a teen hearing a text message beep, a shot of possibility.

Due north off Long Island where the Sound mixes with the ocean, I can tell the barometric pressure is dropping rather suddenly, and I become uncertain about the weather. Something is stirring, is it me? Sounds?

One of the most powerful and mysterious aspects of the sea is sound. I love to play ocean waves (or baroque music) in my classes, at least for the first few minutes and between classes. "Alpha" or "MU" sound waves, like a military helicopter in the distance, are conducive to good behavior; they calm people down and make them receptive.

I'm listening to them.

Through infrasonics, the study of sound waves, we can learn about a whole set of sounds we normally disregard, sounds we cannot or can barely hear. This frequency range, beneath 20 Hz and down to 0.001 Hz, is utilized for things like monitoring earthquakes and charting rock or petroleum formations below the earth. It is also used to study the mechanics of the human heart.

Storms.

As I sense wind picking up and clouds moving much more quickly, I feel a bit anxious, almost as though there is something supernatural taking place.

Weather that builds over long distances results naturally in severe wind and surf. Just the impact they have on our hearing alone can be profound. Leaving the calm whooshing of alpha waves, as the wind and weather pick up, beta waves of maybe 18 Hz (or in the 12-19 Hz range) are its messengers, and we should sense some agitated brain waves, not consciously at first; when beta waves are coming, we sense them well before we hear them. Just like distant sounds of weather, infrasound can cause feelings of awe or fear in humans. The military chopper is approaching, deepening, or is it the rival soccer team and we have the boom box cranked? Passion. Your breathing deepens. Single-handing in times like these, you're managing so many things at once that there is nothing to spare, you need every faculty, and any slip-up or error could cost you dearly. All this, and the pounding wind and rain to orchestrate it. You can hardly see where you're going, but that just enhances every other sense. You don't know when it's going to end, when you'll come out of it or, when it gets real bad, if you'll come out of it at all. That's what I call being alive!

I can no longer see stars, and the clouds are gathered dark and leaden above. Within moments of my noticing this, my pulse is quickening. Waves begin pitching up raucous and crazy, some over the bow or slapping hard over the gunwales, and had anyone else been at the helm, I certainly would have taken shelter in the cabin. No one is here, the sound track is changing and I am alert and tightly focused.

I become uncertain about whether to stay my planned course for the open ocean or to hug the Connecticut shore. In this situation, winds can reach as high as seventy knots and tornados are possible. High alert.

Squalls like these are the subject of both scientific research and Sunday sermons, in equal reverence. For my uncle Roderick, a seafaring Episcopalian minister, the difference meant absolutely nothing, a point of pride and subtle fury.

Before these uncertainties awaken in me much longer, lightening comes, angry, and storm winds whip up the waves. Then the rain comes, and now so heavily that my visibility grows dim as it pounds the ship. Now lightning bolts crack all around so intensely I start to wonder if there is a way to get out of this situation and if I'm going to be okay. How could this be happening to me! I could be waking up soon at the Green Inn.

Much like a video game, elementary and secondary school classrooms present a virtual reality, not an authentic experience like a storm. It's a simulated life which ends at the bell. Virtual as they may be, they have their ups and downs, which may seem very real indeed. In bad classes, and I've taught my share, we may orally experience something called "the cocktail party effect," where various sound frequencies compete from different locations making collective thought impossible for many, and sensible students take cover in multitasking or other forms of superficial compliance. Kids were not meant to sit still and listen in an environment like that. At my worst as a teacher, I have tried to force or demand or even blame my way through parties like this—not so great. Like great seamen, great teachers somehow embrace and engage and shape all these sounds and energy sources, and they channel them into a sense of unity and flow. Mastery like this is a wonderful, beautiful thing to observe or, on your best days, to achieve.

The elements press on. I can hardly see anything, and it is very hard to keep a steady course because of the wind and waves. For a while, I cannot see twenty feet in any direction.

Dead Reckoning: Setting Intentions and Tracking Them

Just recently, sailing on a classic ninety-seven-foot schooner, I pointed out two constellations to the captain, who was a recent college grad. I was puzzled for a while at his disinterest in the stars. How could a young ship's captain have no regard for the stars? And then it dawned on me: we have entered the first century, the first millennium, in all of human existence where, for those coming of age, the stars no longer have any bearing on their life paths. The stars that guided the Magi and the Phoenicians, the stars that have played a visual and spiritual symphony for the sages through the ages, are now window dressing. To our millennial captain, the whole of the cosmos is surpassed in output by an electronic GPS screen the size of a car radio. At the risk of sounding old and romantic, I still think it bears asking: *how will sages find their way?*

Dead reckoning has everything in common with great schooling. Worthy principals (and ship's captains)[9] chart their courses constantly, using everything they can get in the feedback loop so they can see if they are on course for the outcomes they aim for.[10] Like all the most important aspects of education, the principle that we must be intimately in touch with the feelings and thoughts of our students is one which should remain beyond documentation—it must be an assumption. At sea, it is an urgent matter when you are off course or, worse yet, if you are uncertain of it. In many schools I visit, doors mostly closed and departments siloed, superintendents caught between state, district and school site agendas, it is hard to find a captain's intended bearing. It can be impossible to discern a true philosophy in action, a guiding star. Cocktail party effect. Unfortunately, but understandably, most organizations tend to press on anyway, "coalitions of the willing," as Harlan Cleveland, a true captain if ever there was one, captured in *Nobody in Charge*.

The lightening intensifies. I heave-to for a while, stabilizing the vessel in its position so I can study the charts, hoping the storm will pass. But in the end all bets are off on the storm passing any time soon. My charting has been consistent and I can estimate my position within reason. I plot it again, this time within a triangle of possibility, then add a vector line for an estimated drift in these conditions. After a few minutes, I make an assumption about whether or not I am lost, and this assumption becomes my best dead reckoning: a thin pencil line amidst almost infinite complexity.

Today, thirty-five years later, my daughter would have just pulled out her iPhone for a GPS fix, checked the weather map app for a clearing in the storm, and then maybe held it to the sky for star or planet positions, just for fun. What she would have missed! My tools were: a compass, depth sounder, tide table, good chart with a pencil and some parallel rules, pair of eyes, pair of ears.

I keep the ship inside the north fork of Long Island, hugging the Connecticut coast so that I can try to maintain sight of landmarks. No luck. The visibility is such that, if I squint, I can make out the coast now and then, but not consistently. I note my speed and distance and reckon in the currents about every ten minutes on the chart. Torrents of rain sound like sand being blasted into aluminum sheets, terrifying and incredibly beautiful.

We (the ship and I) are now somewhere off Fisher's Island, but the actual charting of vectors accounting for wind, current, tide, estimated boat speed, heading, compass correction, and time could put us only along a sizeable stretch of coastline, most of it rocky, meaning that if we land poorly, our little ship will surely be dashed into rocks. (If you're reading this by a computer, Google up Winslow Homer's "Summer Squall" and you'll get the feeling.) It is then that, through the rain and haze, a small patch of coast appears, as a rubbing, whiter than the dark shading of the rocky coastline and, through examination of the vector lines I had penciled onto the charts, my best guess is that this is a tiny, sandy crescent where I can safely beach the boat.

The destination in many situations is something that can be sensed intuitively even though is not yet visible. I have tried for years to persuade our school trustees of this reality. They have come to find intuitive leadership a quaint notion, especially since the accuracy of my gut financial impressions has surpassed that of their own complex calculations, year after year. Not to brag.

It is only the slightest, grayed-out impression but it seems to lack the crude, darkened shapes of a rocky coast. Then suddenly it opens up, this rubbing, only for a moment, before the weather grays it out again, and it is gone. I have the bearing now! If I approach it too closely, but drift too much with the surges of water and wind, I will surely miss the landing and be knocked down into the shore, drawn into the rocks, and ruin the ship's hull.

Luckily, as sages assured us throughout the ages, despite our skepticism and fear of intuition, when we are attuned to our business properly and with acceptance, our intuitions have a way of lining up with reality.

I draw a final line of dead reckoning, put on the auxiliary motor, and head toward the assumed spot, which soon comes into clear view. I feel heroic. The sloop slides up onto the sand with a soft grinding and I jump out, drenched, with bow and stern lines in hand—preoccupied by doing all of these things at once. Three islanders are there to receive the lines and, with the boat beached and a high tide, ebbing, the vessel would stay high and dry for the night.

In almost all of our lives, when we are ready, we may encounter the far-sighted, the storytellers we traditionally have known as "teachers," who show us not only that a test is when you are facing a storm, but also that a storm is the most natural thing in the world. These teachers are not doing three things at once, are rarely surprised by weather, and I'm guessing they never feel heroic; they receive us simply and with the faith that only one without a closed agenda can have.

"The lightening . . ." I say. "Come on up to the house," says an elderly woman with an ample body, knowing eyes, and the largest pair of binoculars I've ever seen.

Perspective: The Real Teacher

Laird Hamilton of Hawaii was towed on a surfboard by a jet ski into a sixty-foot monster wave, dropped in, engulfed in blackness by the giant, crunching curl, then spit out like a watermelon pit squeezed between the thumb and forefinger, out into the open, making the wave, safe. He observed this: "It helps to have that little jolt of perspective that life's fragile."[11] We could tell sea stories for hours, but what the good ones keep showing is that there isn't a sailor or surfer worth being at sea with who hasn't played out his own imaginary death, been knocked down, humiliated, and seemingly betrayed by natural forces and then—and here is the worth—gone on in life a little humbler with a brighter glint in his eye. *That little jolt of perspective.*

The thought of risk in education, the role of the classroom in developing courageous people, has occurred to me many times since first landing on Fishers Island, back then at the start of my teaching career. Since the new millennium, we have entered into an age of fear, an age when parenting seems to mean moving aside any obstacle that could lead children from the linear path of the right grades, right college, and right job slot. Maybe those parents want to be heroes.

In school, becoming lost and alone, experiencing what we can never plan—single-handing it—is considered bad planning. In school, being lost is an unacceptable departure from the "real world" which schools pretend to offer us; it is the storm fearful parents demand their children be sheltered from. I am so sorry that there seems to be so much to fear in this new millennium. We are used to controlled experiments, scenarios that we can report accurately on. And so, understandably, unwittingly, we eschew freedom and discretion in education. Our school systems red-pencil the fragility and risk of authentic experience. The list of examples detailing this is long and dreary: more content standards per course than experts believe a teacher can cover in over a year and a half, "demos" being falsely called "labs," physical education time crowded out in favor of standardized test preparation, accountability for set outcomes at the expense of discovery, virtual reality being confused with reality, devaluation of teachers who have mentoring relationships with students and commit to the time that takes, homework that crowds out the opportunity for the development of intrinsic passions, more math tutoring and support classes at the expense of high school electives and clubs, and the abandonment of time-honed, qualitative evaluation strategies in favor of one-dimensional metrics. Confusion about what it means to be a *real teacher* versus a student manager. Total confusion about the whole idea of free time. Heavy backpacks. With wheels. These are the faces of fear and, as I travel the American Southwest and beyond, I've seen them in every community I've visited since the turn of the millennium. I see joy and passion and talent, too, but there is always fear. Fear narrows our peripheral vision. We see straight ahead only the enemy and we lose sight of our larger world.

Out in the open ocean, some don't make it, but let that never lead us to conclude that we were wrong to go out there or that all of our striving has been in vain. Life is fragile. At school, I suspect there will be continued efforts to remove what we cannot control: field trips, individually-paced curriculum, open-ended projects, small classes, recess, problem solving, team building, outdoor education, Socratic discussion, inductive thought, the arts. Given epidemic levels of plagiary, we may be entering a time where a substantial portion of the writing process consists of students cutting and pasting digital text into essays which are scored electronically by computers. And how can we blame them? As more controls are placed on human institutions, our players become increasingly passive and the quietly subversive is awakened in our future leaders. If the institution is school, the less ownership our students have, the more they retreat or form cliques or multitask themselves into virtual worlds or receive labels like "ADD" and the subsequent medications; and the more drop-out rates increase. Some day these drop-out rates may be seen as good news, as the unconquerable spirit of human freedom.

The sturdy Molly Chandler walked us all up to her house on the hill, led us into her bay-windowed kitchen which had overlooked the Long Island Sound and Atlantic Ocean for generations. She had seen me long before I could see her. She set down the binoculars. Studying them, they appeared to be the kind of old family treasure that contained epic tales. We ate.

Chandler was the oldest remaining family name on the island. Molly's early ancestors had died when two ships went down in a squall two hundred years ago. From this kitchen, she had waited years for her husband to return from voyages until, one day, he did not. There is no longer anything sad or moving about her solitude now. Any fear of being lost or alone, such as I might have felt, was two hundred years buried in her, unspoken and unthought, stated only in the way she held her coffee mug and looked out her kitchen window across the Sound, saying: *Where you belong is where you are. We are never lost.*

> *I made no plans for the boat that night and did not know what I would do—call the Coast Guard, call the owner of the ship and get him to fetch his damn yacht, something else? My shadow self, the weak one, was tempting me to give up on what I had started. Amidst this internal debate, Molly mentioned that high tide was at ten o'clock the next morning. My ship would be in high enough water to shove off by eight.*

> *Molly was already up with coffee by 7:00 a.m. and did not need to ask what I was doing. Her presumption that I would persevere was unspoken, yet so undoubting that it became my own.*

This life and death drama was a small thing in Molly's perspective. No ship was rolled or dismasted, the rigging was undamaged, no one drowned, there was no hurricane, we hadn't harpooned anything. I had not sailed away from England and the known world forever, bound for Plymouth Rock in the 1600s. Molly's stoicism honed through generations tendered me all the courage I needed. Studying this all in years later, I learned I had visited the home built by one of New England's legendary seaman.

Mike Marshman was sailing in the legendary 1998 Sydney to Hobart Race in sixty to eighty knot winds with spray ripping into him when a sixty-foot rogue wave engulfed the yacht and rolled it, snapping the mast and cracking the deck, trapping him under the rigging. He was pummeled this way through a pitch-black night, losing a crewmate and lifelong friend overboard. Returning home, he said: "I've been a pretty selfish bastard—just ask my wife. But all the emotions I faced out there stunned me. All my values in life have changed . . . The house is fun again. I want to spend more time with my kids, and I'm actually enjoying my work again." This, after a brutal, nightmarish, thirty-six-hour battle. [12]

My entire squall episode, from onset to beaching, took about four hours, less than the time "Millennial" generation children spend in front of a computer and/or television screen daily, on average (versus two hours a week exercising).[13] Molly easily could have given me a C- in seamanship, but why complicate things? She found a hungry sailor, and she fed him—a Fishers Island routine. I was in equal parts humiliated by my own weakness and empowered by this older, larger world view.

Maybe Molly Chandler wasn't a dreamer, but that only meant she would never fathom the ways we might conspire in the very dark shadows of our little hearts to abandon our dire situation, to bail. Her presumption that our only possible option was to complete our personal journeys somehow became manifest because of its very nature.

Similarly, great teachers do not really create learning, they only open up a space for it, and this can be a lot to face up to. When it's real and lasting, that space can expose the crack in our souls, the weakness and longing, the soft matter. A real teacher takes our vulnerability for granted, knows that this soft matter is where the passion resides, and that we will move on with greater humility and a wider perspective. As the trail guide says in Reinhart's wonderful film, *Meek's Cutoff,* "We're not lost. We're just finding our way."

To experience teaching like this is to tap into a force of nature; it is life changing and life affirming, and I cannot imagine wishing a summer squall had never jolted me off course and exposed the weak sailor in me, and the strong one. What many squalls strangely have in common is that they often end as they started, with a beautiful, peaceful day. The day was great, blue and dark, and I felt like I could see 360 degrees around me. The after-storm air was a mix of smells, with the stirring hint of ozone. The tide was rising. We ambled back down to the beach, and I shoved off the coarse sand along with some neighbors, hopped on, and hoisted sails, bearing towards Montauk Point.

Encinitas, CA; Martha's Vineyard, MA

10

~

Who Gets Grandpa's Tools?

Wᵉ were sitting in the small parlor after the burial. Staring at the luster of the mahogany banister across the room, I became lost in images of the last time I was with Howard, my old teacher. I love wood, and Howard was the first person I'd known who felt the same way. Now here he was, draped in wood with satin-finish trim that matched the banister, beyond judgment. I was lost.

It was several months ago, I thought. He had become sort of like a grandpa to me by then. I was just launching my young teaching career while his had been over for nearly a generation. After an outing downtown to the hardware store, not something you often do with a teacher, we had gone down to his basement for some small thing.

The basement was dark, with a clammy feeling about it—choked light filtered down from the kitchen above. There was a coal bin that made you think the basement smelled like coal. It didn't any more (electricity now heated their home), but you could almost hear the dry anthracite scraping down the aluminum chute with a month's supply in 1938, kicking up black dust. Around the other side of the bin, in the back corner of the basement, was set a very separate part of Howard's cluttered grotto.

After trade school at Capitol Radio College, he had apprenticed at Bell Labs, where he'd actually met William Shockley. Then, as the war years

183

dragged on, he did the sensible thing and applied for a job upstate teaching math in a local public junior high. The deferment.

My mother always admired his gentleness and one time, for his birthday, brought him a camel hair sport jacket. The jacket made his shoulders look falsely broad, and the large hands with thin wrists jutting out of the sleeves made his whole body look frail—Charlie McCarthy-esque. He never seemed like a teacher. He seemed like an electrician.

He reached up with his arthritic hand and pulled a chain that led to a bare bulb. The light made his large, pink hands look translucent. Howard, short, shrunken, and a little bent over, seemed like he was where he belonged. He cast his ever-hopeful looking, pale blue eyes downward, and I was a little moved—he had dug the foundation of this house himself and now, more than fifty years later, he stood securely in the cradle of his own hands: his workshop.

The dull shine of three power drills and the glare of a dozen glass jars filled with nuts and bolts and miscellany was attractive. Ball and spaghetti jars were smudged with grease on the lids and labels. Spread out deliberately across the shelf and the wallboard were hammers and screwdrivers of all sizes, mechanical wrenches, hand-carved wooden planes, all dark and oily from the hands that had seasoned them for ten thousand hours. Howard's hands could no longer plane or twist, they were knotted into an ancient burl.

I struck up conversations about the tools I admired, especially the large power drill that I really could have used. A reamer, a circular saw, table saw, a sander. Shadowed under the workbench were sets of socket wrenches (one English, in a leather pouch), cans of oils and solvents, and machine parts.

Howard took all these tools for granted and saw no point in discussing them with me. He had always been a plain man and, through his austerity, I know that to him, my enthusiasm was plain. Hanging from the pegboard, he saw me eying his precision tools, inside and outside calipers, and reached for one. "That one there, Stuart, this here, this one's an odd-leg jenny."

He conceded a vernier caliper that he claimed to have used in his first job at Bell, before he got the calling to teach, and a nail puller made of pig iron that must have been over a hundred years old. I took them. As we began to walk out, I took my last chance to scan the bench and there, too late, saw a thing that made me forever appreciate the art and soul of the shop. It was a genuine, depression-era, classic hand tool with adjustable gearing and polished wooden handle: a Yankee screwdriver. We walked upstairs to the kitchen and while I fumbled with my new instruments Howard, always a teacher, said: "Stuart, do you know how a refrigerator works?" It was pure philosophy. Later, around the house, I made paltry references to grandpa's generosity and his exemplary tools.

Despite my fondness for him, Howard had never struck me as any kind of teacher role model. I was just setting out on my career and admittedly my toolbox was pretty empty. And yet, it seemed he'd never used much more method or educational philosophy than his presence and patience. He was deliberate and contemplative, the kind of man whose aspiration later in life is to take long walks. He had never pushed students. If they wanted to work, he would give them things to do, and if they were curious he would show them interesting objects or even start taking them apart.

If they had no goals or motivation, he didn't seem to mind either. He had none of the urgency and force I grew to expect everywhere in schools, and he was never exhausted or angry, as I grew to witness elsewhere among teachers, even in myself. Of course, some kids took advantage and did nothing or made up false errands to go on. Howard allowed for this. As an eager young teacher looking back at his methods I thought, "But that's not teaching." In those days, I thought saying something profound about education was the same as saying something useful or true. I was young and sure about a lot of theories, and I didn't know what I was talking about.

In the parlor, I became aware of studying the polished wooden banister across the room, and of a little sadness, and realized I was in a daydream. I pictured the polish of his fruitwood casket. In the room only the wood—a credenza, a dining table, a salad bowl, an RCA tube radio console—retained their gloss. All else was vague and stale looking, evoking a dull odor memory that was sour. I was remembering what was real about grandpa. The sweat-honed, wood luster of his planes and hammer handles. The richness and thick polish of his casket.

Across from me sat Howard's three, plain daughters from a long-ago first marriage. I had never spent any time at all getting to know them, even though I went to college nearby. I sensed that now might be the time to spread my nostalgic frame of mind to them. Crossing the room, I smiled and greeted them. They, realistically, would be his benefactors, not me or my mom. Two of the daughters lived across the street, a couple houses down, and I had always found them grave.

Still I wondered what my mother would get, after all her generosity. And some things might get to me, the starting-out teacher who'd been like a grandson. Probably get nothing. These are just thoughts people have. I dearly liked Howard. I admired his practicality and simple wisdom. His gray, broad-shouldered suit which must have fit years ago, his white, Brylcreem hair, the deep pouches under his eyes which could never conceal his constant pain. His Yankee screwdriver. Would there even be people like that left in the schools now, teachers who pass along what's real about our lives and folklore?

"He was a gentle and a good man," I said, as though it were doctrine. "He had a life of perseverance," I said, "and that was enough." I couldn't believe I'd said that, and I pressed on, tentative and humiliated. I told them about the refrigerator lessons he gave me. And about the tools, how Howard had so wanted me to have some of them down there in the basement that day, how special that connection was. The sisters seemed to agree about all this—his practicality, his kindness, his good life, his good tool collection. One of them added that she did a lot of work around the house. She looked forward to putting those tools to work again, Howard's tools, just the way he would have wanted it to be.

Northport, New York

Appendix

Key Issues for Educators, by Chapter

1. Real Teachers: Oil on Canvas

Issues: Defining teaching

Big Questions: What does it mean to be a teacher? What is *educational determinism*? How do classroom teachers unknowingly prevent learning? How is the school teaching role changing?

2. Digging a Hole

Issues: Service learning, the clinical teaching model (lesson planning)

Big Questions: How do the stated and unstated goals of service learning compare? What are the stages of a lesson plan?

3. Leaving the John Muir Trail

Issues: Arts education, experiential education, outdoor education

Big Question: What is authentic education?

4. Hostile Indians Attack Schoolhouse

Issues: Class size, school size, group dynamics, team building, *the small schools movement*, regional education, leadership

Big Question: What are the real reasons classes and schools are sized the way they are, and what are the optimal sizes?

5. The Seventh Generation

Issues: Regional education versus national standards, No Child Left Behind and Common Core Standards, standardized testing, *the small schools movement*

Big Questions: Can schools, like fast food outlets, lose their regional distinctions? What is the impact of standardized testing on student and community development?

6. Chief Tayuk, Guy the Bear Hunter, and Me

Issues: Cross-generational learning and elder wisdom in the school, experiential education

Big Questions: Why are our elders so uninvolved in our schools, and how can they be involved? What other community members do you think should be regulars in the schools?

7. The Awakeners

Issues: Authentic evaluation and action research, cross cultural education

Big Questions: How does our culture bias impact the way we evaluate our schools? What authentic traditions are furthered at your local school?

8. Men in Decline

Issues: Gender literacy, the generation divide, a new millennial consciousness

Big Question: Are our students really our teachers? What issues, beyond gender identity, are on the horizon for the coming generation of students?

9. Single-Handing It in an Age of Fear

Issues: Creating the conditions for learning, digital literacy, outdoor education, mind and brain research in classroom instruction

Big Questions: What is the role of fear in the American school? Can perseverance be taught in the classroom?

10. Who Gets Grandpa's Tools?

Issues: Teacher mentoring, starting out as a teacher

Big Questions: Is there an essential role for authentic mentors in new teacher development? Are mentors found or assigned?

Notes

Chapter One

1 W. Isaacs, *Dialogue and the Art of Thinking Together* (New York: Doubleday, 1999).

2 H. Fischer-Wright, J. P. King, and D. Logan, *Tribal Leadership: Leveraging Natural Groups to Build a Thriving Organization* (New York: Collins, 2008).

3 D. Schoeberlein, *Mindful Teaching and Teaching Mindfulness Boston* (Australia: Wisdom Pub, 2009).

4 C. Jackson, "How to Spot a Real Rembrandt," *The Wall Street Journal*, December 18, 2009.

Chapter Two

No References.

Chapter Three

1 Elliot W. Eisner, "What Can Education Learn from the Arts about the Practice of Education?," *International Journal of Education & the Arts* 5, no. 4 (October 14, 2004), http://www.ijea.org/v5n4/.

2 R. Barth, "Improving Relationships within the Schoolhouse," *Educational Leadership* 63, no. 6 (March, 2006): 8–13.

3 S. Grauer, "Coalition of Small Preparatory Schools," "Small Schools, Very Big Gains—A White Paper," http://smallschoolscoalition.com.

4 Eisner, "What Can Education Learn from the Arts about the Practice of Education?"

5 C. Estes, "Promoting Student-Centered Learning in Experiential Education," *Journal of Experiential Education* 27, no. 2 (2004): 141–161.

6 I. Mergel and W. Greeves, *Social Media in the Public Sector Field Guide: Designing and Implementing Strategies and Policies*, (Hoboken, New Jersey: Jossey-Bass, 2012).

7 N. Owen, G. O N. Healy, C. E. Matthews, and D. W. Dunstan, "Too Much Sitting: The Population Health Science of Sedentary Behavior," *Exercise and Sport Science Reviews* 38, no. 3 (2010): 105–113.

8 Peter Gary, "The Decline of Play and the Rise of Psychopathology in Children and Adolescents," *American Journal of Play* 3, no. 4 (2011): 443–463.

9 Diane Spiegel, *The Gen Y Handbook: Applying Relationship Leadership to Engage Millennials* (New York: SelectBooks, 2013).

10 Dale Carnegie, *How to Win Friends & Influence People* (New York: Pocket Books, 1990).

11 Y. Jackson and V. McDermott, "Fearless Leading," *Educational Leadership* 67, no. 2 (October 2009): 34–39.

12 Eisner, "What Can Education Learn from the Arts about the Practice of Education?"

13 N. Goud, "Courage: Its Nature and Development," *Journal of Humanistic Counseling, Education and Development* 44, (2005): 102–116.

14 R. Barth, "Improving Relationships within the Schoolhouse," 8–13.

Chapter Four

1 W. K. Powers, *Yuwipi: Vision and Experience in Oglala Ritual* (Lincoln: University of Nebraska Press, 1982).

2 Dax Dämon, "The Lodge of Šungmanitu-Išna," http://1onewolf.com/lakota/index.htm.

3 M. T. Archambault, *Black Elk-Living in the Sacred Hoop* (Cincinnati, Ohio: St. Anthony Messenger Press, 1998).

4 Fischer-Wright, King, and Logan. *Tribal Leadership.*

5 We found empirical research from sources including the Gates Foundation, Larry Cuban at Stanford, Tennessee's Project STAR, and others, all indicating something special going on with less than fifteen students in a classroom. Astonishingly, in U.S. News and World Report's Best Schools of 2010 and again in 2011, two of the top five featured classes in the less than fifteen range, and seven of the top twenty-five schools on the 2011 Newsweek's "America's Best High Schools" had classes of less than fifteen.

6 J. Benbow, et al., "Large Class Sizes in the Developing World: What Do We Know and What Can We Do?" American Institutes for Research under the EQUIP1 LWA (2007).

7 R. Hanson, *Buddha's Brain: The Practical Neuroscience of Happiness, Love, and Wisdom* (Oakland, CA: New Harbinger Publications, 2009).

8 W. Moondance, *Spirit Medicine: Native American Teachings to Awaken the Spirit* (New York: Sterling, 1995), 26.

9 R. Dunbar, "You've Got to Have (150) Friends," *The New York Times*, December 25, 2010.

10 M. Gladwell, *The Tipping Point, How Little Things Can Make a Big Difference* (Boston: Little, Brown and Company, 2000).

11 J. Matthews, "Small Schools Rising," *Newsweek*, May 17, 2008.

12 S. Mitchell, "Jack and the Giant School," *New Rules Journal* (2000).

13 J. McRobbie, "Are Small Schools Better? School Size Considerations for Safety and Learning," *WestEd Policy Brief*, October, 2001.

14 Sherman Alexie, *The Lone Ranger and Tonto Fistfight in Heaven* (New York: Grove Press, 2005).

15 "A Hidden America: Children of the Plains," ABC News, Good Morning America, 2011.

16 J. DeCory, personal communication, January 12, 2012.

17 A. Coulson, "The Real Cost of Public Schools," *Washington Post*, April 6, 2008.

Chapter Five

1 D. R. Reynolds, *There Goes the Neighborhood: Rural School Consolidation at the Grass Roots in Early Twentieth Century Iowa* (Iowa City, Iowa: University of Iowa Press, 1999).

2 In fact, there is practically no physical geography at all in the California high school "History and Geography" curriculum. The way it is written, students would spend the whole year analyzing things, as though analysis were the only form of thought. (California Department of Public Schools, 140–167)

3 In the 1980s, the prolific E. D. Hirsh published his books on cultural literacy. It was like an educational swan song, a last-ditch effort to hang on to what Hirsh saw as our heritage, our classics. According to Hirsh, 80 percent of the material in his book on "cultural literacy," written in 1987, had been in regular use in schools for more than a century. Commonality of heritage is lost in textbook committees consisting of those who represent the kaleidoscope of competing American interest groups. The classic literature and historical legends of the twentieth century are rapidly disappearing. It is natural for textbooks to be updated and reordered every three or four years in schools, but the pace of change set by the millennial, digital generation (witness: Wikipedia, Google rankings, online publications) enabled even the most legendary literature to be replaced almost on the fly. By the end of the first decade of the 2000s, far less than 20 percent of the stories covered in school literature textbooks had been around for a hundred years. Clearly, new forces were at work in determining "cultural literacy" and the content of a basic education.

4 "Farmville," Facebook, http://www.facebook.com/pages/WWWFARMVILLECOM/ 203350228350.

5 P. Zimbardo, director, *RSA Animate—the Secret Powers of Time*, 2010.

Chapter Six

1 N. Klouda, "The Beginning of a Beautiful Friendship," *Homer Tribune*, September 30, 2009, http://homertribune.com/2009/09/the-beginning-of-a-beautiful-friendship/.

2 N. Klouda, "Elders Pass Along Self-Reliance to Nanwalek Youth," Indian Country News, August 14, 2008, http://indiancountrynews.net/index.php?option=com_content&task= view&id=4334&Itemid=33.

3 Catherine Rampell, "Why a Big Mac Costs Less Than a Salad," *New York Times*, March 9, 2010, http://economix.blogs.nytimes.com/2010/03/09/why-a-big-mac-costs-less-than-a-salad/.

4 "About Sugpiaq," http://www.sugpiaq.com/about-sugpiaq/.

5 E. Woody, "Recalling Celilo," *Salmon Nation: People and Fish at the Edge* (Portland, Oregon: Ecotrust, 1999).

6 Klouda, "Elders Pass Along Self-Reliance to Nanwalek Youth."

7 "Tribes," Chugachmiut, http://www.chugachmiut.org/tribes/nanwalek.html.

8 "The History of Nursing Homes," Fate Foundation Aiding the Elderly, http://www.4fate. org/history.html.

9 "2010 Report Card to the Public," Nanwalek School, http://www.edline.net/pages/ Nanwalek_School.

10 John Tabasnikoff, personal communication, September 27, 2011.

11 Klouda, "Elders Pass Along Self-Reliance to Nanwalek Youth."

12 Ibid.

13 Dunbar, R.I.M., "Coevolution of Neocortical Size, Group Size and Language in Humans," *Behavioral and Brain Sciences* 16 (4) 1993: 681–735.

14 R. Nash, "Clique Formation among Primary and Secondary School Children," *British Journal of Sociology* 24, no. 3 (1973): 375–398.

15 G. E. Conway, "Small Scale and School Culture: The Experience of Private Schools," *ERIC Digest*, 1994.

Chapter Seven

1 P. Freire, "Participatory Action Research: Renaming the World," Literate Voices, http://literatevoices.com/?page_id=51.

2 Nelly Robles Garcia, "Monte Alban," Society for American Archaeology, http://www.saa.org/AbouttheSociety/Publications/TheManagementofArchaeologicalResourcesinMexi/MonteAlban/tabid/1112/Default.aspx

3 "Organic Shade Grown Mexico," Starbucks, http://www.starbucks.com/blog/organic-shade-grown-mexico.

4 Mike Sholders, "Water Supply Development in San Diego and a Review of Related Outstanding Projects," *The Journal of San Diego History* 48, no. 1 (Winter 2002), http://www.sandiegohistory.org/journal/2002-1/sholders.htm.

5 Victor Philip, "Starbucks Wasting More Than 6 Million Gallons of Water a Day," ABC News, October 6, 2008, http://abcnews.go.com/International/SmartHome/story?id=5964908&page=1#.UEpSwdZmSy8.

6 Luigi Giussani, *At the Origin of the Christian Claim*, trans. Viviane Hewitt (Montreal: McGill-Queen's University Press, 1998).

7 Luigi Giussani, *The Religious Sense*, trans. John Zucchi (Montreal: McGill-Queen's University Press, 1997).

8 Andrew King, Israel Nelken, and Jan Schnupp, *Auditory Neuroscience* (Cambridge, Massachusetts: The MIT Press, 2010).

9 Giussani, *At the Origin of the Christian Claim*.

Chapter Eight

1 O. Handlin, "Living in the Valley," *The American Scholar* (Summer, 1977), 301.

2 D. Espelage and J. Robinson, "Inequities in Educational and Psychological Outcomes between LGBTQ and Straight Students in Middle and High School," *Educational Researcher* 40, no. 7 (2011): 315–330.

3 S. Pinker, "How Attitudes to Boys with ADD Are Changing." *The Sunday Times*, February 17, 2008.

4 D. Kindlon and M. Thompson, *Raising Cain: Protecting the Emotional Life of Boys* (New York: Random House, 2000).

5 L. Sax, *Why Gender Matters: What Parents and Teachers Need to Know about the Emerging Science of Sex Differences* (New York: Doubleday, 2005).

6 L. Feuer, "Arthur O. Lovejoy," *The American Scholar* (Summer, 1977), 358.

7 W. Whitman, "I Sing the Body Electric," *Leaves of Grass*, 1855.

Chapter Nine

1 R. Smith, "Parents' Fears about Child Safety is Fuelling Obesity, Survey Finds," *Telegraph*, March 3, 2009, http://www.telegraph.co.uk/health/healthnews/4927028/Parents-fears-about-child-safety-is-fuelling-obesity-survey-finds.html.

2 Grace Llewellyn, "The Natural Child Project: School is Not for Learning," The Natural Child Project, 1991, http://www.naturalchild.org/guest/grace_llewellyn.html.

3 Robert J. Marzano, *Classroom Assessment and Grading That Work* (Alexandria, VA: ASCD, 2006), 13–14.

4 James Steyer, *Talking Back to Facebook* (New York: Scribner, 2012).

5 T. Frey, "Curiosity-Driven Education," Futurist Speaker, accessed January 27, 2011, http://www.futuristspeaker.com/2011/01/curiosity-driven-education/.

6 Margaret Wheatley, *So Far from Home: Lost and found in Our Brave New World* (San Francisco, CA: Berrett-Koehler Publishers, 2012), 14–15.

7 D. Schoeberlein, *Mindful Teaching and Teaching Mindfulness* (Australia: Wisdom Pub, 2009).

8 T. Wagner, *The Global Achievement Gap* (New York: Basic Books, 2008), 8–42.

9 S. Benjamin, "Simple Leadership Techniques: Rubrics, Checklists, and Structured Collaboration," *Phi Delta Kappan* 92, no. 8 (2011): 25–31

10 T. Williams et al., *Gaining Ground in the Middle Grades: Why Some Schools Do Better* (Mountain View, CA: EdSource, 2010), 14–18.

11 S. Casey, *The Wave* (New York: Random House, 2010), 68–69.

12 R. Mundle, *Fatal Storm: The Inside Story of the Tagic Synney-Hobart Race* (Camden, ME: Australia International Marine/McGraw Hill, 1999).

13 L. Thomas, "Screen Addicts," *Daily Mail*, February 1, 2011, http://www.dailymail.co.uk/sciencetech/article-1352361/Children-spend-time-computers-TV-exercising-week.html.

Chapter Ten

No references

Bibliography and References

"2010 Report Card to the Public." Nanwalek School. http://www.edline.net/pages/Nanwalek_School.

"About Sugpiaq." http://www.sugpiaq.com/about-sugpiaq/.

"Alaska: Plane Crash Hits Schools Hard." *New York Times*, August 15, 2011. http://www.nytimes.com/2011/08/16/us/16brfs-PLANECRASHHI_BRF.html.

Alexie, Sherman. *The Lone Ranger and Tonto Fistfight in Heaven*. New York: Grove Press, 2005.

"America's Best High Schools." *Newsweek*. http://www.thedailybeast.com/newsweek/features/2011/americas-best-high-schools.html.

Anderson, P. "Tribes." Chugachmiut. http://www.chugachmiut.org/tribes/nanwalek.html.

Archambault, M. T. *Black Elk-Living in the Sacred Hoop*. Cincinnati, Ohio: St. Anthony Messenger Press, 1998.

Asher, James. "Send in the Drums." *Feet in the Soil*. New Earth Records, 1996.

Barth, R. "The Culture Builder." *Educational Leadership* 59, no. 8 (May, 2002): 6–11.

———. "Improving Relationships within the Schoolhouse." *Educational Leadership* 63, no. 6 (March, 2006): 8–13.

Benbow, J., A. Mizrachi, D. Oliver, and L. Said-Moshir. *Large Class Sizes in the Developing World: What Do We Know and What Can We Do?* American Institutes for Research under the EQUIP1 LWA, 2007.

Benjamin, S. "Simple Leadership Techniques: Rubrics, Checklists, and Structured Collaboration." *Phi Delta Kappan* 92, no. 8 (2011): 25–31.

Bronson, P. and A. Merryman. "The Creativity Crisis." Accessed July 10, 2010. http://www.newsweek.com/2010/07/10/the-creativity-crisis.html.

"California State Curriculum Frameworks." California Department of Education. http://www.cde.ca.gov/ci/hs/cf/index.asp.

Carnegie, Dale. *How to Win Friends & Influence People*. New York: Pocket Books, 1990.

Casey, S. *The Wave*. New York: Random House, 2010.

Casteneda, Carlos. *The Teachings of Don Juan*. New York: Ballentine, 1968.

Coe, Sophie D. and Michael D. Coe. *The True History of Chocolate*. New York: Thames & Hudson, 1996.

Conway, G. E. "Small Scale and School Culture: The Experience of Private Schools." *ERIC Digest* (1994).

Coulson, A. "The Real Cost of Public Schools." *Washington Post*, April 6, 2008.

Cowan, Eliot. *Plant Spirit Medicine*. San Francisco: Swan, Raven and Co., 1995.

Cuban, L. "Institute of Educational Sciences, Fast Facts." *The New York Times*, September 4, 2011.

Dämon, Dax. "The Lodge of Šungmanitu-Išna." http://1onewolf.com/lakota/index. htm.

DeCory, J. Personal communication, 2012.

Dillon, S. "As Classroom Budgets Are Trimmed, Time in Classes Is Shortened." *New York Times*, July 5, 2011. http://www.nytimes.com/2011/07/06/education/ 06time.html?_r=1&nl=afternoonupdate&emc=aua2.

The Doors. "The End." *Apocalypse Now Redux*. Nonesuch, 1979.

Dunbar, R. "You've Got to Have (150) Friends." *The New York Times*, December 25, 2010.

Eisner, Elliot W. "What Can Education Learn from the Arts about the Practice of Education?" *International Journal of Education & the Arts* 5, no. 4 (October 14, 2004). http://www.ijea.org/v5n4/.

Emoto, Masaru. *The Hidden Messages of Water*. New York: Atria, 2001.

Estes, C. "Promoting Student-Centered Learning in Experiential Education." *Journal of Experiential Education* 27, no. 2 (2004): 141–161.

"Farmville." Facebook. http://www.facebook.com/pages/WWWFARMVILLECOM/ 203350228350.

Feuer, L. "Arthur O. Lovejoy." *The American Scholar* (Summer, 1977): 358.

Fischer-Wright, H., J. P. King, and D. Logan. *Tribal Leadership: Leveraging Natural Groups to Build a Thriving Organization*. New York: Collins, 2008.

Freire, P. "Participatory Action Research: Renaming the World." Literate Voices. http://literatevoices.com/?page_id=51.

Frey, T. "Curiosity-Driven Education." Futurist Speaker. Accessed January 27, 2011. http://www.futuristspeaker.com/2011/01/curiosity-driven-education/.

Gait, J. A., et al. "Map of Exxon Valdez Oil Spill." Exxon Valdez oil Spill Trustee Council. http://www.evostc.state.ak.us/facts/spillmap.cfm.

Garcia, Nelly R. "Monte Alban." Society for American Archaeology. http://www. saa.org/AbouttheSociety/Publications/TheManagementofArchaeological ResourcesinMexi/MonteAlban/tabid/1112/Default.aspx.

Giussani, Luigi. *At the Origin of the Christian Claim*. Translated by Viviane Hewitt. Montreal: McGill-Queen's University Press, 1998.

———. *The Religious Sense*. Translated by John Zucchi. Montreal: McGill-Queen's University Press, 1997.

Gladwell, M. *The Tipping Point, How Little Things Can Make a Big Difference*. Boston: Little, Brown and Company, 2000.

Grauer, S. "Coalition of Small Preparatory Schools." http://smallschoolscoalition. com.

————. "Small Schools, Very Big Gains—A White Paper." http://smallschoolscoalition.com.

Gray, Peter. "The Decline of Play and the Rise of Psychopathology in Children and Adolescents." *American Journal of Play* 3, no. 4 (2011): 443–463.

Gregory, T. "Breaking Up Large High Schools: Five Common (and Understandable) Errors of Execution." *ERIC Digest* (2001).

Goud, N. "Courage: Its Nature and Development." *Journal of Humanistic Counseling, Education and Development* 44, (2005): 102–116.

Halpern, Steven. "In the Theta Zone." *Enhancing Creativity—Beautiful Music Plus Subliminal Suggestions.* Steven Halpern's Inner Peace Music, 1996.

Handlin, O. "Living in the Valley." *The American Scholar* (Summer, 1977): 301–312.

Hanson, R. *Buddha's Brain: The Practical Neuroscience of Happiness, Love, and Wisdom.* Oakland, CA: New Harbinger Publications, 2009.

————. *Personal communication,* 2011.

Herman, C. "The History of Nursing Homes." Fate Foundation Aiding the Elderly. http://www.4fate.org/history.html.

"A Hidden America: Children of the Plains." ABC News, Good Morning America, 2011.

Hirsch Jr., E. D. *Cultural Literacy: What Every American Needs to Know.* New York, NY: Houghton Mifflin, 1987.

Isaacs, W. *Dialogue and the Art of Thinking Together.* New York: Doubleday, 1999.

Jackson, C. "How to Spot a Real Rembrandt." *The Wall Street Journal,* December 18, 2009.

Jackson, Y. and V. McDermott. "Fearless Leading." *Educational Leadership* 67, no. 2 (October 2009): 34–39.

Jenkins, Philip. *Dream Catchers: How Mainstream America Discovered Native Spirituality.* New York: Oxford, 2004.

Kennedy, David. *The Dark Sides of Virtue.* New Jersey: Princeton University Press, 2005.

Kindlon, D. and M. Thompson. *Raising Cain: Protecting the Emotional Life of Boys.* New York: Random House, 2000.

Klouda, N. "The Beginning of a Beautiful Friendship." *Homer Tribune,* September 30, 2009. http://homertribune.com/2009/09/the-beginning-of-a-beautiful-friendship/.

————. "Elders Pass Along Self-Reliance to Nanwalek Youth." Indian Country News, August 14, 2008. http://indiancountrynews.net/index.php?option=com_content&task=view&id=4334&Itemid=33.

Lavallee, C. F., S. A. Koren, and M. A. Persinger. "A Quantitative Electroencephalographic Study of Meditation and Binaural Beat Entrainment." *Journal of Alternative and Complementary Medicine* 17, no. 4 (April, 2011): 351–355.

Lloyd, Marion. "Evolution Revolution Falls Short in Mexico." *Houston Chronicle* (March 29, 2008): 1.

Malkin, Elisabeth. "As Gangs Move In on Mexico's Schools, Teachers Say 'Enough.'" *New York Times*, September 25, 2011. http://www.nytimes.com/2011/09/26/world/americas/mexican-teachers-push-back-against-gangs-extortion-attempts.html?emc=tnt&tntemail1=y.

Marshall, J. M. *The Lakota Way*. New York, NY: Penguin Compass, 2001.

Marzano, Robert J. *Classroom Assessment and Grading That Work*. Alexandria, VA: ASCD, 2006.

Matthews, J. "Small Schools Rising." *Newsweek*, May 17, 2008.

McNeil, M. "Bill Gates to Govs: Raise Class Size, Avoid Furloughs." *Education Week*, February 28, 2011.

McRobbie, J. "Are Small Schools Better? School Size Considerations for Safety and Learning." *WestEd Policy Brief*, October, 2001.

"Meditation Hakalau." Ancient Huna. www.ancienthuna.com/hakalau.htm.

Mergel, I. and W. Greeves. "The Public Manager 2.0: A Social Media Field Guide for the Public Sector." Jossey-Bass/Wiley.

Mitchell, S. "Jack and the Giant School." *New Rules Project*, 2000.

Moondance, W. *Spirit Medicine: Native American Teachings to Awaken the Spirit*. New York: Sterling, 1995.

Mundle, R. *Fatal Storm: The Inside Story of the Tragic Sydney-Hobart Race*. Camden, ME: Australia International Marine/McGraw Hill, 1999.

Narby, Jeremy and Francis Huxley, eds. *Shamans through Time*. New York: Tarcher, 2001.

Nash, R. "Clique Formation among Primary and Secondary School Children." *British Journal of Sociology* 24, no. 3 (1973): 375–398.

"Overweight and Obesity Statistics." Weight-control Information Network (WIN), U.S. Department of Health and Human Services. http://www.win.niddk.nih.gov/statistics/index.htm.

Owen, N., G. N. Healy, C. E. Matthews, and D. W. Dunstan. "Too Much Sitting: The Population Health Science of Sedentary Behavior." *Exercise and Sport Science Review* 38, no. 3 (2010): 105–113.

Pallack, B. "More Native Americans make Grades for College." *Arizona Daily Star*, 2011.

Paxson, Diana L. *Trance-Portation: Learning to Navigate the Inner World*. San Francisco: Red Wheel/Weiser, 2008.

Pinker, S. "How Attitudes to Boys with ADD are Changing." *The Sunday Times*, February 17, 2008.

Powers, W. K. *Yuwipi: Vision and Experience in Oglala Ritual*. Lincoln: University of Nebraska Press, 1982.

Preston, Julia. "Fewer Latino Immigrants Sending Money Home." *New York Times*, May 1, 2008.

Rampell, C. "Why a Big Mac Costs Less than a Salad." *New York Times*, March 9, 2010. http://economix.blogs.nytimes.com/2010/03/09/why-a-big-mac-costs-less-than-a-salad/.

Reynolds, D. R. *There Goes the Neighborhood: Rural School Consolidation at the Grass Roots in Early Twentieth Century Iowa*. Iowa City, Iowa: University of Iowa Press, 1999.

Robinson, J. and D. Espelage. "Inequities in Educational and Psychological Outcomes between LGBTQ and Straight Students in Middle and High School." *Educational Researcher* 40, no. 7 (2011): 315–330.

Sack, Kevin. "Illegal Immigrants Turn to Traditional Healing." *New York Times*, May 10, 2008.

Sax, L. *Why Gender Matters: What Parents and Teachers Need to Know about the Emerging Science of Sex Differences*. New York: Doubleday, 2005.

Schjeldahl, P. "Spot on." *The New Yorker*, January 23, 2012, 84.

Schnupp, Jan, Israel Nelken, and Andrew King. *Auditory Neuroscience*. Cambridge, Massachusetts: The MIT Press, 2010.

Schoeberlein, D. *Mindful Teaching and Teaching Mindfulness Boston*. Australia: Wisdom Pub, 2009.

Shapiro, F. *The Yale Book of Quotations*. New Haven, CT: Yale University Press, 2009.

Sizer, T. R. *National Association of Secondary School Principals (U.S.), & National Association of Independent Schools*. Boston: Houghton Mifflin Co., 2004.

Slocum, J. "Sailing Alone Around the World." *The Voyages of Joshua Slocum*. Translated and edited by W. M. Teller. Dobbs Ferry, New York: Sheridan House Inc, 1985.

Smith, R. "Parents' Fears about Child Safety is Fuelling Obesity, Survey Finds." *Telegraph*, March 3, 2009. http://www.telegraph.co.uk/health/healthnews/4927028/Parents-fears-about-child-safety-is-fuelling-obesity-survey-finds.html.

Spiegel, Diane. "The Gen Y Handbook: Applying Relationship Leadership to Engage Millennials." New York: SelectBooks, 2013.

Starbucks. "Organic Shade Grown Mexico." http://www.starbucks.com/coffee/whole-bean-coffee/latin-america/organic-shade-grown-mexico.

Steyer, James. *Talking Back to Facebook*. New York: Scribner, 2012.

"STRYVE: Striving to Reduce Youth Violence Everywhere." Centers for Disease Control and Prevention. http://www.cdc.gov/violenceprevention/stryve/.

Tabasnikoff, John. *Personal communication*, 2011.

Thomas, L. "*ScreenAddicts.*" *Daily Mail*, February 1, 2011. http://www.dailymail.co.uk/ sciencetech/article-1352361/Children-spend-time-computers-TV-exercising-week.html.

Trilling, Susanna. *My Search for the Seventh Mole: A Story with Recipes from Oaxaca, Mexico*. Oaxaca, Mexico: 1997.

———. Seasons of My Heart. http://seasonsofmyheart.com/.

Wagner, T. *The Global Achievement Gap*. New York: Basic Books, 2008.

Walberg, Herbert J. and Herbert J. III Walberg. "Losing Local Control." *Educational Researcher* 23, no. 5 (1994): 19–26.

Wheatley, Margaret. *So Far from Home: Lost and Found in Our Brave New World*. San Francisco, CA: Berrett-Koehler Publishers, 2012.

Williams, D. T. "The Dimensions of Education: Recent Research on School Size." *ERIC Working Paper Series*, 1990.

Williams, T., K. Michael, and E. Haertel et al., *Gaining Ground in the Middle Grades: Why Some Schools Do Better*. Mountain View, CA: EdSource, 2010.

Woody, E. "Recalling Celilo." *Salmon Nation: People and Fish at the Edge*. Edited by E. Wolf and S. Zuckerman. Portland, Oregon: Ecotrust, 1999.

Zimbardo, P., director. *RSA Animate—the Secret Powers of Time*. 2010.

Acknowledgments

Some of these ideas and stories were originally introduced in *The Grauer School Weekly Newsletter*, but when readership of that in-house publication reached 123 cities around the world, I determined the most helpful course of action would be to gather and develop the best material into a well researched and cohesive body of work.

A core group of scrutinizing readers and editors was established at The Grauer School, the school I founded in 1991. Deserving great thanks among those students, teachers, and alumni are Morgan Brown, Stephane Deuvaert, Mike Branon, Lisa Ezzard, Chris Ahrens, Elizabeth Braymen (and family), Jingya Zhong, and Sam Mullinax. Student Keanan Gottlieb opened my eyes to refined ways of understanding gender. Sean Hauze patiently helped arm me with the technology I needed to function globally and Dana Abplanalp-Diggs made a thousand things possible.

Doug Katz, author, marketing and management consultant, literary connoisseur, and great friend, first envisioned these essays as a unified series, and he subsequently critiqued each one. My research associate, Christina Ryan (M.A., Peace Studies), was utterly incapable of divining anything but joy and understanding from all I wrote, whatever it was.

Generously underwriting my work and global investigations were Harley Sefton and the Sefton Family of San Diego, and the Board of Trustees of the Grauer Foundation for Education.

Along the trail I met extraordinary individuals who made the stories possible: Darryl Kreun of Nanwalek, Alaska; Roger and Vida White Eyes from Pine Ridge, South Dakota; Jace DeCory of South Dakota State University's Indian Studies Department. Pastor Bill Harman led us into schools and youth centers of Botswana and the sanctuaries of Israel, where pain and hope coexist. Mary and Chris Ellis underwrote my work in Monte Albán, Mexico. John and Reggie Rowe supported my travels to the South Seas; Moorea educator and surfer Patrick Bourligeaux gave me local access to remote venues, all because I was a teacher. The generous people at the Scorpion Bay Club in San Juanico opened up their grounds for me to work in seclusion for some weeks, many of them during a power outage, which served to reveal the moon and stars and howling dogs. Christina Baldwin of Peer Spirit opened up both her talent and the soulful Whidbey Island retreat to me. Small schools legend Deborah Meier and national educational change agent Diane Ravitch weighed in with support and encouragement. There were many more.

I thank my daughter Audrey Grauer, born and raised on a school and now a Bates College student, for her careful, loving, and sensible readings, and Susan Nestor for her appreciation and critiques. Thanks to Priscilla Grauer, my mother, for a lifetime of supporting artistic endeavor at the expense of all else. Brothers David and Bill both helped clarify my concepts. Perhaps my trickiest critic, my wife of twenty-two years, Sally Grauer, deserves endless gratitude for unconditionally and constantly supporting both the stories and the unpredictable lifestyle that they illustrate.

Thanks to my agent Bill Gladstone at Waterside Productions. Thanks to my publisher at SelectBooks, who made it possible for this book to be shared widely. I always wrote better because I knew they were reading.

Last and most, I thank my students present and past, who have breathed life into the most alluring places on earth, both in and out of the classroom. It is not our travels or even our best teachers that make teachers out of us; only our students can do that.

About the Author

Dr. Stuart Grauer, a teacher, is the founding Head of School, The Grauer School. He also holds positions as President of The Grauer Foundation for Education and Founder of The Coalition for Small Preparatory Schools.

The author has been interested in education since he was a young man, becoming the Principal of the International School of Basel, Switzerland at the age of twenty-nine.

In 1991 Dr. Grauer founded The Grauer School (www.grauerschool.com) in order to establish humanitarian secondary education in Southern California. He is considered one of the nation's top authorities on small schools and community education and consults and speaks widely on this area. He has evaluated many schools worldwide, taught graduate education courses, and was awarded with a Fulbright Administrator Exchange to Argentina and, in 2012, an Ameson Foundation exchange to China.

Dr. Grauer's writings and work have been covered widely, including by The Discovery Channel, *The New York Times, International Education Review, Community Works Journal,* and frequently in the local press in his home town of Encinitas, California, where he has been named "Peacemaker of the Year" and a "Legendary Local." He holds a bachelor's degree from Syracuse University, a master's degree from Long Island University, and a doctorate from the University of San Diego.